HAMM

L

"The
days, a
it was is

115 A

-6.

L

COMPETITIVE SWIMMING AND DIVING

COMPETITIVE
SWIMMING & DIVING

D. A. Armbruster, M.A.

Associate Professor of
Education and Head Swimming
Coach, University of Iowa

NICHOLAS KAYE

LONDON

First published in Great Britain 1948
by Nicholas Kaye, Ltd., 1 Trebeck
Street, London, W.1.

Printed in Great Britain for Nicholas Kaye, Ltd.,
by Jarrold & Sons, Norwich

PREFACE

Source material in the field of competitive swimming and diving is amazingly limited. Mindful of this situation, the material in this book has been presented with the idea of aiding beginning coaches and beginning competitors, as well as improving the performances of advanced swimmers and divers. To this end, the technique of each stroke and dive is presented in some detail. Where technique and form are somewhat involved, the author has attempted to present each phase in a clear, logical and orderly sequence so that both the high school and college athlete can easily understand the discussion.

The author recognizes the differences of opinion as to what constitutes good form in swimming. Kinesiologic principles and physical laws were the guiding factors in presenting the material. An attempt is made to fit the discussion to conform to practices which are recognized as being correct. Some new studies and techniques have been advanced as a result of experiments carried out at the University of Iowa. Where opinion was the only source material available, practices which are generally considered as being correct are given.

The diagrams presented in this book were secured almost entirely from an underwater movie study of some of the world's greatest swimmers. These underwater motion picture studies, taken through underwater observation windows, have opened a new technique in the competitive swimming world.

Comparative records have been presented. The schedules of work which are given represent a mean load of work for college men. Personalities were intentionally omitted.

Unfortunately it is impossible to mention everyone to whom the author owes a grateful debt of thanks for advice and encouragement. However, I do wish to single out two individuals. First, the author wishes to express his sincere thanks to Dr. W. W. Tuttle, Professor of Physiology, University of Iowa, for his inspiration and guidance throughout the preparation of the entire book. His counsel pertaining to matters of a physiologic nature is appreciated. And second, I wish to express my debt of gratitude to Dr. Laurence Morehouse, Director of Physical Education and Athletics, Wichita University, for his assistance in preparing the manuscript, as well as for his advice in technical matters pertaining to the field of swimming and to physiology.

Much inspiration and encouragement were received from Professor E. G. Schroeder, Director of the Division of Physical Education and Athletics, and Dr. C. H. McCloy, Professor of Physical Education, University of Iowa.

To those champions who performed before the cameras and to the many former and present members of the University of Iowa swimming teams whom the author has had the privilege and pleasure of coaching, much credit is due.

The artistic ability of Mr. Lee Allen, Medical Illustrator, Department of Ophthalmology, University of Iowa Hospital, in creating the figures for the diagrams is a real contribution for which the author is grateful.

The author wishes to thank Mr. Lee W. Cochran, Supervisor of Visual Instruction, University of Iowa, for his patient and accurate services in filming the motion pictures used. The Dolphin, national honorary swimming fraternity, has rendered invaluable service in the promotion of swimming studies at the University of Iowa and has also further aided by supplying moving picture materials for the filming of underwater pictures.

Much credit is due to the leading swimming and diving coaches in the United States for their suggestions and discussions throughout these many pleasant years to advance and improve swimming and diving.

D. A. A.

Iowa City, Iowa
January 1, 1942

CONTENTS

CHAPTER I

CHAPTER II

CHAPTER III

CHAPTER IV

CHAPTER VIII

CHAPTER IX

ILLUSTRATIONS

COMPETITIVE SWIMMING AND DIVING

Competitive Swimming and Diving

CHAPTER I

INTRODUCTION

The development of speed in swimming can be traced from writings dating to the sixteenth century. Prior to that time, accounts by the Greek, Roman, Anglo-Saxon, and Scandinavian classics, deal only with great feats of swimming prowess of the heroes of their day and leave the type of swimming stroke used by these heroes to the reader's imagination. Other ancient narratives mention swimming in connection with religious rites, but these practices usually included dousing or bathing and not the art of moving progressively in the water.[1]

The first book on swimming was written by Nicolaus Wynman, a German professor of languages, in 1538.[2] A more scientific treatise was later written by Thevenot, a Frenchman, in a book entitled *The Art of Swimming*.[3] The method Thevenot described resembles closely that which we now designate as the breast stroke. The arms stroked sideward, like the oars in rowing a boat, except that they were recovered under the water. The legs also stroked sideward in unison, similar to the kick of a frog. Although the breast stroke was not adapted to speed swimming, it had many advantages which caused it to remain popular. The stroke gave the swimmer unobstructed forward vision and permitted free and natural breathing. Stroking the arms under the surface prevented splashing the swimmer's face. The stroke thus gave the swimmer a feeling of stability, even in rough water. The pioneers constructed this stroke so well that it established the foundation of all strokes. Two and a half centuries after its origin, this method of swimming retains its original characteristics. It is still the most seaworthy of all our present strokes.

[1]For a more complete account of historical swimming literature, see Cureton, T. K.: How to Teach Swimming and Diving, Association Press, 1934, Chapter IV, p. 85.

[2]Wynman, Nicolaus: Colymbetes, Sive de Arte Natanli Dialogus et Festivus et Incundus Lectu (Dutch Copy), Ingolstdt. Bavana, 1538. The title of this book is translated literally as follows: "The Diver, or a Dialogue Concerning the Art of Swimming, both Pleasant and Joyful to Read."

[3]Thevenot, M.: L'Art de Nager, Paris, 1696.

2

With the advance of competitive swimming in Europe, some of the utilitarian values of the breast stroke had to be sacrificed to speed. English coaches experimented to reduce the resistance of arm and leg recovery movements under water. They found that if the swimmer changed his position from prone to side, he could lift one arm out over the water on the recovery of that arm, thus speeding the recovery and reducing the water resistance to his forward motion. This necessitated a change of the leg action, and a movement like that of scissor blades, in which the principles of the frog-kick are used in the prone position, was adopted. The stroke was called the ''English-over-arm'' or ''side-over-arm'' and the best recorded time for 100 yards by this method was 1 :15.0 set by W. Cole of England at the first English championships in 1871. In the next twenty years this stroke was refined and in 1895 J. H. Tyers of England reduced the time to 1 :02.5. British coaches are given credit for devising this stroke, on which J. Trudgeon, also an Englishman, built his famous Trudgeon stroke, and they deserve great credit for their pioneering contribution to the swimming world.

Swimming experimenters then reasoned that if by lifting one arm out of the water at each stroke greater speed was obtained, then further speed might be expected by recovering both arms out of the water. The first practical use of this principle was made by J. Trudgeon. Each arm was permitted to recover out of the water by rolling the body from side to side. The ''scissors'' kick was retained and occurred following each arm stroke. The stroke was named after its originator, Trudgeon, but was sometimes called the ''alternating-over-arm'' stroke. The success of this innovation as a speed stroke was proved by further time reductions for swimming 100 yards. In 1901, F. V. C. Lane, of England, used the Trudgeon stroke and achieved the astounding time of one minute flat.

In thirty years the record for swimming 100 yards had been lowered 15 seconds. The first two eras in the history of speed swimming had produced considerable headway. During the English-over-arm era of twenty-three years, from 1871 to 1894, the swimming time for 100 yards improved 12.5 seconds. During the seven-year Trudgeon era from 1894 to 1901 there was a further time improvement of :02.5.[4]

---

[4]Note: Although other distances were also being swum, the 100 yard event is alluded to as records are most complete in this event.

So far, attention had been given only to the arm action. The legs had been only a little more than just trailing members. An analysis of the leg action employed by swimmers using the Trudgeon stroke reveals three factors which had to be revised before the leg action could make a contribution to speed. First, the recovery phase of the Trudgeon kick involved too much resistance to forward progression. The doubling up of the legs and their lateral spread preliminary to the drive of the kick presented an opposing force that materially discounted the drive of the power phase of the kick. This counter force had to be reduced. Second, the Trudgeon kick had only one single unit of power for each arm stroke. A leg action that provided a continuous series of forward drives to each arm stroke was, therefore, sought. Third, the rhythm of the Trudgeon kick did not synchronize with the alternating-over-arm stroke. The body had to be rolled from side to side in order to deliver a good scissors kick. This rolling movement retarded the action of the arms and had to be eliminated before better timing could be attained.

The delivery of one kick with each arm stroke in the refined Trudgeon technique was an advance over the single kick for each arm cycle as employed by the English side-over-arm swimmers. In order to double the number of leg kicks for each arm cycle, the width of the leg spread in the recovery phase was reduced. With this, the resistance to forward progression was also somewhat reduced.

The pause after each scissors kick in the English-over-arm stroke was eliminated in the Trudgeon stroke. Although the leg action in the latter stroke was slow and each kick was performed in an alternatingly different position, the kick was somewhat continuous and resembled a "fluttering" action. The increase in leg kicks from one to two beats for each arm cycle in the change from the English-over-arm to the Trudgeon stroke did not improve the timing as the leg movement still had to be arrested in order to correspond with the recovery of the arm out of water. The action of the legs thus had to undergo the greatest change. A higher ratio of kicks to arm cycles had to be established before swimmers could "shift into a higher gear" and thereby increase their speed in swimming.

In far-off Australia, a man named Richard Cavill came to these same conclusions. Cavill observed a race between his brother, Tum, and a friend named Syd Davis. Both used the alternating-over-arm stroke but Tum swam with his legs tied while Syd used the regular Trudgeon kick. Tum was able to beat Syd. When Tum's legs were untied and they raced over the same distance again, this time both of them using both arms and legs, Syd beat Tum. Here was a demonstration that the Trudgeon kick was a retarding rather than an advancing factor! Richard Cavill recalled a rapid, vertical action of the legs used by Alec Wickham of Colombo, Ceylon. He combined this leg action with the alternating-over-arm stroke and found that greater speed could thus be attained. This "Australian Crawl" was first introduced by Richard Cavill at the international championships in 1902. He lowered the world record for swimming 100 yards to :58.4. This new style immediately gained in popularity among the coaches of all nations and soon the Australian crawl was being swum in many parts of the world. The new leg action provided solutions to the three recognized drawbacks present in the Trudgeon stroke. The kick was called the "flutter" kick, its name descriptive of the thrashing action of the legs. The recovery phase of this leg action offered only a small resistance to forward progression. It provided a continuous series of four power units for each arm cycle and was easily synchronized with the alternating-over-arm stroke. The reciprocal succession of acceleration and deceleration had been eliminated and now the forward progression was steady and more economically derived. The increased power from the legs in using the flutter kick permitted the body to maintain a position at the surface of the water which reduced the resistance of the water to the body considerably. The introduction of the flutter kick in 1902 established a new era in speed swimming.

There were still a few mechanical mysteries pertaining to the flutter kick that remained to be solved. The theory that the straightening of the bent leg at the knee pushed the water backward and provided the main propulsive force which drove the swimmer forward was still held. This propelling force was also thought to be supplemented by the water being squeezed out from between the legs as they came together. That phase of the leg action in which the legs are thrust vertically apart was considered to be a recovery phase only and, as such, provided no forward propelling force. The emphasis was therefore placed upon the extension of the knee and the adduction of the legs.

The face was held down in the water and the arms were moved in a crawling fashion. Because of the peculiar appearance of this stroke it was first called the "creeping crawl."

American coaches sought to meet the keen competition by revising this new speed stroke. They increased the leg action from four to six beats to each arm cycle. An eight-beat kick was tried but was found to be too fatiguing and was soon abandoned. The crawl stroke was confined to use in short distances only as the swimmers were soon out of breath. A system of breath control was developed in which the swimmer raised his head forward for a gasp of air and then slowly bubbled it out under water. This so-called "underwater breathing" contributed to swimming performance over greater distances. Later it was found that breathing could be further improved by turning the face to the side for the inhalation.

A slightly "pigeon-toe" position of the feet was introduced in order to present a greater surface area to the water during the vertical kick. A further refinement by American coaches included a brief relaxation period for the arms. This occurred during the recovery phase while the arm was above the surface of the water. The coaches in the United States termed this revised edition of the Australian crawl the "American crawl."

The results attained by the American coaches in perfecting the crawl stroke soon became evident. In 1906, Charles M. Daniels became the first United States speed swimming champion of the world. He lowered the 100-yard swimming record to :55.4. The crawl became so popular that it was the first stroke taught to beginners. "Duke" Kahanamoku, a Hawaiian, using the American crawl, lowered Daniels' record to :54.6 for 100 yards. This record was made in 1913 and remained unbroken until 1921. Kahanamoku's chief asset was a pair of long, broad feet which provided a large surface for propulsive action. He was tall and powerful and used a tremendous leg action. He was one of the first great swimmers to develop a purely vertical, full measured, six-beat, flutter kick.

The leg action that was generally used at that time was the "trudge-crawl" kick, developed by Frank Sullivan of Chicago for distance swimmers. Six beats for each arm cycle were used. The first and the fourth beats were wide and scissors-like. These were called the major beats. The second and third and the fifth and sixth were narrow and faster. These were called the minor beats. The popular use of the trudge-crawl kick was gradually replaced by the faster, evenly measured, vertical flutter kick.

In 1923, a youth 17 years of age, named Johnny Weissmuller, lowered Kahanamoku's record to :52.8. In 1927, he lowered it again to 51.0. During this same year, Weissmuller, in a 20-yard course, swam 100 yards in :49.8. In seven years he established over fifty American and world records. Many of his records remain unbroken today.

Weissmuller introduced four new and significant developments in the speed crawl stroke.[5]

1. The pull-and-push power arm stroke in which the pull starts from a straight arm action as soon as the arm enters the water. The arm is pressed down and slightly inward until the arm reaches a point just ahead of the shoulder. Here the arm is bent slightly at the elbow, resembling a boomerang, and from this point continues in a pushing delivery.

2. The turning of the head for breathing was independent of the arm action.

3. A deep leg action for the flutter kick was used in order to obtain greater traction in the water.

4. The deeper leg action allowed the chest and shoulders to be carried higher.

In the 1928 Olympic Games, Weissmuller captured nearly all of the sprint swimming championship titles. His style was generally accepted by American swimmers and coaches as the best speed swimming stroke in existence. The youth of this country set about to master this stroke with the aid of a special device which was soon to aid in again revolutionizing the speed swimming stroke. This special device was the slow-motion picture camera. Many miles of film were being distributed which showed both out-of-the-water and underwater shots of Weissmuller's speed swimming style.

The use of these films was not limited to the Americans, however. Weissmuller and other American and European swimmers were photographed in action from all directions by the Japanese swimming technicians. These films were taken to Japan and were widely exhibited among the Japanese schools. These school children thus observed and were coached the best styles from early youth, and through intensive training, some of them were able to overcome all competition in speed swimming at the 1932 Olympic Games. Four

[5]Weissmuller, John, and Bush, Clarence: Swimming the American Crawl, Houghton Mifflin Co., Boston, 1930.

years before, in the 1928 Olympics, they won only the 200 meters breast stroke. In 1932 they won every swimming event except the 400 meters freestyle.

The Japanese style contained nothing new, but was essentially a combination of the best speed swimming mechanics used by previous champions. The essential features of their arm action were the quick recovery and long glide of each arm after it entered the water. This style was introduced by Buster Crabbe and his coach "Dad" Center from Hawaii at the 1928 U. S. Olympic tryouts.

A great portion of the success of the Japanese could be ascribed to their superb physical condition. This condition was due to a careful control of their diet, exercise, and rest as well as their rigorous training regime.

Although overshadowed by Japanese successes, two other styles of the crawl were seen at the 1932 Olympics. Many European swimmers used a peculiar arm action in which the arms recovered with a low, lateral, straight arm sweep above the surface of the water. The arm action of this European crawl resembled the sweep of a scythe. Another crawl style was used by the women's team from Holland who employed a high arm recovery, and smashed the arms into the water as the recovery was completed.

American swimmers and their coaches returned from the 1932 games with a determination to develop their style and condition in order to recover the swimming crowns lost to the Japanese. Their efforts were rewarded at the 1936 games in Berlin where they were successful in winning two swimming titles and in winning the Olympic swimming and diving championships.

Champions have always had a large following. Some swimmers have become champions in spite of an arm stroke or leg kick that was mechanically unsound. A great many swimmers and some coaches have sought to copy the style of a champion with the theory that if it was good for the champion it was good enough for them. Others believed that certain styles should be adapted to athletes of a certain build. Many coaches contended that Weissmuller's style could be used by tall swimmers, but that it was not suitable to those of less height.

The development of the technique of swimming the American crawl has evolved from the trial-and-error method of experimentation, the criterion of the success of certain innovations being the increase in speed in swimming. The constant lowering of records is a good indication that the mechanics of the swimming strokes are still being improved.

In the development of speed swimming, attention has been focused on the crawl, the fastest of all strokes. Two other competitive strokes, however, were retained and they have undergone a development which is also interesting to note.

The breast stroke, outmoded as a speed stroke by the English-over-arm, was never eliminated from the competitive swimming program. In fact, because of its utility it was placed on each program as a special event and was the only stroke in which a prescribed style was required.

The underwater recovery of the arms and legs was the retarding factor in this stroke. The time for swimming 100 yards using the breast stroke was 1:07.0 until in 1934 an arm stroke which complied with the rules and yet employed an out-of-the-water recovery was discovered. The recovery was a double, over-arm stroke in which the arms were simultaneously swung laterally and then forward. The swimmer resembled a butterfly in flight and the name ''butterfly'' was given to this stroke.

Using the new butterfly breast stroke, 100 yards was swum in 1:05, a new record for the breast stroke. Although this stroke did not violate any of the rules pertaining to the breast stroke, it was a departure from the orthodox method and it met with disapproval among many coaches and officials. The butterfly breast stroke is at present ruled out in the high schools of certain sections of the United States. The International Swimming Federation gave it sanction for universal use in 1937.

With this new and faster arm action, the retarded recovery action of the legs became an even greater matter of attention. In 1935, Jack Sieg, a University of Iowa swimmer, developed the skill of swimming on his side and beating his legs in unison similar to the action of a fish's tail. He then tried the same leg action while swimming face down. With a little practice Sieg could perform the leg action as efficiently in this position. Finally Sieg combined the butterfly arm action with this leg action and found that the two could be synchronized. Swimming with two leg beats to each butterfly arm action, Sieg swam 100 yards in 60.2 seconds. This kick was named the "dolphin-fishtail" kick.[6]

The dolphin kick was ruled illegal because the legs moved in a vertical plane. This illegality was corrected by Jack Kasley of the University of Michigan. The knees were slightly spread and the toes were turned slightly outward as the legs were thrust downward and upward as they closed and completed the kick. The feet engaged the water on this thrust and continued to do so as the knees were straightened and the legs prescribed an upward sweeping kick similar to the dolphin kick. This kick resembled the lateral orthodox breast stroke kick and was declared legal. Kasley used the butterfly breast stroke with the revised dolphin leg action and in 1936 set a new world's record for the 100-yard breast stroke at 1:02.7.

The development of the third competitive stroke, the back crawl, dates back to 1902, at about the time that Richard Cavill was combining the flutter kick with the Trudgeon crawl. The back crawl, in fact, is a by-product of the crawl. In its early form it was also a by-product of the breast stroke, since the breast stroke kick and double over-arm action were used. This inverted breast stroke was soon abandoned as a possible competitive stroke since it was too slow and served only to duplicate the regular breast stroke.

Previous to 1902, the back stroke had been nothing more than a trick combining a sculling action of the hands with a leg action similar to a flutter kick. Following an attempt to make the back stroke a speed swimming event by inverting the breast stroke, it was noticed that an inverted reverse over-arm crawl combined with the inverted flutter kick resulted in a stroke which gave more speed than the breast stroke. In 1912 the back crawl was established as a competitive swimming event and was gradually improved by many refinements.

In 1935, a Chicago schoolboy, Adolph Kiefer, swam the back crawl for 100 yards in :57.6. The technique developed by Kiefer contained three features that distinguished Kiefer's back crawl from the generally used form. First, the recovery of the arms was made in a very low, lateral fashion with the arms held straight. Second, the arms entered the water just above a line opposite the shoulders instead of straight up from the shoulders, alongside the head. Third,

[6]Armbruster, David A.: The Dolphin Breast Stroke, Journal of Health and Physical Education 6: No. 4, April, 1935.

the arms were drawn through the water just below the surface as contrasted with the deep pull employed generally.

The quest for speed has brought about revolutionary changes in swimming styles in the past two and one-half centuries. It is expected that this improvement will be continued. With the increase in the knowledge and study of kinesiology and body mechanics as well as the study of water resistance and other physical and physiologic problems related to speed swimming, this sport is being developed through scientific investigation.

Competitive diving is an outgrowth of aerial acrobatics and tumbling. The first recorded diving competition took place in England in 1905. Since that time, diving has been an integral part of the competitive water sports program. Feats of diving have been recorded as early as 1871, when divers were reported to have plunged from the London Bridge and other high places.

From the simple head first and feet first dives, there have been developed nearly one hundred fancy dives. These are combinations of forward, backward, handstands and twists, somersaults, gainers, and jackknives. They are performed in either a straight, pike, or tuck position. They are executed from either the low or high board, or from a platform.

With the present interest in the advancement of swimming and diving through scientific investigation, the records for swimming the various strokes for different distances are being lowered, and the skill of the divers is improving constantly.

CHAPTER II

THE START

The competitors with the fastest starting times have a significant advantage over those who are slow in leaving the marks. Likewise, a fast swimmer may see his efforts go for nought if for some reason he fails to leave his mark with precise, forceful, and well-timed movements. The mechanics of the start and the physiologic and psychologic factors entering into its performance are indeed complex.

The swimming start is defined as including the events which take place between the command "Take your marks" and the beginning of the first swimming stroke.

The description of the start of a race in which the crawl stroke is used is presented in this chapter. The start of all distances of crawl swimming races is essentially the same, but the importance of having a good start is magnified as the swimming distance becomes shorter. The start of the breast stroke race is the same as that of the crawl until the body enters the water. The events which take place in the breast stroke race after the entry into the water are described in Chapter VIII.

Since the start of the backstroke race is altogether different from that of the start of the crawl or breast stroke, it is discussed in detail in Chapter VII.

The take-off platform is 18 inches above the surface of the water. It is flat and parallel to the water's surface. At the signal "Take your marks" the swimmer steps to the starting mark and assumes his starting position with his toes gripped over the edge of the pool. After holding a steady balance in this position for an appreciable length of time a pistol is fired. The swimmer throws his center of gravity in front of his base of support and then supplies the thrust which projects him forward from his mark with as much force as he can generate. He leaves the mark at the angle which will give him the greatest distance from his mark.

The start may be divided into the following components: (1) The preparatory position, (2) the step to the starting mark, (3) assuming the starting position, (4) leaving the mark, (5) the flight, (6) the entry, (7) the glide, and (8) the initial strokes.

1. **The Preparatory Position.**—After the contestant is in his proper lane and starting station, adequate warning is given by the

Fig. 1.—A, B.

Fig. 1.—A series of ideal form for the crawl stroke start. A. The preliminary stance. B. Coming "on the mark." C. On the mark in the momentary steadiness position. D. Preliminary movements for executing the drop after the gun is fired. E. The position for the drive. F. Position of the body leaving the mark. G. Position of the body in flight. H. Position of the body entering the water. I. Position of the body in the glide under the surface. J. Position of the body showing the start of the stroke at the end of the glide under the surface. K. Position of the body swimming to the surface.

Fig. 1.—C, D, E.

Fig. 1.—F, G, H.

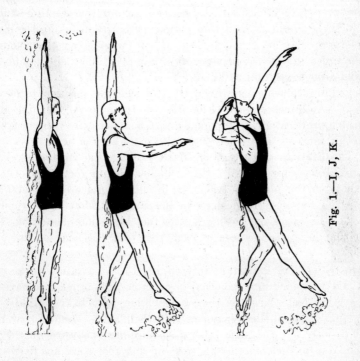

Fig. 1—I, J, K.

official starter that in a few moments the race will be under way. In these few brief moments, the swimmer must concentrate on the events which are to follow. In preparing himself for his race he can stretch, swing the arms in circles, and, by a few quick vibrating shakes, loosen the leg and arm muscles generally for relaxation and proper tonus. The swimmer should take several deep breaths, emphasizing the expiration phase, so as to insure adequate ventilation at the beginning of the race.

The preparatory position is assumed behind the starting station and in such proximity to it that little time is lost in taking the mark. This stance may be taken in one of two ways: (a) the swimmer stands erect in the preparatory position (Fig. 1A) and assumes a relaxed crouch position as he goes to his mark (Fig. 1B), and (b) a crouched stance which approximates the starting position to be employed. An erect stance (Fig. 1A) is recommended as the most favorable preparatory position since the swimmer can ventilate freely, shake his muscles, and easily sight down the course he is to swim.

2. **The Step to the Starting Mark.**—When the starter gives the signal "Take your marks," the swimmer should focus the eyes on the spots on the platform where he intends to place each foot (Fig. 1B). The swimmer then steps to the starting mark in a crouched posture. He steps on the mark, one foot at a time, watching carefully that he curls the toes of each foot over the edge of the platform.

Two factors are important in stepping to the starting mark: One is to take the mark in a crouched position and the other is to have the eyes see the feet placed on the marks rather than to feel blindly for the grip. Many sprint swimmers ruin their starts because they take off with only one foot, the other foot slipping backward on the flat surface due to the fact that the toes of that foot were not fixed over the edge of the pool.

Some competitors purposely come to their marks slowly with the intention of causing an overanxious swimmer to break from his marks before the pistol is fired.

3. **Assuming the Starting Position.**—A study of the starting positions used by competitive swimmers reveals a wide variation in techniques. The major differences occur in the position of the trunk. Two of the most commonly used types are described as follows:

(a) *The Full-Crouch Start.*—The trunk in this starting position is bent forward to an angle approximating a right angle with the

upright position (Fig. 1C). The full-crouch start is used by nearly all of the best swimmers since it allows a more "gathered" position for the spring.

(b) *The Semi-Crouch Start.*—This position is defined as one in which the trunk is bent forward at an angle of approximately 45° from the perpendicular. The semi-crouch position permits greater relaxation and has less tendency to cramp the swimmer if he becomes too tense on his mark.

Once the sprint swimmer has adopted his best starting posture he must next consider the position of his feet, knees, head and eyes, and arms.

The Position of the Feet.—The feet are parallel with each other and at right angles to the starting line (Fig. 1C). The lateral spacing of the feet depends upon the width of the hips and the structure of the bones of the legs. The foot position which seems most natural and presents the most stability is commonly one in which the feet are from three to six inches apart. This position places the ankle and knee joints directly below the hip joints and places the leg muscles in the optimum position for the dive. The feet are parallel to each other and at right angles to the starting line. The force of the ankle and leg drive is exerted directly over the toes which grip the edge of the platform. The mechanical advantage of the straight pull of the muscles in this position is diminished when the legs are overspread and the toes turned out. The weight of the body rests mainly on the balls of the feet. The heels rest lightly on the platform to give support while the swimmer is holding a steady balance in the starting position awaiting the pistol shot (Fig. 1C).

The grip of the toes is made with the second joint of the great toe flexed over the edge of the platform, the second toe curled slightly over. The third, fourth, and fifth toes assist slightly in the drive but give mainly lateral support. The grip of the toes also inhibits forward loss of balance.

The swimmer should never permit his body to sway on the mark. If the body is swaying backward at the pistol shot, the swimmer cannot project his body forward until the body has reached the end of the backward sway and has again recovered to the point of balance. This accounts for some swimmers being caught flat-footed. If a swimmer is caught back on his heels when the pistol is fired, he may partially overcome it by lifting his toes and the balls of his feet, thus shifting the point of support from behind the center of weight, so

3

that a forward motion can be started sooner. This shift of the base of support will result in a much faster start than would otherwise have been made.

It has always been the custom for swimmers to start from a flat-footed position on the edge of the pool. The success which sprint runners met with the use of inclined starting blocks on top of the track suggested that an inclined starting block might be of advantage to the swimmer. An investigation of the use of starting blocks in the swimming start showed quite conclusively that inclined starting blocks are a disadvantage to swimmers in leaving the mark, as far as starting time is concerned.[1]

The Position of the Knees.—The proper amount of flexion of the knees in the starting position is one in which a straight line passing from the acromion process of the shoulder to the malleolus, or ankle bone, will pass just in front of the kneecap (Fig. 1C). A greater knee-flexion would cause the heels to be lifted and the center of weight to be shifted forward to a position over the toes. In this forward position the swimmer is less stable and is effecting too great a tension on his extensor muscles. The knees should be so bent that the heels can rest lightly on the platform and further flexion and extension can take place freely. In this position the swimmer is well poised and is ready to execute a powerful drive from his mark.

The Position of the Hips.—The degree of flexion of the hips depends upon the choice of starting position. If the full-crouch position is used, the flexion is nearly complete, causing the trunk to be held in a horizontal plane, the hips held at about the same level as the shoulders (Fig. 1C). If the semi-crouch position is used the shoulders are held above the level of the hips. In both positions the hips are held far enough behind the center of support so that that portion of the body in front of the base is counterbalanced.

The Position of the Head and Eyes.—In the starting position when the swimmer has placed the feet on the mark, he then looks down the course of the pool to a point near the water level at the end of his lane on the opposite side of the pool. The head should be raised high enough so that the swimmer can easily see this point (Fig. 1C). In this position the eyes aid in holding a steady balance for an appreciable length of time, and also guide the flight of the body when leaving the mark.

[1]Tuttle, W. W., Morehouse, Laurence E., and Armbruster, David A.: Two Studies in Swimming Starts. I. The Use of Starting Blocks in Swimming Sprints, Research Quarterly **10**: 1 (March), 89-92, 1939.

The Position of the Arms (Fig. 1C).—The position of the arms depends upon the type of take-off technique employed and is designed in order to obtain the greatest speed possible, since the speed of the arm action in the drop phase of the start is of paramount importance. It may be said that the speed of the start can be no faster than the speed of the arms. If the arms are to act as stabilizers and are to control body balance, their action must coincide with the tremendously rapid action of the legs.

If the arms are to make the commonly used slightly upward and backward circular motion, it is best to have them slightly flexed in a downward hanging position. If merely a pump-handle swing is to be used, then the arms should be extended backward at approximately hip level. The elbows should be slightly flexed which shortens the radius and decreases the range of movement. This increases the speed of the arms in the get-away phase of the start. This technique allows more speed in starting and is especially advantageous to individuals who have a slower reaction time.

Now that the swimmer has assumed his starting position and is holding a steady balance, two further factors must be considered. They are, namely, breathing and attention.

Breathing.—While the swimmer is awaiting the command "Take your marks," he should be breathing deeply. During this period of increased ventilation, forceful expiration should be made in order to reduce the carbon dioxide content of the air in the lungs. When this is accomplished, the swimmer can hold his breath for a longer period of time and thus breathing does not interfere with his arm mechanics in the early part of the race.

Some experimenters have demonstrated that a few deep breaths of oxygen before a race will increase the performance over short distances. This experiment met with the same success when regular air was substituted for the oxygen and the swimmers kept ignorant of the change. Deep breathing (washing out the excess carbon dioxide) plus a psychologic factor (faith in the beneficial effects of oxygen) were evidently the causes of increased performance.

It requires approximately from 20 to 30 seconds to swim the 40, 50, or 60 yard dash. With adequate ventilation previous to the start, only a few breaths are required during the race.

If conditions were such that forced respiration could be continued until the moment before the swimmer entered the water, the beneficial effects of overventilation would be augmented. However, in order to maintain his equilibrium in a delicately balanced starting position while awaiting the pistol shot, the swimmer must halt the heaving movements of his thorax which accompany forced respiration.

In addition to aiding the swimmer to maintain a steady balance in the "set" position, cessation of respiration also aids the swimmer to give maximum attention while waiting for the pistol shot.

If a swimmer frequently loses his balance while in the starting position or is a slow starter, the coach may check the swimmer's breathing habits to find if he is properly holding his breath in the starting position while awaiting the pistol shot.

A short and deep inhalation at the take-off acts to increase the swimmer's buoyancy and prevents him from sinking too deep during the plunge and glide. It also provides air which further aids him to hold his breath without distress during the glide and the first few strokes.

A study of the respiratory habits of trained swimmers during the start of a race supports the following conclusions[2]:

(a) Prior to the starter's command, "Take your marks," trained swimmers either use forced respiration or breathe normally. After the command "Take your marks," as the swimmers assume the starting position and maintain a steady balance while awaiting the pistol shot, the breath is held at the end of a normal inspiration. After the pistol shot, as the swimmers prepare to leave their marks, a deep inspiration is made and is held.

(b) The respiratory habits of trained swimmers are similar to those of trained track runners. The adaptation of respiratory habits to race situations is, in most cases, so natural that the athlete acquires proper habits through practice and without advice from the coach.

Attention.—When the contestant is behind his starting station awaiting the starter's instructions, he sets about the task in the following brief moments to prepare himself for the race at hand: The swimmer's attention becomes closely fixed on the words of the starter as the instructions are given. He then makes the bodily adjustments in preparation for the signal "Take your marks." At this signal he carefully steps to the starting mark and assumes his starting position which he then holds for a period of momentary steadiness. It is during this period that attention must reach its peak. The swimmer is "set" for the gun; his breathing ceases, extraneous

---

[2]Morehouse, Laurence E.: The Respiratory Habits of Trained Swimmers During the Start of a Race, Research Quarterly 12: 2 (May), 186, 1941.

stimuli such as the noises and movements of the spectators and other contestants are shut out, and his entire organism is in a state of readiness for the pistol shot.

Attention occurs in waves, reaching a peak and subsiding continuously. Thus, the length of time the starter holds the swimmers at a steady balance in the starting position will affect the start.

It is a well-known fact that the interval of time that a starter holds swimmers on their marks is subject to individual variation. Some starters allow only a short interval and start the swimmers before they are ready, and others prolong the holding time so that the swimmers have passed their peaks of attention and the initiation of performance is prolonged when the pistol is finally fired.

The optimum interval of time that a swimmer should hold a steady balance in a starting position on his mark has been found to be 1.5 seconds.[3] Attention should be fixed on the act of starting rather than on the report of the gun. In the first condition, known as motor mindedness, the swimmer is responding automatically with a minimum of response time. If his attention is fixed on the report of the gun, a condition known as sensory mindedness, he must spend an additional time in starting by shifting his attention to the act of leaving his mark.

The starter who is "set" is similar to the powder in the shell of the pistol that is about to be discharged. When the powder is ignited by the spark it bursts forth with sudden violence and likewise the swimmer's energy is exploded by the pistol shot and he springs forward with a tremendous drive.

4. Leaving the Mark.—The act of leaving the mark may be divided into two parts, (a) the drop, and (b) the drive.

(a) *The Drop.*—The drop may be defined as that portion of leaving the mark which is concerned with shifting the center of the body weight to a position in front of the base of support so that force applied behind the center of weight in this position will drive the body forward. A well-executed drop requires skillful and rapid movements of the arms and legs to overcome the inertia of the swimmer in the steady balanced position. At the pistol shot, the arms, which have been either hanging downward or extended backward to a small degree, are flung backward and upward (Fig. 1D). This action aids

---

[3]Tuttle, W. W., Morehouse, Laurence E., and Armbruster, David A.: A Further Study of the Optimum Time for Holding a Swimmer on His Mark, Research Quarterly **11**: 1 (March), 53-56, 1940.

the body in moving forward. At the same time the body is continued forward by a slight extension of the knees and hips. At this moment a deep breath is taken and held.

The arms next reverse the swing from backward to forward. This is followed by a rapid body drop caused by a flexion at the hips, knees, and ankles. The heels now rest firmly on the platform until the body has almost reached the drive position and the ankles have been full flexed.

(b) *The Drive.*—The end of the drop occurs when the hips, knees, and ankles are flexed, and the arms have been swung forward as far as the knees (Fig. 1E). The body is leaning forward at a 60° angle when the drive is started. At this point the body is crouched and ready for an explosive forward spring. If the arms are too far forward or too far backward at this point, much power will be lost.

The drive now commences with a powerful action of both the legs and arms. The legs propel the body forward by an extension of the knees and hips. The arms are swung forward from the knees until they reach a position slightly below eye level. At this point the swing is suddenly halted.

The ankle is not extended until the arms are stopped near eye level. The ankles, being weaker joints than the knees or hips, are used to push the body forward after it is well under way. In this advantageous position they are snapped into extension adding considerable force to the forward speed at the end of the drive.

One of the simplest and most commonly used starts has been described above. There are variations in this form of starting which have proved to be equally as successful and deserve consideration here. The swimmer would benefit by practicing all the good forms of starts and selecting the one which advances him to a ten-yard distance in the shortest interval of time. An experiment devised to seek the best start revealed that among expert swimmers the start which was regularly used by each proved to be the best for him and that variations in arm or leg action of the style he had learned tended only to inhibit him. A similar experiment with inexperienced swimmers showed that the start which contained the simplest movements was the most successful.[4]

---

[4]Morehouse, Laurence E.: A Comparison of the Starting Times of Various Forms of Competitive Swimming Starts, Official Aquatic Guide, A. S. Barnes and Company, New York, 1941-42, page 66.

Variations in the Start.—There are numerous variations in starting technique which are worthy of consideration.

(a) *Circular Arm Action.*—This start was designed to move the body forward from the balanced position with greater rapidity than the former method. This extensively used technique employs a circular arm action and in this manner adds power to the arms in both the drop and the drive portions of the start.

In this starting position the arms hang downward along the sides of the hips. At the pistol shot, the knees and hips are extended slightly, lifting the body a little less than in the full crouch. At the same time the arms are moved forward with tremendous speed and are caught quickly directly below the shoulder level. The sudden check of the forward motion of the arms is conducive to a rapid forward movement of the body. The arms then continue in an outward and upward circular sweep and the body drops. The body is now nearly in a position for the drive. The arms are now carried downward with great force to gather speed so that when the hands reach the point opposite the knees and the body, they are in a position to facilitate a vicious drive off the mark (Fig. 1E). The drive is then performed as described in the standard start.

The chief criticism of this manner of starting is that the arms perform too great a range of movement to allow a fast start.

(b) *Knee Action Technique.*—The swimmer using this technique fixes his hips and uses only his knees in the maneuver of the legs in the drop to the drive position. This start is suited for relay races as the head is held downward and the swimmer can see his teammate approach the finish mark under him.

The starting position of the swimmer employing the knee action technique is similar to the full-crouch start. Following the pistol shot, the circular arm action is applied. The head is held low to keep the trunk from rising. At the instant the arms swing forward following the pistol shot, the knees straighten and the body is extended forward. The knees are then rapidly flexed and the forward speed of the body is increased due to the shortened radius. By the time the knees have dropped to a position of full flexion, the arms have completed their circular movement and have arrived opposite the knees. The body is now ready for the drive which is executed as described in the full-crouch start (Fig. 1E).

The knee action technique can also be accompanied by the standard arm swing.

(c) *Knee Flexion Technique.*—Although this type of start considerably reduces stability in the starting position, it yields a very fast start when it is once mastered. Some swimmers with a slow response time but with good equilibrium find that whereas they were always the last to leave their marks with other starts, they are now among the first with the knee-flexion technique.

In the starting position the knees are held straight, not hyperextended, and the body is bent forward at the hips. The arms are held backward at a level slightly above that of the hips. The head is held well up.

In this stance the weight is carried further forward to a point at the front of the balls of the feet and just behind the toes. The body is held at a steady balance in this precarious position.

At the pistol shot the knees are promptly flexed causing the body to drop forward toward the drive position. The arms are held backward as the body drops under them. When the body has nearly reached the drive position, the arms are swept downward. When the arms coincide with the knees, the drive is started and is carried out in the standard manner.

An additional speed-imparting skill can be added to this and other starts for use by those gifted with a high degree of equilibrium. While holding the steady balance awaiting the pistol shot, the swimmer can slowly lower the trunk so that when the pistol is discharged the body is already in motion. The force will be applied, then, in changing the direction of the motion instead of starting the motion from a position at rest. A steady balance must be held during this slow lowering of the body as the competitor will be charged with a false start if he has gained unfair advantage by being off balance in the direction of the start when the pistol is discharged.

(d) *The Toe-Lift Technique.*—The skills which are included in this start are still in the experimental stage but favorable results from repeated trials have indicated that they are well worth while considering. The essential merit of this technique is its simplicity. The leg action is so fast, however, that any arm action yet devised cannot gather satisfactory momentum in so short a time as to be able to coincide with it.

This technique can be employed from the full-crouch position. The body is inclined forward, head up, arms back just below hip level, knees slightly flexed, and the toes in the regular gripping position. The center of weight is over the balls of the feet. At the pistol shot, the toe muscles are relaxed and the support is removed from the front of the feet and transferred to the heels. This transfer of support to a point behind the center of weight causes the body to fall forward at a rapid rate.

As the body commences to drop, the knees are flexed and the arms are then quickly swung forward so that their action coincides with that of the knees at the initial stage of the drive (Fig. 1E).

Some power is lost during the drive since the arms have not gained sufficient speed. This deficit may be somewhat compensated for by the additional power gained from the swiftly falling body as the impetus is changed to a forward direction by the drive.

Motion picture studies show that nearly all sprint swimmers slightly relax the great toe and allow the weight to fall somewhat backward to the heels during the drop. This shift occurs naturally during all types of starts. The toe-lift technique is merely an exaggeration of this natural tendency.

When the body reaches the beginning of the drive position, the toes again forcefully grip the edge of the pool. This prevents slipping and also provides a firm support for the drive from the edge of the starting station.

5. **The Flight.**—The swimmer leaves the 18-inch take-off with his body in a nearly horizontal position. His body follows a regular parabolic curve as it is projected forward through the air.

The extension of the ankle during the final part of the drive tends to throw the legs upward. If this is allowed to occur, the body will be projected toward the water at too sharp an angle and the swimmer will enter too soon and in a disadvantageous position. In order to avoid throwing the legs upward the toes should remain in contact with the take-off until the ankles are fully extended (Fig. 1F).

The angle of the take-off should be nearly horizontal, never being more than 20 degrees above the horizontal. A take-off at an angle below the horizontal from the take-off will result in an entry that is too near the starting mark, too deep, and lacking in momentum. On the other hand, if the take-off is nearly horizontal the entry will be at a greater distance from the mark, the body will remain near the surface of the water, and will result in a longer and faster glide due to the advantageous application of force (Fig. 1F).

As the swimmer leaves the mark, his head is held up and his eyes are looking forward. Care must be exercised that the head is not held so high that the body becomes arched. When an alignment is attempted from an arched position, the swimmer frequently overcompensates and enters the water with his arms and legs dragging which results in retarding his forward motion.

If the swimmer keeps his head up until near the end of the flight and then drops it between his arms, he has a tendency to raise his arms and lower his legs. This type of entry is thought by some to facilitate the first strokes because the shoulders are not submerged and thus the arms are free to start stroking. Repeated observations have shown, however, that the extended shallow glide is faster than the leg drag and early arm action.

The head should be lowered to a position between the arms in the early period of the flight (Fig. 1F). In this position the body is held steady on a horizontal level which facilitates a proper entry (Fig. 1G and H).

6. **The Entry.**—If the take-off has been performed at a level approaching the horizontal and the body parts of the swimmer have been held in a good alignment, the entry will be made at a maximum distance from the mark. The finger tips are first to enter and the rest of the body follows at an angle of from 8 to 10 degrees, following the same opening the finger tips have made in the surface (Fig. 1H).

If the swimmer enters the water in a horizontal position, he will remain at the surface. The forward momentum in this position would be retarded by contracurrents of water set up by the parts of the body which present a lateral surface to the water. If the entry is too angular, the swimmer will submerge too deeply and his course will be curvilinear and time-consuming.

As the body enters the water, it should be held rigid. The fingers and palms are held in line with the arms, and the feet and toes in line with the legs. The head is held low between the arms, and the back of the head in line with the upper surface of the arms. The arms are to be pressed against the sides of the head and the thumbs and index fingers of the hands are held together. The whole body is in a streamlined position (Fig. 1H).

Upon striking the water the arms must be pressed downward in order to keep their alignment in the presence of the force of the water.

Observations have been made of the effectiveness of entering the water with the feet held in a narrow stride position so that the flutter kick can be commenced in the air or as soon as the legs are submerged.

This early leg action was found to retard the forward motion instead of accelerating it. An early arm action was found to be a detriment also.

7. The Glide.—As the body disappears through the surface, it is held stretched in the same streamlined position as during the flight (Fig. 1I). The distance and speed of the glide depend upon the impetus given by the drive from the mark, the extent of the trajectory to the water, and the resistance of the water to the body in its forward motion.

The water resistance is greatest at the surface and is heightened by the whirling or eddying motion of choppy water. The glide, then, should be just far enough below the surface to allow all parts of the body to escape these swirls.

The fingers do not have to be planed upward in order to guide the body toward the surface. As momentum is lost the body rises toward the surface due to the specific gravity of the water which is higher than that of most individuals who are holding their breath.

8. The Initial Strokes.—When the speed at the glide is reduced to a point where it is no greater than the maximum swimming speed, the initial strokes should be made. The swimmer can cultivate the feel of the speed by noting the sensation caused by the friction of the water against the surface of the body at various rates.

At this point, the legs start their drive and the arm opposite from the breathing side executes the first arm pull (Fig. 1J). This prevents the temptation to turn the head for air after the first arm pull. Turning the head is detrimental to arm action and body balance at this point as the body is still low in the water and the head would have to be raised too high to get a breath. The swimmer should learn to hold his breath until he is well under way and his pace has been set. If adequate ventilation has occurred just before the start, this breath-holding will not be uncomfortable.

The first arm pull is started while the body is still about 8 to 12 inches below the water's surface. The arm movement is started by depressing the hand and starting the pull backward. The elbow is then flexed and the arm is drawn backward. The arm action does not start with a strong down stroke as this would cause the body to be driven upward instead of forward, resulting in a loss of speed. The body is pushed forward and breaks to the surface with great speed (Fig. 1K).

The head is held down during the first arm pull. It is then gradually raised to the swimming position with each succeeding arm stroke until the third arm stroke is reached. While the initial arm is pulling, slight supporting pressure is exerted on the other arm. This places it in readiness at the proper depth to start the arm pull as soon as the other arm has finished its stroke.

A forceful kick during the initial strokes lends stability to the arm action and aids in driving the body forward to the surface. The rhythm of the legs must coincide with the arm action from the beginning. A narrow, fast kick tends to cause a swimmer to speed up his arm action to a faster rate than that which he has been accustomed to using. He then often finds it difficult to reduce this rhythm to his natural pace. The optimum speed of the initial leg and arm strokes is that which approaches the rate of the regular swimming rhythm.

CHAPTER III

THE SPRINT CRAWL

The modern crawl stroke is the fastest and the most efficient stroke used by competitive swimmers today. In all freestyle events from the short 50 or 60 yard dash to the 1500 meters race, the crawl stroke is universally used.

There are two forms of swimming the modern crawl. The first, the sprint crawl stroke, is used for short dashes in which the conservation of energy is not a factor, and the second, the distance crawl stroke, is used in races in which energy must be conserved and distributed over the course of the race. In the freestyle, races of 100 yards and less are generally considered as sprints. According to this definition, competitors who must conserve their energy by swimming at a speed slower than their maximum in order to complete a 100 yard swim must consider this race as a distance swim. Until they have improved their condition to such an extent that they can swim the 100 yards at their top speed, the race, to them, is not a sprint.

The essential differences between the methods of swimming the sprint and the distance crawl lie in the duration of the arm and leg cycles and the manner in which each arm performs the first act of the pull after it has entered the water. In order to lengthen the duration of the arm and leg cycles for distance swimming, there is a sliding movement added to the arm stroke. The slide occurs just after the arm enters the water and before the pull is started. The duration of the slide depends upon the pace desired. In swimming the sprint crawl, the slide is reduced to a minimum, and the arm is pressed downward into the driving position as soon as it enters the water.

In order to obtain maximum speed, the modern crawl is swum in the sprint style. This style is described in full in this chapter. Modifications of the sprint crawl which adapt it to middle distance and distance swimming are discussed later.

Characteristics of Sprint Swimmers.—A wide range of difference will be found among top-flight sprint swimmers. Competitors with only one leg have been among the place winners in county and state championships. In general, though, one will find top-ranking swimmers to be examples of physical perfection. A large number of these have developed from weaklings and poorly skilled individuals to powerful and smooth performers.

There are certain characteristics which will aid in sprint swimming performance. These can be divided into three classes, anatomic, physiologic, and psychologic.

The anatomic qualifications are probably the most important. These represent the equipment of the swimmer. The efficiency with which he uses this equipment depends upon his physiologic and psychologic functions. The oft-repeated rule that a good big man has the advantage over a good little man still applies in top-flight swimming.

A long hand will provide a good lever, but it must be accompanied by powerful wrist and arm muscles if this lever is to be effective. Due to the wide range of movement of the shoulder girdle during sprint swimming, the muscles attached to this girdle must be flexible. The arm depressors, especially, must be supple.

The muscles of the back and abdomen must be powerful as they are the muscles of fixation of the thorax and pelvis. The vigorous arm and shoulder movements and the driving leg action must originate from stable bases, if these movements are to be effective. The body which sags in the middle and wobbles during the swimming action will not be streamlined and greater resistance will be met in the water.

The hips should be thin and yet powerful. The buttocks should slope from the back to the thighs. A buttock which is undercut presents an abrupt surface which causes a drag in the water. In other words, the body should be shaped more like a torpedo than like a rowboat.

The legs should be long and slender with flexible and strong muscles. An item of great importance is the ankle. This joint must be of the type which allows a large range of extension. Such an ankle is usually slender and the joints in the ankle and foot are loose. A simple test of ankle flexibility is made by sitting on the floor with the legs extended forward and turning the feet inward and downward in a pigeon-toed fashion in an attempt to touch the floor with all the toes. Full efficiency in swimming the crawl cannot be realized until this degree of extension can be reached. This movement can be developed in most individuals through constant application of a few simple exercises which are presented in Chapter X.

The feet should be long, slender, and flexible in order to achieve a free fishtail action. A foot that presents a long lever will be an efficient paddle as the leg muscles are capable of providing powerful action to it as the leg completes the upward and downward drive.

Individuals with short necks have difficulty in turning the head in breathing in the crawl stroke. The long-necked individual seems to tie-up less. In full-speed swimming the individual with the long neck can lift the head better in acquiring the desired planed position.

The foremost physiologic qualification is speed. A sprint swimmer must be a quick mover. He must have a fast response at the start and at the turn, and he must be capable of moving his legs at a high rate of speed in order to coordinate them with his driving arm action.

The muscles must be powerful in order to develop the tremendous horsepower needed to overcome the water resistance. As the speed is increased the resistance of the water becomes greater and consequently more power is required to keep the swimmer moving at a high rate of speed.

The recovery phase operates mainly after the sprint race is over. Still, the condition must be such that energy-yielding foods are readily available for muscular contraction during the race and the waste carrying mechanisms must be able to remove the excess products of fatigue which would inhibit the action of the working muscles were they allowed to remain. The heart must be capable of moving large amounts of blood and the lungs must be able to transfer the gases to and from the blood at a high rate in order to ward off fatigue.

The sprint swimmer who must move his arms and legs at a continuous rapid rate over a distance often becomes tied-up. This occurs most frequently in those who are poorly coordinated. These individuals require more energy to overcome the waste movements. The sprint swimmer must train rigidly in order to derive a perfect stroke coordination. Some swimmers are faster learners than others and achieve this measure of skill in a relatively short time. Others must devote hours of conscientious practice in order to reach this stage of training.

Comparative Marks in Freestyle Sprint Competition.—The distances in the sprint events for both high school and college differ accordingly as the length of the course differs. In either high school or college, distances remain the same in sprinting events.

	WORLD'S RECORD	AMERICAN RECORD	INTERCOLLEGIATE RECORD	HIGH SCHOOL RECORD
Twenty-yard Course				
40 yards freestyle		:17.6[1]		:18.0
60 yards freestyle		:28.4	:28.6	
100 yards freestyle		:49.8	:51.4	:52.6
Short Course (25 yards)				
50 yards freestyle		:22.6	:22.9	:23.5
100 yards freestyle	:51.0	:51.0	:51.6	:52.6
Long Course (50 yards and over)				
50 yards freestyle		:22.8	:23.1	
100 yards freestyle		:52.0	:53.1	

It is well to note that world records are not acceptable which are made in the twenty-yards course. This is due to the advantage gained by additional turns. However, American records are acceptable. World records can be established in either the short course (25 yards) or the long course (50 yards and over).[2] The 40-yards event has been discontinued in major college competition and the 60-yards event has been substituted.

The Technique of the Sprint Crawl

The components of the sprint crawl will be discussed in the following order: (1) the body position, (2) the leg action, (3) the arm action, (4) coordination of the arms, (5) coordination of the legs and arms, (6) breathing, (7) coordination of breathing with the sprint crawl stroke, (8) the sprint crawl turn, and (9) the finish.

1. **The Body Position.**—Nature has given streamline bodies to fish, but the human body must be held in a position to follow the natural lines of streamline flow in order to eliminate the turbulence which retards the motion of the swimmer.

(a) *The Position of the Head and Neck.*—The head is carried well up with the face only in the water (Fig. 2A). The water level varies from a position just below the eyes to one at the level of the hairline. This variation is in accordance with the height of the bow wave in front of the head and the buoyancy of the swimmer.

---

[1]Noteworthy performances, not records.

[2]See Rules, Amateur Athletic Union of U. S. Official Swimming Rules. Published by Amateur Athletic Union of U. S., 233 Broadway, New York, N. Y.

Also, National Collegiate Athletic Association, Intercollegiate and Interscholastic Swimming Guide, Official Rules Swimming and Diving. American Sports Publishing Co., New York, N. Y.

The bow wave will be higher as the swimmer increases his speed and will lower as the speed diminishes. When the swimmer is towed at full speed through the water with his body assuming a swimming position, the bow wave is near the hairline and when this speed is reduced the water level will be near the eyebrows.

A difference in buoyancy will also affect the optimum height at which the head is carried. A great many sprinters are exceedingly muscular and have a heavy skeleton. This type of swimmer does not float as high in the water as do individuals with lighter skeletons, less musculature, and more adipose tissue. The less buoyant individuals will thus swim lower in the water with the water level near the eyebrows, even at maximum speed.

In all events the head should be held high enough so that the water is permitted to slip under the face and body. The bow wave should wash around the sides of the head and shoulders, not over them.

The eyes are directed forward in a natural position and are not peering upward from under the eyebrows or sideward from the corners of the eyes. The eyes are the main aids in the control of the body position. If they are directed in an upward or sideward position the body will be easily thrown out of equilibrium and the propelling motion of the arms and legs will be inhibited. The eyes are centered on the forward plane of progression. When the head is turned for an inhalation, the eyes move with it but quickly return to the centered position and remained fixed in this position until the next inhalation. Any sideward rolling motion of the body should not alter the stability of the vision.

The nose and chin are also held in a centered position and excepting for the turn of the head for breathing, they do not oscillate with any rolling movement of the body. After the inhalation they also recover to the center. The head cannot be held steady if the neck is too rigid. In this condition, any movement of the trunk is transmitted to the head.

It is commonly observed that if the head is turned from side to side during the exhalation phase of the crawl stroke, an unbalanced leg action will result. This reduces the driving power of the legs and thus should be avoided.

The chin is carried forward, away from the throat, except when turning for air. When the head is turned for air, the chin is tucked into a position in front of the shoulders and in line with the arm pit

4

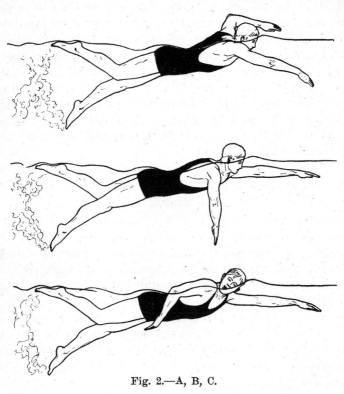

Fig. 2.—A, B, C.

Fig. 2.—A series of ideal form for the modern sprint crawl stroke showing the six leg beats and one revolution of the arm stroke. These figures also show the counterbalance of arm and leg action, the turning of the head for air in the stroke, and the body position in relation to the surface. A. Beat 1. B. Beat 2. C. Beat 3. D. Beat 4. E. Beat 5. F. Beat 6.

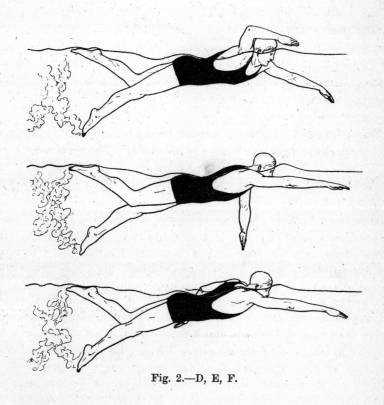

Fig. 2.—D, E, F.

so that a relatively smooth surface is presented by the side of the face, neck, and chest wall (Fig. 2C) so that the water can flow under them with little resistance.

The chin should not be held so far forward that wrinkles appear in the back of the neck. This rigid posture is most apt to be found, especially, in individuals with short necks. A strained position of the neck will result in early fatigue as constant turning of the head in this position requires a greater effort. A rigid neck position usually is accompanied by a rigid body position also. In this condition muscles must work against each other as well as against the resistance of the water and additional work must be done to overcome this additional load.

Although the head moves independently of the shoulder girdle and upper spine, the proper position of the head is aided by an accommodating posture of the shoulder girdle and upper spine. Likewise, a good body position is dependent upon the posture of the head and neck.

The speed developed by the powerful movements of the sprint crawl will naturally elevate the head and shoulders. The swimmer, therefore, does not need to lift his head and shoulders. In fact, they are pressed somewhat forward and downward, giving the impression of swimming downhill.

A common fault of sprint swimmers attempting to get a good head position is to raise the head and neck too high. In this position too much energy must be dissipated by exerting the downward force of the arms which is necessary to hold the head high. Such a position also causes the lower trunk to compensate by sinking into the water. The stream of water flowing past the body in motion then offers additional resistance as it is broken into turbulence as large volumes of water close in over the back and are sent whirling off in eddies.

(b) *The Position of the Shoulder Girdle and Upper Spine.*—The shoulder girdle serves as a base for the action of the arms. It is formed by the scapulae and clavicles. The girdle is incomplete behind, the scapulae being connected to the trunk by muscles only. It is light and very mobile.

The position of the shoulder girdle during the sprint crawl is designed to permit the maximum power and efficiency of the arm strokes. The scapulae should be held flat and the clavicles held as level as is possible during the race. The upper level of the shoulder is slightly below that of the top of the head (Fig. 2B).

The shoulders are raised forward in the direction of the movement of the body. In this position the arms are able to execute a stronger pull and the scapulae can articulate freely during the recovery.

The upper spine is also flexed slightly forward. In this position the sprint crawl swimmer presents the appearance of being somewhat hunchbacked (Fig. 2B). This position not only affords a freer but also a more powerful arm action due to the more mechanically advantageous position of the arm depressor muscles. It also places the trunk in a more streamline position. The whole surface of the thorax and abdomen is flattened and presents a minimum of elevations or depressions. As the swimmer propels himself through the water, his body level under the surface is parallel with the surface of the water and the water can thus pass under this plane with the least amount of resistance due to turbulence.

Resistance is further eliminated by this plane position as the back and hips ride high in the water and a smooth thin stream slithers along the sides and past the hips in an unbroken sheath. The swimmer in this position experiences the sensation of swimming downhill. A common error in the position of the shoulder girdle and upper spine is to exaggerate their forward position. In this overly arched position, mechanical advantage of the arms is decreased and power is therefore diminished. A high position of the upper spine also tends to result in a marked depression of the lower back and hips (Fig. 2B) and large quantities of water are allowed to whirl over them and further energy is lost.

(c) *The Position of the Hips.*—During the sprint crawl the hips, like the shoulders, remain level. They serve as a base for the articulations of the legs. The hips are carried slightly lower than the shoulders and move through the water just below the surface (Fig. 2B).

The position of the hips varies among individuals as the contour of the hips differs widely. Some swimmers' hips are shaped to follow the natural lines of streamline flow. This type has narrow hips and small, flat buttocks. They hold a distinct advantage over those whose hips and buttocks are large and less streamlined. The large hipped swimmers have greater water resistance as the stream of water passing around the wide hips and large buttocks breaks into turbulence and resistance is thus encountered.

The water flows over narrow hips and small buttocks in an unbroken stream which causes much less resistance and allows the water to remain in the most effective condition for the propulsive leg action.

Swimmers with large hips should submerge them more than those with small hips in order to permit the water to flow smoothly over them. Those with smaller streamline hips can carry them higher with the legs well down in the water so that the body is held level and the legs are in the most favorable position for the propelling action of the flutter kick.

(d) *The Position of the Legs.*—The legs are held fully extended. The ankles and knees pass close by each other in a supple movement. An efficient leg action appears as though the legs were made of rubber.

During the sprint crawl the legs move well under the surface (Fig. 2A) in order to gain maximum traction in the water. No propulsive force is gained by any part of the foot when it is out of the water; therefore, the feet should be beneath the surface at all times. If the hips are allowed to sink too low in the water, the heels are apt to be raised too high and they break through to the surface and lose power.

Another common fault in the leg position is to allow the heels to drift apart in order to accommodate the toeing inward. In this spread position the legs lose some of their driving power and the outward surfaces of the legs present a resistance to the forward motion of the swimmer.

In most individuals the proper alignment of the body position can be checked by drawing a straight line from the midpoint of the shoulder joint through the midpoint of the hip joint, the line being extended backward past the feet. If the body is in proper alignment, this line will pass exactly through a point which is midway between the ankle joints when the legs are fully spread in the stride position at the end of each beat (Fig. 2). In this position the legs are operating directly behind the body providing the force in the most effective manner.

2. **The Leg Action.**—The action of the legs in the sprint crawl has been termed the "flutter kick." Because of its general usage and also because no really descriptive term has yet been assigned to it, the leg action will continue in this treatise to be called the "flutter kick."

The legs neither "flutter" nor "kick" but oscillate forcibly and regularly, serving to push the water backward with each vertical abduction and adduction. In order to derive maximum force from the leg action, the swimmer must have trained and strengthened his leg muscles to endure the continuous vigorous motion of the flutter kick. This may be accomplished by daily drills with the aid of the kicking board. While using the kicking board the body position should simulate that of the regular sprint crawl position. Many bad swimming habits can result from careless use of the kicking board. The swimmer should strive not only to get his legs in top condition, but also to train his legs to perform in a manner which will allow him to derive the greatest amount of drive from each beat of the legs.

The most efficient sprint crawl leg action is one which resembles the action of a fish's tail. Although the swimmer's legs move in a vertical plane and the fish's tail in a horizontal plane, their propulsive action is derived from the same principle. The swimmer's leg propels him forward with both the forward and the backward swing just as the fish's tail propels him forward with each sideward swing.

The swimmer's leg, however, possesses a structural limitation which is not present in the tail of the fish. His knee joint restricts movement to a backward one only. If the knee joint allowed movement forward as well as backward, the swimmer could use his legs in the same range as that used by a fish during swimming. In order to compensate for this structural limitation, a slight variation from the fishtail action is made as the downward beat is completed. If the reader would sit on the edge of his chair and, leaning back slightly, go through the motions of pedaling a bicycle, he will get a good concept of what the compensated fishtail action ought to be. Note the action of each joint as well as the movements of the limbs. The pedal is pressed with the ball of the foot on the forward and downward stroke. The knee is straightened on the downward stroke and then the foot is pressed more firmly against the pedal as it is pushed backward and then slightly upward. As the foot presses upward, the knee bends again and the pushing power is diminished.

In the water the swimmer's leg action and range of motion is nearly identical to that of the bicycle rider. In riding a bicycle the pressure is always exerted on the balls of the feet, whereas in swimming the crawl the pressure is exerted alternately, on the soles of the feet in the upward tread and on the instep in the downward tread.

The movement in the flutter kick leg action originates at the hip joint and is transmitted through the thigh to the knee joint. In whiplike motion the wave passes from the knee to the lower leg and next to the ankle and finally to the foot which is lashed like the free end of a rope which is being snapped. The initial movement is in the hips in both the upward and downward beat.

At the beginning of the upward leg movement the hip is slightly flexed and the knee and ankle are extended (Fig. 2A). With the extension of the hip the water is pressed backward by the posterior surface of the thigh and the body is moved forward. This backward flow continues along the back of the leg and is finally whipped behind by the sole of the foot. The flow of water is thus forced backward with ever-increasing speed and, as it leaves the foot, the snap of the ankle sends it backward with a tremendous driving force thus propelling the body forward.

When the leg finishes its upward beat, the hips and knees are slightly flexed and the ankles are extended (Fig. 2A). The downward beat of the leg starts with the leg in this position. As in the upward leg beat the action starts from the hips. A small flexion at the hips sends the water washing backward along the anterior surface of the thigh. The knee is then extended (Fig. 3A). The water is thus driven backward along the anterior surface of the leg and down over the ankles as the body is driven forward.

The toes are turned inward in a pigeon-toed fashion during the down stroke (Fig. 3A[3]) in order to contact more water with the tops of the feet. Toeing in during the down stroke pushes the water backward at a more effective angle as the foot can be farther extended in this position, and thus the body gains forward speed.

In order to execute an efficient leg drive in this fashion, the leg muscles must be flexible, powerful, and able to relax to such an extent that they exert only a minimum of tension upon the joints which are being moved by their reciprocal muscles. Swimmers' muscles, when relaxed, give the appearance of being loose and elastic.

The advantage of possessing large feet and flexible ankles is apparent when the mechanics of the flutter kick are considered. The effectiveness of the kick will be limited by the degree of extension of the ankles. The lashing action of the foot provides the major propulsive action of the legs. If the ankle is stiff and movement limited, this lashing action is lost and the legs do not provide their share of the propelling force.

The feet act as paddles and swimmers with the largest feet naturally have the most effective paddles. The ideal foot for swimming is long, thin, and flexible.

The ankles, however, can be made more flexible by stretching and limbering exercises such as those described in Chapter X.

The upward leg action is more effective in propelling the crawl swimmer forward than is the downward action. The greater propulsive force on the up-beat is due to the more favorable mechanical action of the joints in the movement. The slight knee flexion and powerful ankle extension as the leg completes its upward sweep contributes to the fishtail action which is capable of sending large amounts of water backward from the sole of the foot. This fishtail action is inhibited on the downward kick as the lashing motion is restricted by the inability of the knee to bend forward. The small amount of propelling surface presented by the instep as compared with that of the sole of the foot is also a restricting factor.

The width of the flutter kick stride should be from 18 to 26 inches, depending on the length of the swimmer's legs and the speed with which he moves. Due to the refraction of the water, the stride appears much narrower and appears to be from 12 to 18 inches wide. Since observation windows have been erected,[3] the swimming strokes can be analyzed with less refractive error.

Observations have been made of one-legged swimmers and swimmers using the dolphin breast stroke kick in which the legs are held together and move up and down in unison. These have shown that propulsion from the flutter kick is not a result of a series of vertical scissors kicks which served to squeeze the water out from the wedges formed by the legs approaching each other, but rather, each leg forces the water backward from its anterior and posterior surfaces while acting as individual propulsive units, the result being a forward propulsion of the body.

Turbulent water that is swirling and eddying is an inhibiting factor to the driving force of the legs. The legs act best well below the surface of the water because water agitated by other swimmers or by waves striking against the side of the pool is less effectual than water that is smooth and quiet.

The water disturbed by one leg detracts from the efficiency of the other leg in the flutter kick. This may be the reason why swimmers

[3]Armbruster, David A.: Under-Water Observation Windows, Intercollegiate and Interscholastic Swimming Guide, Spalding's Athletic Library, No. 491, pp. 71-73, 1940.

can progress faster using the dolphin kick than by using the flutter kick. A further advance in speed in freestyle sprint swimming may result from a combination of the dolphin kick with the crawl arm stroke. The best arm-stroke rhythm yet found for the dolphin kick is the butterfly—the alternating arm stroke does not coordinate with rhythm because of less counteraction force.

Common faults in the sprint crawl leg action are: (a) kicking with the legs too near the surface, (b) spreading the legs laterally so that the heels are beyond hip width, (c) kicking away from the vertical plane, especially during inhalation, (d) holding the ankles in a rigid extended position, (e) holding the feet, toed inward during the upward stroke, and (f) holding the knees in a rigid extended position.

3. **The Arm Action.**—In the sprint crawl, the arms alternately reach forward into the water and pull the body forward over the surface. The arm is then quickly recovered out of the water and placed in position in the water for the next stroke. For the purpose of analysis the sprint crawl arm stroke may be classified into seven components: (a) entry, (b) support, (c) catch, (d) pull, (e) push, (f) release, and (g) recovery.

(a) *Entry.*—The arm must enter the water in such a manner that it is immediately placed in the most favorable position for a forceful stroke as well as taking hold of as much water as possible. In the sprint crawl the hand begins its propulsive action as soon as it penetrates through the water's surface.

For the purpose of this discussion the arm entry will be defined as that period in the crawl arm cycle which starts when the hand passes in front of the shoulder following the recovery and ends when the arm is finally in the supporting position.

If the arm has been recovered with the elbow flexed and carried high, the elbow is usually slightly in advance of the hand when the arm passes over the shoulder. The forearm hangs in a nearly vertical position. The wrist is flexed or laterally flexed and the palm and fingers are directed backward in order to pass over the water. Before the hand enters the water it must be straightened so that the fingers are parallel to the line of progression and the palm is held horizontal to the surface of the water. If the hand enters the water with the thumb side or little finger side inclined downward, the hand loses its supporting and propulsive effectiveness.

If the arm has recovered in a low flat plane, the hand is in advance of the elbow as the hand passes over the shoulder. The forearm is carried almost horizontal to the water's surface. In both types of recovery the elbow is held higher than the hand (Fig. 2D).

Following the "high" recovery, the forearm is swung straight forward from a vertical position to a horizontal position in front of the shoulder. After the "low" recovery, however, the forearm is continued to be swung forward from a sideward horizontal position until it is directed forward in front of the shoulder.

As the hand reaches forward and the arm is extended for the entry, the shoulder girdle is held high and not allowed to extend forward with the reach. Although the forward displacement of the swimmer's shoulder girdle would increase the extent of the reach several inches, this displacement places the shoulder in a distinct mechanical disadvantage for the propulsive arm action. A shoulder displacement also tends to result in a lateral movement of the body which impedes forward progression.

With the shoulder in a fixed position, more of the body weight is held over the arm and represents potential energy for the arm drive. The shoulder and arm muscles are also in a better position to draw the arm downward and backward through the water.

The straight arm is dropped into the water directly in front of the shoulder. The shoulder remains high (Fig. 2E) and as the arm contacts the water, the hand and forearm are pressed downward. The tip of the elbow is pointing sideward and is held in this position to prevent hyperextension of the elbow and also to prevent the shoulder from dropping as the arm is pressed downward.

As the arm is pressed below the surface of the water, the swimmer's shoulder moves slightly forward, not downward, so that as pressure is applied to the hand and forearm, the body weight is shifted over the arm until the catch is made. This action gives the sprinter the sensation of swimming downhill. Actually, however, the shoulder and the rest of the body are moving straight forward on a level with the surface of the water.

When the sprint crawl swimmer is at full speed, the wave in front of his head and shoulders causes the surface water in front of him to be swelled up into an inclined plane (Fig. 2D, also Fig. 3A). It is along the surface of this plane that the arm enters the water. The angle that the arm drops into the water depends, therefore, upon the height of this wave which, in turn, depends upon the velocity, size, and body position of the swimmer.

Common faults in the sprint crawl arm entry are (1) smashing the arm into the water which splits the water and allows a great deal of slip, (2) pressing the hand into the water with either the thumb or the little finger leading, (3) turning the elbow downward as the arm is pressed into the water, thus allowing the shoulder to drop, (4) reaching too far forward by displacing the shoulder which results in a loss of power and a disadvantageous position for the use of the body weight, and (5) reaching forward with the hand too high above the surface of the water, or (6) dropping the hand into the water too soon before the arm is extended.

(b) *The Support.*—In the sprint crawl, the arm and hand serve to propel the swimmer forward as soon as they enter the water and continue this propulsive action until they are removed for the recovery. The main propulsive action does not begin until the arm is in a favorable driving position below the surface of the water. The interval elapsing between the entry and the position at which the arm starts its major propulsive action is the supporting phase of the sprint crawl arm action. This supporting phase of the stroke serves to maintain the head and shoulders at the proper elevation above the surface of the water.

As the arm enters the water it slides forward on a line parallel to the center line of progression. The fingers are forward and slightly downward. The tip of the elbow is pointing outward and the elbow joint is slightly flexed so that there is approximately a hand's length of extension remaining as the arm slides forward and downward into the water. The shoulder is held high and somewhat drawn inward (Fig. 2F).

The angle at which the arm slides through the water during the supporting phase of the arm stroke depends upon the swimmer's speed. If the speed is slow, the angle is less and the arm glides at a depth just below the water's surface. If the speed is fast the elbow is bent further and the arm is thrust into the water at a slightly deeper angle. Each variation is very slight but very essential and important. The reason for this variance is obvious. At slower speeds a greater support is needed to maintain the body elevation, therefore, a more shallow slide should be used to prevent bobbing up and down with each stroke. At faster speeds the water pressure on the face and chest is greater, and the body elevation does not need to be supplemented by as much additional support by the arms.

In the sprint crawl this supporting phase is reduced to the minimum required to stabilize the body position. The arm is thrust into the water in a manner in which but very little emphasis is given to support, but much is given to propulsion.

During the brief slide the fingers and palm are pressed downward, and the water beneath them is forced backward under the forearm thus generating propelling power. By pressing downward with the hand and slightly elevating the elbow tip and shoulder, the widest portion of the forearm is presented to the water. In this position the arm is sliding downward with the weight of the body moving forward over it. The water is forced up the arm and is passed under the chest. This action produces the effect of rolling a barrel under the arm. The press of the hand and forearm on the water as the arm is extended into the water serves to propel the body forward without actually pulling the arm backward.

The arm does not slide into the same place through the surface which the hand has entered, but is pressed forward and downward into the water.

Common errors in the supporting phase of the sprint arm action are: (1) extending the elbow fully, (2) completely elevating the shoulder girdle, (3) dropping the elbow and shoulder to a position below the hand level, (4) rotating the elbow downward, (5) over-cupping the hand, (6) holding the wrist "set," (7) abducting the hand to the right or left so that the fingers are not in forward alignment at all times, and (8) pressing the arm sideward instead of directly downward and forward.

(c) *The Catch.*—During the supporting phase, the arm is pressing downward and backward. The major force is directed downward. As the arm is further depressed, the major force is directed backward and the propulsive action of the arm is increased. At the point at which the major force of the arm action thus shifts from downward to backward, the catch is made. In most sprint swimmers, the catch takes place when the hand is from 5 to 8 inches below the surface of the water.

The catch is a quick inward movement of the hand and arm devised to place the arm in the most advantageous position for the large depressor muscles to act during the following pull and push phases of the sprint arm stroke. The large muscles which draw the arm downward, forward, and backward are the latissimus dorsi and the pectoralis major. The latissimus dorsi originates at the vertebrae and the lower ribs and inserts on the humerus. The pectoralis major originates at the clavicle and sternum and also inserts on the humerus.

To observe this muscle action, place the right arm in a position about 10 inches in front of a line directly above the shoulder. Grasp the pectoralis major muscle with the left hand and feel its action as the right arm is drawn downward and forward in various positions against some resistance. If the right hand and elbow are held slightly to the left of a position in front of the right shoulder, the pectoralis major will be felt to contract very strongly. If the right arm is depressed in a position directly in front of the right shoulder, only a feeble contraction is felt. By holding the arm in a position at the right of a line in front of the shoulder, hardly any of the pectoralis major muscle is used when the arm is depressed. The most powerful arm action results from a teamwork of both the pectoralis and the latissimus muscles. This is accomplished when the arm is held toward a line in front of the axis of the body.

While the arm is being placed in the position which results in maximum muscle teamwork, the pressure on the water which has been obtained during the supporting phase must not be lost. This is accomplished by a quick inward movement of the hand followed immediately by a similar movement of the forearm and then likewise with the upper arm. This motion results in turbulence behind the hand which increases the water resistance and thus adds to the frictional force which prevents the arm from slipping through the water. If the hand and arm are pulled too slowly, they will travel too far before traction is gained and the effectiveness of the arm pull will be diminished.

The catch brings the hand to a position in front of the axis of the body (Fig. 2A) so that the center of body weight is balanced over the driving arm. If the body weight is carried to one side of the driving arm, it will result in an inefficient lateral motion similar to the sway of the body while walking with the feet widely spread.

The elbow is continued to be directed sideward so that the widest part of the forearm remains in contact with the water that is being forced backward. The upper arm is brought to an approximately vertical position in front of the shoulder so that the large muscles can best act to draw the arm downward and backward.

(d) *The Pull.*—At the end of the catch the arm has gained traction in the water and has been brought into position for the most propulsive phases of the arm stroke. From the point of the catch until the arm is below the top of the head, the arm pulls the body forward. If the swimmer allows his arm to be pulled under the shoulder before the push and drive are started, the shoulder passes over the hand and the arm is in a disadvantageous position to deliver a powerful drive. During the pull as well as during the push which follows, the water is forced directly backward. The arm is acting nearly vertically to the forward direction of the swimmer and, in this manner, is in the most advantageous position to deliver the forward drive. When the arm is in this position, the muscular energy used in swimming is most efficiently applied. The powerful team of swimming muscles, the pectoralis major and the latissimus dorsi, are here called upon to exert their maximum tension to pull the arm downward. As the arm is depressed the hand is pulled along a line below the axis of the body and the elbow is gradually flexed in order to maintain the movement of the hand in this plane. The arm in this position closely resembles a boomerang (Fig. 2B). The hand and forearm are swept downward and serve as a base of anchorage for the shoulder to be pulled forward over them. While the shoulder is riding forward over the anchored hand and forearm, the traction must not be lost by allowing the depression of the hand and forearm to lose speed through the water. In order not to yield its hold on the water, the hand describes a feathering action by an increased flexion of the elbow which moves the arm and hand inward and slightly upward toward the chest. The broad part of the forearm continues to remain in contact with the water which is being forced backward.

There are three reasons why the elbow should be flexed during the pull. First, it places the hand and forearm beneath the body where they can exert their force more nearly in a line with the body, thus reducing lateral motion. Second, the lever arm is shortened so that more speed can be attained. With the shortened lever, the weight to be moved is nearer to the fulcrum and thus less energy has to be expended in order to move the weight. Third, the transition from the pull to the push is more easily made.

Swimmers of the stocky type, with short arms and a heavy and powerful shoulder girdle, may reduce the amount of elbow flexion in order to obtain a longer and more propulsive stroke. A slight elbow flexion and feathering action during the pull is necessary to maintain balance and to prepare for the transitional movement.

(e) *The Push.*—The transitional movement from the pull to the push is accomplished by shifting the head of the humerus into the articular capsule of the shoulder joint and strengthening it so that the pectoralis major and the latissimus dorsi can draw the arm powerfully downward and backward. This adjustment is made just before the arm passes under the shoulder so that it is in the proper position for the drive, or push.

The arm has maintained traction in the water so that when the powerful push is made, the arm will meet with sufficient resistance to drive the body forward. As the arm is brought downward and backward under the shoulder, the upper arm remains vertical to the surface and the forearm is gradually extended (Fig. 2C). As the arm approaches the front of the hip in completion of the push, the hand is whipped backward to give a last additional drive to the arm stroke. The propulsive action of the arm thus ends with the hand opposite the middle of the thigh, just below the hip.

(f) *The Release.*—At the completion of the push the arm is lifted from the water. In the sprint crawl the water is released at the point at which the propulsive force of the arm stroke is progressively diminishing. If the arm is pushed backward too far, the body will be forced downward and its level will be lowered.

The propulsive force of the arm stroke starts to diminish when the hand is opposite the hip. The hand is well below the surface and must be deftly lifted from the water without impeding forward progression. At the termination of the hand whip, the elbow is near the surface and the hand is beneath and slightly behind the elbow with the palm facing upward. As the forearm and hand relax their pressure upon the water, the elbow is raised from the water and is elevated until the hand leaves the water. As the elbow is raised the hand is rotated one-quarter turn inward so that the little finger is upward and the hand and forearm are raised in a backward motion. The narrow surface of the arm and hand is thus presented to the water and only small resistance is encountered.

If the arm stroke is ended after only a short drive and the release is made in front of the hip, much propulsive power is lost and the recovery is opposed by a great deal of water resistance. Likewise, if the hand is carried upward past the hip joint before the release is made, the body will be pulled under the water and the arm will be inhibited in its recovery.

(g) *The Recovery.*—The action of the arm from the release to the entry is termed the recovery. During the recovery the arm is carried forward out of the water from a position with the hand near the hip to a position with the hand ahead of its shoulder in preparation for the entry.

The action of the arms is continuous throughout the crawl stroke although the speed of the arms varies during the different portions of the arm cycle. At no point are the arms arrested in their movement. A common fault is to pause the arms at the end of the release and at the beginning of the press. This practice causes momentum to be lost with a concurring loss of propulsion.

During the sprint crawl, the recovery must be well controlled and executed in such a manner that the head and body position are not altered and that no lateral motion is effected. The driving action of the legs and opposite arm, likewise, must not be inhibited by the recovery.

At the completion of the propulsive action of the arm stroke, the water is released. The arm is immediately lifted from the water by raising the elbow until the hand clears the surface. The forearm and hand are then elevated in an outward and forward circular motion with the elbow remaining relatively stable and acting as the axis. The forearm executes a quarter turn and the hand is carried forward with the palm downward and the thumb forward (Fig. 2A). As the elbow is carried forward its elevation is maintained above the level of the hand for the remainder of the recovery and the entry. The forearm is nearly horizontal as the arm is carried forward past the shoulder. The hand remains in a line with the forearm. As the hand passes the head, the arm reaches forward. The upper arm is brought forward near, but not touching, the side of the head. As the arm thus reaches for the entry, the shoulder girdle is somewhat elevated, the tip of the elbow is carried high and the elbow is slightly flexed. The fingers are reaching forward into the water with the palm parallel with the water's surface (Fig. 3A). The arm is now in a position preparatory to the entry.

There are many other styles in which the arm is recovered during the sprint crawl stroke. Other styles include those in which the elbow is carried either high or low and the arm is recovered with the elbow either high above the shoulder or close to the surface of the

5

water. These low, high, and medium recoveries with both the flexed and extended elbow have been used by different record-breaking sprint swimmers.

4. **The Timing of the Arms.**—In the sprint crawl, as the catch is made with one arm, the opposite hand has reached a point in its recovery approximately lateral to the side of the face (Fig. 2A). This figure shows one arm well in the pull phase, while the recovery hand has just passed the side of the face. As the arm, which has been recovered, presses into the water at the entry, the opposite arm is propelling the body forward in the pulling phase of the arm cycle (Fig. 2A). While the arm which has just entered the water is pressed into position for the catch, the swimmer glides forward on that arm as he executes the powerful pulling phase with the other arm. As the catch is started with the arm which is now forward, the water is released by the arm which has finished its drive and it is recovered out of the water. The recovery arm completes its forward swing and its hand is at the side of the swimmer's face as the opposite arm makes the catch. The first half of the arm cycle is now completed and the second half follows the same sequence in regular alternate succession.

As one arm is pulling backward the other moves forward. When both arms are in the water, as one arm presses downward, the other is driving backward (Fig. 2B). The pulling arm drives the body forward onto the supporting arm and the body rests upon this supporting arm until the pulling arm completes the drive and partially recovers. Then the pulling arm becomes the supporting arm while the arm which was formerly acting to support the body now does the pulling. This reciprocal arm action sustains the body balance as well as affords a continuous propulsive force which maintains steady forward progress.

5. **The Timing of the Arms and Legs.**—In swimming the sprint crawl, the cadence of the legs is faster than that of the arms. This results in a motion which, at first, appears to be an unnatural one as it is unlike that used by man while walking and running. In walking and running the arms serve to counterbalance the driving action of the legs by swinging in the opposite direction as the legs. The legs and arms thus move in a 1 to 1 ratio during walking and running. In swimming the crawl, however, the leg to arm ratio is 3 to 1. The legs perform 3 beats to each arm movement, or 6 beats to each arm cycle.

An analysis of the mechanics of the six-beat crawl stroke reveals that it is as truly balanced as is the counterbalancing action of the arms and legs in walking. In order to facilitate a description of the timing of the arms with the legs in the sprint crawl, the stroke will be divided into six parts and each part discussed as a separate unit. The part of the stroke that is performed with the most regular rhythm is the leg action. Although the arms also move in cycles, their rhythm is a peculiar one as during one complete arm cycle each arm is out of the water during one-third of the cycle and both arms are in the water during the remaining two-thirds of the cycle.

The legs move upward and downward in uniform periods and each upward and downward beat of the legs marks a certain regular phase of the stroke. For the purpose of uniformity, the timing of the arms in relation to the legs will be described in 6 parts. Each part will commence with the instant the legs are completely spread in the stride position at the end of each beat.

Beat 1.—The right leg has completed the kick upward and the left has completed the kick downward. The left arm has nearly completed the recovery and is in a position with the hand in front of the face and ready to press into the water. The right arm is forward and moving downward in the water and is at the end of the catch and ready to begin the pull (Fig. 2A).

As the left arm penetrates the water, the right leg travels downward. In this, the forces on the opposite side of the body are balanced and body rotation is eliminated. As the right arm catches the water and gathers it and pulls the body forward, the left leg offsets a rotation due to this action by its upward drive.

Beat 2.—The left leg has completed the kick upward and the right has kicked downward. The left arm begins to press into the water and the right has completed the pull and is at the beginning of the push (Fig. 2B).

As the left arm thrusts into the water, the right leg stabilizes this action by a downward beat. The backward and somewhat upward drive of the right arm during the push is equalized by the upward movement of the left leg.

Beat 3.—The right leg is again upward and the left downward. The left arm has completed the entry and has been pressed into a position for the beginning of the catch. The right arm has completed the push and is finishing the release in preparation for the recovery (Fig. 2C).

As the left arm is forced sharply inward and downward during the catch, the right leg counteracts by its downward kick. As the right arm is lifted upward from the water, following the release, the left leg maintains equilibrium by lifting upward also.

Beat 4.—The left leg is now upward and the right is downward. The left arm has completed the catch and is beginning to pull. The right hand is in front of the face and ready to press into the water. The action is now comparable with that in beat 1, except that it is the opposite arm and leg which are acting (Fig. 2D).

The counteraction of the arms and legs is the same as in beat 1 except that the action is occurring in opposite arm and leg. It will be noticed that beats 5 and 6 are also mirror images of beats 2 and 3, respectively. Therefore, each action described in beats 1, 2, and 3 will be applicable to each of beats 4, 5, and 6.

Beat 5.—The arms and legs in this position are the mirror image of those in beat 2. The right foot is upward and the left is downward. The left arm begins the push and the right is pressing downward (Fig. 2E).

Beat 6.—At the completion of the 6 beat cycle the left leg is upward and the right downward. The left arm has released the water at the end of the pull and is ready to recover and swing forward into the position described in beat 1. The right arm is beginning to catch and will finish the catch as the legs are again in the position for beat 1 (Fig. 2F).

It is impossible for the coach to detect errors in timing of the arms and legs of a swimmer sprinting at full speed by simply trotting by his side and watching his coordination. By the use of slow motion and still movies, however, an analysis is made possible. Many of the newer pools are equipped with underwater observation windows through which such pictures may be taken.[4] Many coaches have made use of a diving bell for this purpose. If such equipment is not available, photographic records must be made above the water's surface. Above-water pictures are valuable even though the splashing and turbulence disrupts the actual movements and analysis is made difficult by this procedure.

Once the record is obtained a comparison may be made with the illustrations presented in Fig. 2 and the action of the swimmer compared with that described in the text. The underwater movie method

[4]Op. cit. See footnote 3, page 57.

has been effectively used by the author in coaching. The coach and swimmer can study the timing and other mechanics of the stroke and determine objectively where the fault lies.

If the underwater movie method is not used, the coach must resort to an analysis of the arm action alone and then the leg action alone while the swimmer swims and attempts to detect an unbalance due to faulty mechanics. For example, the coach may watch the arms during a certain phase of the crawl such as the action of the arms as one arm enters and the other presses into the catch. As the left arm enters, the right arm should be pressing forward into the catch. The most common error in this phase is to allow the right arm to start the pull before the left arm enters. In this manner the arms will be moved too fast and will race ahead of the legs. The propulsive action of both the arms and legs is diminished by this error in timing.

6. **The Technique of Breathing.**—Expiration through the nose under the surface and inspiration through the mouth above the surface is the traditional form of breathing in swimming the sprint crawl. However, expiration may be made through the mouth under surface as well as above. The two types may be modified by exhaling out of both nose and mouth. Although the nose is a natural inlet as well as outlet in the breathing mechanism, there are several objections to expiring under water through the nose alone. The nasal openings are very small to exhale all the air against water pressure. To exhale against the water, a forceful expiratory pressure would be required. This forceful expiration through the nose against the water resistance causes mucus discharge to pass toward the nasal and frontal sinuses and the middle ear and increases the liability to autoinfection.[5] When air is forced out through the mouth, the pressure against the ears and sinus regions is practically eliminated.

Expiration under surface, therefore, may be made through the nose, through the mouth, and through both the nose and the mouth simultaneously. A method actually used by sprint swimmers in releasing the air from the lungs was found to occur simultaneously with the closing of the lips after the inspiration.[6] Air was released slowly through the lips or nose until just an instant before the head was turned out for the next inhalation and a forceful expulsion was made through the mouth. This is often called the ''explosive'' method.

[5]Taylor, H. Marshall: Otitis and Sinusitis in the Swimmer, Journal of American Medical Assn. **113**: 891 (September), 1939.
[6]Aycock, T., Graaff, L., and Tuttle, W. W.: An Analysis of the Respiratory Habits of Trained Swimmers, Research Quarterly **3**: 199 (May), 1932.

During inhalation, air should be taken rapidly through the mouth. As a general rule, inexperienced swimmers swimming the crawl will fix the abdominal and back muscles, thus interfering with the function of the diaphragm in expiring air properly. Rigidity of the abdominal muscles during the sprint crawl interferes with expiration. This rigidity occurs most frequently among swimmers who depress the hips too far causing the fixation not only in the abdominal region, but also in the lumbar region. The fixed tension of these groups of muscles is relieved by lifting the hips which in turn relieves this tension and permits deeper breathing.

Breathing may disturb the leg kick and arm rhythm because during expiration the abdominal muscles have a tendency to relax. The abdominal muscles aid in fixing the pelvis during flexion or extension of the thigh upon the pelvis. In water the extent of the fixation is diminished because of pressure of water on all sides. One can lie face down in the water and swim with the legs alone for some distance while releasing the air with the head under the surface even after the air is expelled and find no interference with the force of the leg kick. The same is found to be true when both arms and legs are used in the same manner. The interference occurs not from diminishing the fixing action of the abdominal muscles, but from either faulty head turning mechanics or from depressing the hips.

One seldom has difficulty in inspiring if the mouth can be turned easily above the surface. In fact, usually too much air is breathed in too early in a race and not enough is expired. If the swimmer breathes regularly early in a race, he should not breathe as deeply, but should increase the depth in proportion to the air requirement. The expiration should be adequate, otherwise carbon dioxide soon builds up within the tissues and fatigue sets in early in the race. Expert swimmers who have skillfully mastered breathing and relaxation of the abdominal muscles seldom have difficulty in breathing when under the exertion of swimming at great speed.

The question as to the number of breaths to take in a sprint race has always been a point of debate. It is a foregone conclusion that in turning the head less often the fast rhythm of the arms and legs is least disturbed and, therefore, greater speed is developed.

The number of breaths to take during the sprint races depends upon individual differences such as breath-holding ability, relaxation, and the ability to accumulate an oxygen debt. One cannot lay down a "hard and fast" rule as to the number of breaths to take. However, in a 40- or 50-yard sprint, almost any good swimmer can cover the first length with one breath, and take only one breath coming back. Some swimmers need to breathe with every other stroke after the first length. Others can breathe with every third arm stroke which is a very good method if the swimmer can breathe properly on both sides. This method also tends to impart greater relaxation to the shoulder stabilizer muscles and maintain greater balance. The breath-holding interval should not be long enough to cause the swimmer to fight for air. This fault is recognized by a "wild-eyed," taut, drawn expression upon the swimmer's face as his mouth is lifted high out of the water to get air.

In distance crawl swimming the swimmer breathes with every arm cycle. However, the ventilation is greater and a longer time is expended in taking in the air when the mouth is turned out to obtain air. Some attempts have been made to breathe on every third arm stroke, but this makes breathing too slow, and inadequate for such strenuous exercise. Another method in distance swimming is to increase the speed of the stroke rhythm so that the swimmer is able to breathe oftener. The increase in the speed of the stroke rhythm is aided by the added oxygen fed to the lungs, thus permitting greater speed to be developed in distance events. The slide phase of the stroke is diminished and the swimmer is more able to withstand the driving pace because he is provided with more frequent breathing intervals. Working muscles become oxygen hungry and unless fed adequately at proper intervals under working conditions, they will become prematurely fatigued.

Lifting the head out of the water for air at the turn slows the sprinter down from 0.3 to 0.5 of a second. At the start, and in coming out of the water after the glide, the head should not be turned for air on the first arm pull as his head is then too far below the surface. The swimmer should first get under way with at least 4 to 6 arm pulls. The head must rotate on its central axis and should not be raised backward or lifted sideward during breath taking. The most important duty of the head other than the part which it plays in breathing, is to keep the body on an even keel and maintain symmetrically balanced arm and leg strokes. The head must be turned for air and recovered as quickly as possible. For this reason the face is held below the surface most of the time to maintain equilibrium. At the proper moment in the stroke, the head is turned so that the least amount of interruption to the stroke balance will occur and the least amount of time will be consumed.

Between inhalations the face should be directly forward (Fig. 2B). This plane should not be disturbed during the stroke other than during inhalation regardless of what the arms or shoulders are doing. The neck must be relaxed in order to isolate the movement of the head from that of the shoulder girdle. Many swimmers have the sensation of having their head aligned with the spine, when in reality it is turned toward the breathing side. This often causes swimmers to bear toward that direction, across the racing lanes. Then too, some swimmers will permit the chin to oscillate back and forth with the movements of the shoulder girdle while the arms are stroking and recovering. Relaxing the neck and holding the chin and nose on dead center will remedy this fault. Another fault commonly committed by the swimmer is to fail to recover the chin and nose fully to the center. Such a fault will inhibit the action of the opposite arm, especially in the push phase. The eyes should be on a horizontal plane so that the eyes can look ahead in almost normal forward vision. The tips of the shoulders should also be raised and the upper spine should bend to conform to the planing position in sprinting. In the distance races, the bend in the neck and the spine is not quite as pronounced as in sprint racing. In the distance stroke, the eyes are just able to see straight forward by looking out from under the eyebrows.

As the body gains in speed, and considerable friction occurs under the face, neck, and body, the swimmer should experience and actually feel that he is pressing down upon the water as he pulls and pushes his body forward over the water. The friction under the body created by the speed attained should not actually be permitted to force the body too high, but high enough to keep the water off the back as far down as the hips. When this position is assumed, then breathing is a simple matter. With the body in this position, a bow wave is created that curves around the head and sweeps in a graceful downward curve on either side of the head at an outward angle. This in turn creates a deep trough inside the bow wave next to the body. The aim in turning the head to get air is to get the mouth into this trough and not into the bow wave. To accomplish this purpose, the head must turn on its longitudinal axis. The chin is turned to the side and pressed in close to the throat as the mouth is opened. The eyes play an important part in turning the head correctly to this point. They must sweep from the forward line of vision and focus on the surface of the water just in front of the chin and mouth. Many swimmers make the mistake of looking forward while turning the head. This causes the chin to move out into the bow wave and for this reason it must be lifted further to the side in order to get air. As the body rolls to the opposite side, and the supporting arm slides from its balanced alignment, the pull and push phases of the arm stroke are shortened. While the head is being turned to the side for air, the water streams down under the chest. While turning the head, the face should be pressed against the resistance of the water to keep the water away from the front of the face (Fig. 2C). If the head is permitted to lift away from the water, the planing effect of the face is lost and the bow wave is broken which causes difficulty in clearing the mouth to take air quickly.

The mouth should not open until the lips are clear of the water. Air is then taken in in the form of a gasp. In distance swimming, inhalation can be slightly slower because deeper breathing is necessary.

The mouth is closed immediately after air has been taken and the head is quickly recovered in order to put the body again on an even balanced keel. During the entire movement of the head, the water level should always be maintained constant. There should neither be a sideward nor an upward or downward movement. To prevent a tendency toward lateral movement while turning the mouth out for air, press the head slightly toward the supporting arm since the head is likely to be moved toward the side to which it is turning to get air. When the head recovers to the center, air is expelled immediately if a breath is to be taken at the next stroke. If more strokes are to be taken before air is again inhaled, the breath should be held and air bubbles should be permitted to escape until just an instant before the head is again turned out for air. Then the air which remains should be forced out in one larger bubble. This release of air should be skillfully timed so that the exhalation is finished as the lips and nose are breaking out to the surface. With the air being released in one large air bubble instead of emitting a series of small bubbles, the water is cleared away from the mouth by the air bubble as the lips break through to get a fresh supply of air.

All crawl stroke swimmers should learn to breathe on both sides. The reasons for this are obvious. A sprinter is not always able to come out even at every turn so that he can turn but one way. Thus, after he completes his turn he can take a breath as soon as the body is aligned at the surface. The habit of breathing on both sides tends to keep a more symmetrically balanced stroke. Finally, turning the head at certain intervals, especially during the fatigue part of the race, releases shoulder girdle and neck tension. After turning the head several times to the right and left, even though air is not always inspired, the competitor feels immediate relief if fatigue and muscular tension have already set in.

The Relation Between Turning the Head for Breathing and the Arm and Leg Cycle.—The novice usually breathes by turning the mouth to the side for air in the same rhythm with the breathing side arm. This seems to be a natural method. The head thus turns for air just as slow or as fast as the cadence of the stroke. This method is inefficient, however, as it causes the head to remain at the side too long for the purpose of getting air. Whenever this unskilled method is used, one can almost always find that the body lies off-keel, principally on the side opposite the breathing side. The body should be flat on the chest with the face forward on front dead center, for a period at least twice as long as the time required to take a breath and return to the swimming position. It is the function of the head to maintain the body on an even keel and this function is impaired if the head spends a large part of its time in getting air. This not only throws the body off balance, but the whole stroke equilibrium is disturbed and speed is reduced.

While turning the head to the side for inhalation, the body must remain stable so that neither the arms nor the legs are caused to deviate from their normal range of movement. In order to accomplish this maneuver, certain adjustments must be made. The neck must be relaxed in order that its movement can be isolated from that of the shoulder girdle, so that the shoulder girdle will not be tilted to the opposite side to permit mouth inspiration. The opposite arm must have just entered the water for countersupport before the head is turned to the side for air. The head should start to recover as the breathing arm is lifted out of the water and should be fully recovered when the breathing-side arm is directly at the side of the head in the recovery. These accommodations permit the head to remain forward and on center four full beats of the legs. This permits the body to ride steadily and gives the arms and legs freedom to function without interference from the head. When improper breathing causes the body to roll, the arms and legs are less propulsive. As in canoeing, if two persons sit in a canoe and paddle and the person in the front seat sits off-keel, the person in the back seat is put at a disadvantage and paddling is very difficult for him. As soon as the person in the bow end sits on center over the keel, the canoe balances and the stern paddler's strokes are more efficient. The same sensations are experienced by the crawl stroke swimmer whose head keeps the shoulders out of keel by faulty breathing mechanics. Poorly timed head mechanics is a detrimental factor to speed. The well-trained swimmer should make every effort to turn his head for air and return it independently of the cadence of his arms. The head must move to and from air at a greater speed than the cadence in which the arms are moving. One can easily test the detriment of breathing by swimming the length of the pool at top speed without turning the head for air over the entire length, and then swim it at top speed and breathe with every stroke cycle. The former method will be very much faster. Note, too, how symmetrically balanced and smooth the arms and legs function when the head is maintained on dead center. If a helmet could be perfected to fit over the face and nose with a breather valve, so that one could breathe without turning the head for air, what a really fast 100 yards a man could swim. Until such an apparatus is constructed and accepted in competition, a breathing method which will reduce this head-turning interference to a minimum must be employed.

The breathing method referred to above may be designated as the two count system. Note how skillfully the head is timed into the whole movement of the arms and legs. If the swimmer breathes on the right side the head is turned at beat 3 (Fig. 2C). The right arm is completing its push. The left leg is driving down for counterbalance in turning the mouth to the surface as well as for lifting the arm out of the water. The left arm is gliding forward and downward for the catch. At beat 4, the right leg beats down while the head quickly recovers all the way to dead center (Fig. 2D). At the beginning of beat 4 the recovery arm is just ready to enter the water. The inhalation has been accomplished in two counts or two beats of the legs. Therefore, the body remains balanced four out of six leg beats. The body on its keel and both legs and arms performing undisturbed for four beats in each stroke revolution is a tremendous factor toward greater speed and less energy expenditure.

If the swimmer breathes on the left side, the head is turned to get air during count 6 (Fig. 2F). Another way to time this method other than by the count is to turn the head to the side the instant the opposite arm is beneath the surface. Care must be taken not to turn the head prematurely, that is, before the hand enters the water. The head is timed with the opposite breathing arm as it is entering the water. In either method the head should be fully recovered when the breathing arm has arrived in its recovery to a point directly at the side of the head. The sliding arm begins its pull as the head is completing its recovery.

A common error in this method is to drop the shoulder downward after the head has been recovered and after the breathing arm has entered the water. A shoulder drop in the crawl stroke violates sound mechanics in speed swimming. The shoulders must remain over the arms during the entry and propulsive phases. A shoulder drop is often caused by failure to maintain the head on dead center during exhalation. In turning the mouth for air, the head should not lift away from the pressure of the water, but both chest and the under side of the face should lie against the pillow of water while air is inhaled.

Common Errors in Breathing Technique.—Other common errors resulting from faulty head turning mechanics are the following: (a) Lifting the chin forward and sideward to get air results in dropping the opposite elbow and shoulder which causes the opposite arm to slide laterally. It also disturbs the leg balance, and propulsive force is dissipated. (b) Turning head in the same rhythm and cadence as the arms results in rolling the body. (c) Not fully recovering the head results in loss of body balance. The opposite shoulder drops and the opposite arm pulls too wide, thus failing to complete the push-drive phase. The pull is premature. The recovery-side arm has a tendency to freeze or lock at the entry. (d) Opening the mouth with the lips stretched back too far results in strangulation due to water entering the mouth. Facial muscles become tense. The lips should aid in guiding the water away from the mouth. (e) Moving the head out of its longitudinal axis results in a loss of symmetric arm and leg action, disturbs body balance, and thus propulsive force is lost. (f) Breathing on one side only results in the neck and shoulder muscles becoming cramped, loss of balance and the inability of the swimmer to see the field on both sides during a race.

8. **The Turn.**—In order to execute a fast turn and one which will not become a mental hazard, the swimmer must be able to turn to either side equally well. When he is within 10 feet of the side of the pool he must be able to judge accurately, with his eyes either above or below the surface, the number of arm strokes necessary to reach the turn. His decision is made before he reaches the end as to which direction he will turn. Some swimmers often become so engrossed in the race itself that they forget the wall, until one arm hits it. Most modern pools have a warning mark four feet from the end, on the bottom. Often this is not seen because the swimmer's eyes are in turbulent surface water. Sometimes a pool wall has a peculiar color of tile on the end wall which is very difficult for the swimmer to distinguish from the water. This makes it hard for him to judge the approximate distance. Sometimes room lighting is very poorly arranged, resulting in shadows being cast on the inside wall so that a white wall looks dark. All lights over a swimming pool should be so arranged that the light directs its rays against all inside pool walls. In order to accomplish this the lights should be set inside the pool wall enclosure at least 5 feet. This eliminates all shadows and, if the water is clear, it gives adequate illumination. Underwater lights should be shut off during competition, since they tend to blind and confuse the swimmer at the turns.

A sprinter should not anticipate his turn and touch by the finger tips because if he does he may miss his touch entirely and thus become disqualified. Neither should he veer to one side as he approaches the wall since this error contributes to a slow turn. The swimmer should come to the wall, head on, and touch with the hand opposite from the direction he is going to turn. The hand should touch the wall in front of the shoulder opposite the direction of the turn.

Mechanics of the Sprint Turns

The Lateral Turn.—As the hand touches the wall, about 6″ to 10″ under the surface of the water, the elbow should bend slightly so that momentum can be utilized (Fig. 3B). Simultaneously with the hand touch, the legs are tucked tightly with the knees together. Then the turn is made with the body remaining flat on the chest. The feet are tucked under to form a pivot upon which the body spins. After the tuck has been completed the head

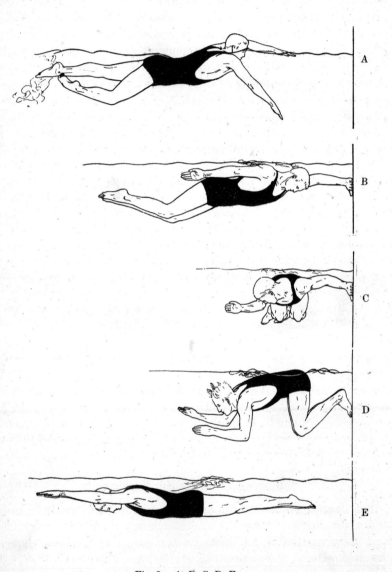

Fig. 3.—A, B, C, D, E.

Fig. 3.—A series of ideal form showing the sprint crawl stroke turn. A. The approach to the wall. B. The start of the turn. C. The position of the body at the quarter turn. D. Body set for push-out. E. The body in the glide position after leaving the wall.

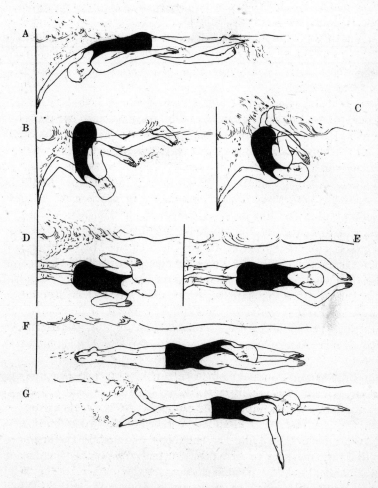

Fig. 3 (a).—A series of ideal form showing the somersault turn. (See description, page 82). A. Showing the start of the turn with hand touch, head tucked down and free hand anchored. B. The position of the body at the quarter turn with free hand assisting the completion of turn and the tuck of the legs. C. Showing the body in the complete tuck position. Note position of free hand assisting completion of upward turn and quarter twist of the body. D. Body set for push-out. E. Body pushing off wall with feet and head completing twist. F. Body in glide-out-position. G. Position of the body swimming to the surface.

and shoulders whip away from the arm which is against the wall and the hips move around toward the wall (Fig. 3C). The free arm assists the turn by whipping the hand in a sculling motion, starting from the side of the hips and sweeping outward and across to the chest in a short, quick, vigorous movement. The touching hand is quickly removed from the wall and tucked close to the body as it is brought to a position alongside the other hand under the head (Fig. 3D). The feet are driven against the wall and the arms are extended with a thrust and the head is lowered between the arms in the glide position.

In the glide, the body must be held straight, not arched (Fig. 3E). It should glide slightly upward. The body should be stretched from toes to finger tips with the legs held close together. The break through to the surface should be executed as described in the start. The swimmer should extend his arms in a line with his spine and press down with his hands as he glides out. The legs should be held straight. Starting the kick prematurely is a waste of effort and slows down the swimmer if the push-off has been powerful. At the end of the glide, the swimmer should come out from under the surface, swimming hard. He should not turn his head for air on the first arm stroke. If the swimmer has a reflex of turning the head, even though he does not take air, he should be trained to pull through his opposite breathing arm first. His first movements should be concentrated in gathering speed or at least maintaining the speed gained from the turn. Many times a good swimmer can advance one, two or even three feet beyond his opponent at each turn.

The body should be tucked before turning. When the body is elongated it cannot be easily turned, but when the radius is shortened, angular motion is accelerated and the body turns faster. The tuck phase is fast. The spine is flexed, placing the body in a ball-like position. Dropping the shoulders or ducking the head too low will cause the hips to lift, then the feet are placed too high on the wall and the body is pushed toward the bottom. The head actually changes its position three times during the turn. When the hand reaches for the wall, it should dive under about ten inches short of the wall, the head and shoulders should go down with the hand. Then as the body starts the turn, the head and shoulders should be lifted slightly. When it is nearly around to the front, it should duck down again as both hands come in to join each other under or just in front of the head. These movements keep the hips under control and do not allow them to lift too high.

Sprinters should not use the scum rail for the turn as this practice usually yields a slow turn. Also, not all pools have scum gutters at the ends.

The feet are set against the wall with ankles fully flexed. The balls of the feet rest against the wall with heels nearly touching. The balls of the feet are set on a level about midpoint between the knee and hip joints. This places the heels slightly below the spine line. The thighs are approximately parallel with the vertical wall against which the feet are pushing. The legs derive the greatest amount of power from a vigorous straightening of the hips and knees. The ankles are the last to straighten just as in the start. However, it is the quick extension of the ankles toward the end of the turn that adds to the power and speed already gained by the extension of the knees and hips.

The elbow of the turning arm should be slightly bent. If the elbow is bent too much, the hips are brought too close to the wall and the feet are placed too low. The body is pushed away from the wall by the legs, not with the turning hand.

When the turn is completed the arms should be thrust out simultaneously with the leg drive. If the arms are set straight before the push-off, the body will go in the direction in which the arms are set. If the arms are pushed out simultaneously with the leg drive, the hand can guide the direction of the push-off more effectively.

The Head-Out Turn.—This type of turn is very fast and is used for middle distances and in the last turn of a sprint where air is needed to finish the race. This turn is executed exactly as the above sprint turn, excepting that as the head turns away from the arm on the wall, the face is turned on its side facing the hand. It is turned as one would turn the face to the side to get air in the crawl stroke. As in the crawl stroke the swimmer should avoid either turning the head too high or lifting it forward and upward. The head is held in line with the spine and the entire body is slightly lifted, just enough for the mouth to reach the surface with the side of the face flat on the surface. The air should be taken as the turn is executed. When the body has completed the turn, the face is still on its side. The body is submerged with a vigorous downward plunge. As the arm is drawn away from the wall, it is tucked in close to the body and thrust forward beneath the water's surface.

If the head and arms alone are thrust downward, the hips will rise above the surface and the feet will be placed against the wall too near the surface and the swimmer will push off toward the bottom.

Many untrained swimmers use this method for the last turns of the 100 yards sprint. However, all turns in the sprint events should be underwater turns if breathing has been properly distributed over the distance.

The Somersault Turn.—The somersault turn for the sprint crawl has been adapted from a similar turn used in the back stroke. Because of its speed it has gained great popularity since its first use by Robert Reed, a University of Iowa swimmer, at the 1938 National Collegiate Athletic Association meet at Rutgers. The use of the somersault turn for the sprint crawl was first used by Jack Seig of Iowa during the two years previous to its formal introduction at the 1938 N.C.A.A. championships.

The turn is dangerous and its use should not be permitted by a sprinter until he is able to perform it consistently. The danger lies in the fact that the hand must touch near enough the surface so that the inspector of turns is able to observe it actually touching the wall. Sometimes the hand drives down and touches the wall about 12 to 14 inches under water. This should not be permitted because of the danger of disqualification by the inspector of turns for failure to touch the wall. The swimmer should be trained to hit the wall near the surface so that his hand can be observed as it hits, and then it should be permitted to slide lower to accommodate the turn.

The somersault turn is faster than the traditional turn by 0.4 to 0.6 of a second. One fact that makes this turn so fast is that the momentum is not lost. The somersault turn is performed by striking the wall a downward glancing blow and simultaneously ducking the head and shoulders straight forward and downward. The heels are then vigorously tucked tightly toward the hips, and the knees are held together as the legs are tucked. At this point, the somersault has progressed slightly farther than just past standing on the head when a quarter twist is made, but the somersault movement is continued until the trunk is in push-off position. As the push-off is made, the body completes the other quarter twist and leaves the wall again righted and facing downward.

The success of the somersault turn depends upon tucking the heels up to the hips tightly as the swimmer goes over and then completes the twist when he is past standing on his head (see Fig. 3(a)).

A variation of the somersault turn is one in which the legs are tucked and thrown over to the wall, but the body turns in more of a lateral motion. This lateral somersault turn may be used successfully by those swimmers whose equilibrium is impaired by a full somersault. This turn is performed in the following manner: the drive into the wall and the tuck and throw of the legs are the same as in the somersault. When the body is in the tuck position, however, the head and shoulders are turned laterally in the direction of the turn. The shoulders and the head lift in order to raise the forepart of the body to the surface. The turn is made with the chest downward at all times.

9. The Finish.—The finish consists of the approach to the finish wall, and finish hand touch.

(a) *The Approach to the Finish Wall.*—In the sprint events, especially in the 100 yards in which the swimmer must rely upon endurance to finish with a burst of speed, too often the finish is made in poor form and the race is lost. A great many swimmers just lower the head and "barrel" in for the finish. This is a grave mistake. Even though the swimmer experiences a sensation of driving harder, in reality his speed is diminished. The reason his stroke feels more powerful is that his arms are going faster. The lowering of the head lets the water support the body, whereas, when swimming with the head and shoulder girdle elevated, the body is to some extent supported by the arms and legs. With the body held in sprinting position, the arms and legs are given additional purchase on the water at a more advantageous angle and the arm speed provides the greatest traction.

In the approach to the finish some swimmers are coached to watch the field to see if gaining or losing. If the field is ahead, an occasional glance should suffice, but he should not look at the field every stroke, especially if he is tired or nearly "spent," because by looking forward he lifts the chin out and turns the head poorly and destroys stroke balance. Good sprinting form must be maintained at any cost in the approach of the finish.

(b) *The Finish Hand Touch.*—In the touch at the finish a swimmer should never reach out and slide in to the touch, but he should come in swimming hard and drive the hand in to the wall above the surface. Many swimming races have been lost by reaching for the finish and stopping short of it only an inch or two with no more slide left. When one reaches, he stops swimming and usually his head lifts up out of the water and the feet sink before the hand has touched. This situation is tragic for the swimmer in a close finish. He should swim until one hand hits and then stop swimming. If the hand touches under water, it is because he was sliding in too far. However, if one does slide in and touches underneath the surface, he then should not drive the other arm in just to make sure the judges will get his finish. If the hand touches in such a situation, the official is bound to judge him by the arm that comes in last, even though he did touch under water with the first. The judge is likely to be influenced by the action of the swimmer himself, by the fact that the swimmer knows whether or not he touched with the first hand. If the other hand is thrust forward, the judge will assume that he did not touch with the first. Even though a judge stands right over a lane and looks down, it is sometimes difficult to see if the touch has actually been made. If the judge is standing at the side, the angle of perception at the finish under the water makes it difficult for him to judge as to where the touch is actually made. It is practically a guess. Should there be a question as to whether the underwater touch beat the opponent's touch above the surface in a close race, the touch above the surface is usually awarded the race.

Racing Fundamentals

The sprint race is one in which the maximum speed is maintained throughout the entire race. For practically everyone who swims in competition, a distance of 25 yards can be considered as a sprint event. The swimmer simply plunges into the water and swims at his top speed over the whole distance.

As the racing distance is extended to 40, 50, or 60 yards, younger and inexperienced boys and girls will have to reduce their speed in order to finish the race. They cannot, therefore, consider these distances as being sprints.

At 100 yards, only seasoned, top-ranking competitors can cover the distance at top speed without regard for conservation of energy. A survey of split times of champions for the 100 yards shows that the time for each consecutive lap becomes greater from the start to the finish. This means that the swimmers had not made any attempt to reduce their speed at any point during the race, but rather attempted to swim at top speed throughout. The cumulative factor of fatigue caused their speed to be reduced as the race progressed.

Swimming as fast as one can go does not mean to make the arms and legs move as fast as possible. There is an optimum rate of movement which produces the greatest swimming speed for the individual. Fast flailing movements of the arms only cut the water open and very little hold on the water is gained.

As soon as the sprint swimmer enters the water he should attain the rate of movement which will produce the maximum speed and attempt to maintain this speed throughout the race. A common tendency among inexperienced swimmers is to break this optimum rhythm when they notice that they are being passed by a competitor or that they are behind the field. To break rhythm invariably results in an easily recognizable decrease in speed and, consequently, the loss of the race.

Thus, the answer to the swimmer's question, "How shall I swim this sprint race?" might well be, "Get off your mark as fast as you can, with a powerful dive. Come out of your glide swimming, not fighting the water, and build up into the rhythm of your greatest swimming speed. Hold your rhythm at this speed throughout the race to the best of your ability."

In order that a swimmer may compare his split times with those of champions, Table I is presented. By referring to this table, the swimmer can notice the part of the race which was swum too slow. The next step to be considered is then, the reason for this reduction in speed. The cause is commonly found to be improper breathing techniques and they should be checked carefully. Improper breathing is usually associated with tying-up and the swimmer often complains of being tired at this point.

The sprinter should not survey the field of competitors during a race. By lifting his eyes and head forward and sideward to look for his competitors he drops his opposite shoulder and throws his body off balance and rhythm of his arm and leg strokes is interrupted and speed is lost.

Sprint swimmers have a tendency to race the arms at a faster rate of speed than is possible to attain with the legs. This causes a loss of rhythm between the arms and legs and can only result in a loss of speed. If a faster rhythm is desired to close a margin, or a burst of speed at the finish, the speed of the leg action should be just as great as that of the arm action. The speed ratio between legs and arms is then balanced and will result in greater propulsive speed.

TABLE I

THIS TABLE SHOWS IDEAL SPLIT TIMES FOR VARIOUS RACING TIMES IN THE 100 YARDS CRAWL (25 YARDS COURSE)

ELAPSED DISTANCE YD.	ELAPSED TIME SEC.	SPLIT TIME SEC.	ELAPSED DISTANCE YD.	ELAPSED TIME SEC.	SPLIT TIME SEC.
25	9.9	9.9	25	11.9	11.9
50	22.0	12.1	50	26.0	14.1
75	34.9	12.9	75	40.9	14.9
100	48.0	13.1	100	56.0	15.1
25	10.4	10.4	25	12.4	12.4
50	23.0	12.6	50	27.0	14.6
75	36.4	13.4	75	42.4	15.4
100	50.0	13.6	100	58.0	15.6
25	10.9	10.9	25	12.9	12.9
50	24.0	13.1	50	28.0	15.1
75	37.9	13.9	75	43.9	15.9
100	52.0	14.1	100	1:00.0	16.1
25	11.4	11.4	25	13.4	13.4
50	25.0	13.6	50	29.0	15.6
75	39.4	14.4	75	45.4	16.4
100	54.0	14.6	100	1:02.0	16.6

How to Use Table I

1. Select your best total time that you now swim for the 100 yards freestyle race, as shown in the above table.

2. Record your own split times from this race and compare them with the split time divisions in the above table as made by swimming champions.

3. To improve your best time for 100 yards use the split times in the table for the next faster total race time.

CHAPTER IV

THE MIDDLE DISTANCE CRAWL

Middle distance races include any swimming event between 150 and 300 yards. There is no sharp distinction between middle, sprint, and long distance events, except in the distance events the swimmer must distribute his efforts so as not to be overcome by fatigue before the prescribed distance is covered.

The 220 yards freestyle is generally considered the ideal middle distance event. The middle distance races also include the 150 yards back stroke and the 200 yards breast stroke.

Characteristics of the Middle Distance Swimmer.—There are some individuals who possess the speed of a sprinter plus the stamina and endurance of a long distance swimmer. These are the ideal qualifications for the middle distance swimmers. Many long distance swimmers have developed into excellent middle distance swimmers.

The wide range of difference in physical characteristics of middle distance swimmers prohibits a description of an "ideal" build. The buoyant individual, however, has an advantage over a heavy muscled and heavy boned competitor. Both sprinters and distance swimmers have achieved a high level of success in the middle distance events.

Most swimmers entering competition for the first time think only of the sprint distances and desire to try nothing else. Many of these will never be a success at sprint swimming because of certain anatomic and physiologic limitations such as the lack of strength and speed of movements. At the middle distances, however, he may develop into a smooth and powerful swimmer and achieve a measure of success far above that he would have gained in sprint crawl competition.

Comparative Marks for the Middle Distance Competition.—The middle distance freestyle event is the 220 yard distance. For high school it may be considered a distance event, since it is the longest distance on the official order of events for both dual and championship competition.

	WORLD'S RECORD	AMERICAN RECORD	INTER-COLLEGIATE	HIGH SCHOOL
Twenty-yard course				
220 yard freestyle		2:07.8	2:09.7	2:13.2
Short course (25 yards)				
220 yard freestyle	2:07.9	2:07.9	2:09.6	2:14.0

Occasionally, in dual meet competition, a sprinter may swim in the middle distances to gain endurance, and a distance swimmer to gain speed. In changing a sprinter to the middle distance race, speed will still be maintained but additional stress is given to endurance and proper distribution of effort. In transforming a distance swimmer to the middle distance, speed will be added to endurance.

Whenever an event is long enough to warrant special emphasis to be placed on endurance, the problem of effort distribution immediately becomes an important factor. The middle and longer distance swimmer must learn to plan his race so that he can efficiently spread his energy over the entire event in accordance with his own energy capacity.

In order to become a successful middle distance swimmer, one must accomplish a powerful, rhythmic stroking action. This action gives the appearance of sprinting all the way rather than a slower distance type of stroking rhythm. The ability to synchronize leg, arm, and head action is fully as important in these swimming events as in sprinting.

Endurance, being an equally important factor in swimming the middle distances, involves the development of powerful muscles and vital organs. The middle and longer distances are not injurious to the swimmer if he is organically prepared for prolonged exertion. This preparation is accomplished through a systematic training and conditioning program of work in which the cardio-respiratory system adjusts itself to the gradually added strain brought about by an increased distance.

The Technique of Middle Distance Swimming.—The shorter of the middle distance events are similar to sprinting races, whereas the longer middle distance events take on an aspect of distance swimming. The middle distance stroke varies somewhat from the sprint stroke. Since speed is diminished in order to distribute the energy over the race, compensations in the stroke must be made.

1. **The Body Position.**—The body rides slightly lower in the surface of the water than in the sprint crawl because the speed is less. The sprint crawl swimmer who enters middle distance competition commonly makes the error of attempting to maintain his body at the same level as during the sprint races. In order to do this he increases the downward pressure of the arms and thus decreases the efficiency of their forward action. The swimmer in the middle distance events should bear in mind that as the speed is reduced, the body position

will naturally be altered and the body level will be deeper in the water as the speed is diminished. As the shoulders are lowered in the water, the hips are somewhat elevated to prevent body sag.

An attempt should be made to carry the shoulders at a level with the water surface. Although the shoulders are elevated slightly during the recovery, they should return to this level position as the arm slides forward in the entry and should not be allowed to drop into the water. By keeping the shoulders level, the chest surface will be kept flat, water resistance will be at a minimum, and the shoulder girdle muscles will be maintained in an optimum position to deliver the arm pull.

In order to maintain the shoulders at a level, the shoulder girdle muscle fixation is less than in the sprint crawl. The muscles are less tense and allow the shoulder girdle to move freely in relation to the trunk.

2. **The Leg Action.**—In the middle distance crawl, the speed of the legs is decreased and the stride becomes wider than that of the sprint crawl. In the sprints, the arms are the major propelling forces but as the racing distance is increased the driving action of the legs becomes increasingly more important.

3. **The Arm Action.**—The arms move slower, they slide more and are held less tense in the middle distances than in the sprints. The arm entry is more shallow, the press diminished and the slide is longer. The catch is made nearer to the surface. The pull is somewhat longer but the arm position remains the same in the middle distance as in the sprints during the pull and push. The arms are pulled through farther and the release is made in the region of the hip joint. The recovery can be either low or high in accordance with the structural limitations, the individual with the wide scapulae using a lower recovery than others with narrower scapulae.

A higher arm recovery is more desirable. The high recovery should be modified if it causes the body to roll.

4. **Coordination of the Arms.**—The recovery arm must extend farther forward before the catch is made because the pulling arm has been delayed during the slide phase of the entry. When the catch is made, the recovery hand is just in front of the face.

5. **Coordination of Arms and Legs.**—The counterbalancing action of the legs and arms is the same in the middle distance as in the sprint crawl (Fig. 2). This counterbalance is maintained by slowing the entire stroke.

6. **Breathing.**—The head may have to be turned to the side a little more to raise the mouth above the water's surface as the body is lower in the water and the bow trough is more shallow in the middle distances than in the sprints. The breath is usually taken with each arm cycle in the middle distance events.

7. **Coordination of Breathing With the Middle Distance Crawl.**—The head is turned for air at the instant the arm opposite the side the breath is taken is submerged. If this is done, the body alignment is maintained and a minimum of roll is produced. The whole movement of turning the head and recovering it to the center after the breath is taken consumes only two beats of the legs.

If the head is not recovered in time, it is usually lowered together with the entry of the breathing side arm and the shoulder invariably drops into the water below the swimming shoulder level and the arm and leg action is inhibited due to an accompanying body roll. Faulty head turning mechanics in breathing are commonly accompanied by a pull which starts too soon on the side opposite the breathing side and an inefficient catch of the breathing side arm.

8. **The Middle Distance Crawl Turn.**—The mechanics of the middle distance crawl turn are the same as those of the sprint crawl turns. The turn must still be fast. A breath may be taken as the swimmer pushes away from the wall with the turning arm. The turn is further discussed in Chapter V.

9. **The Finish.**—The swimmer should not lower the head as he makes his final challenge at the approach to the finish. He should increase the speed of his whole stroke by narrowing the kick, shortening the arm slide and sprinting into the finish. The hand should smash into the wall with the palm forward and the finger tips upward. The eyes should be on the finish wall about two strokes before the wall is reached to judge the arm touch accurately.

Racing Fundamentals

In dual meet competition the pool is divided into four lanes, each team having two lanes on each half of the pool. The two middle lanes are the most favorable because the water is less choppy since it is farther away from the sides of the pool. Also, the competitor is in a better position to watch his opponents, if necessary.

If the team's best swimmer anticipates stiff competition he should be given the inside lane. However, if he is far superior to his opponents he should be given the outside lane so that his teammate will be given the opportunity to place well in the competition. In championship competition the lanes are assigned by chance.

Usually the middle distance swimmer must also swim a distance event in a dual meet. A swimmer who is well trained and is in good condition can swim both races and does not need to harbor the feeling that he must conserve his energy in the first event in order to turn in a good performance in the second. In fact, the seasoned competitor will improve the performance of his second event by the warming-up influences of his first race.

1. **Adjustment to the Pool.**—Swimming pools are usually laid out in lanes. (See rules for outdoor and indoor competition.[1]) In dual competition the swimmer may have the opportunity to select his own lane. In narrow pools choose inside lanes. Outside lanes are not conducive to fast swimming because of constant agitation of water below the surface due to waves reverberating from the walls. Observe before the start of the race in which lane a rival is stationed.

In a strange tank, observe both ends of the tank to see that your turning wall is free of any obstruction. If the tank has lane markers on the bottom of the pool observe if it has a warning mark four feet from the turning wall. If surface lane markers are used and should a swimmer hook an arm over one of them, he should not stop, but continue until he is in the clear. If the swimmer has a balanced arm stroke he will seldom swim out of his lane. Too often a swimmer will forget himself and watch his rival. A swimmer should not glance at the field at every stroke. Such an error causes the stroke to become unbalanced and results in a loss of speed.

2. **Speed in the Early Part of the Race.**—The rate of speed in the early part of a middle distance race usually depends upon how thoroughly the swimmer is schooled in pace. However, it also depends upon the ability of the swimmer.

The rate of speed at the beginning of a race is faster than at any other part but it must not be prolonged beyond the swimmer's ability to carry out his race plan. A burst of speed at the start by an opponent need not be met, since he is bound to revert to a slower rate of speed somewhere just ahead unless he is an exceptional swimmer.

[1]See Swimming Guide, National Collegiate Athletics Association. See also A. A. U. Rules Handbook.

Although the first 100 yards of a middle distance race are important, one cannot win a race in the first 100 yards. The inexperienced swimmer is apt to forget this. He should school himself in pace so thoroughly that he can swim 100 yards at any given speed within his capacity and not misjudge it more than 0.5 of a second. In midseason the middle distance swimmer should be checked many times on the 100 yards at varying speeds, so that he gets a sensation of the speed he is traveling. This will assure him of never being drawn out too far at a greater speed than his endurance will permit. If too little is spent in the first part of the race, he can distribute it over the remaining yards. The inexperienced swimmer is more apt to win with such a plan until confidence and sufficient experience are gained. The loss of a race in the last 100 yards is often due to a misjudgment of the first 100 yards.

The top-flight middle distance swimmers can adopt a race plan of going out with the gun and staying out ahead. The top-flight swimmer is one who has had considerable racing experience and can swim a real "rugged" 100 yards and go well beyond that distance. This depends upon ability and competitive experience. The beginner should adopt a predetermined plan and then perfect it as he gains in experience, ability, and confidence.

3. **Maneuvering for Position.**—If a beginner has hopes of winning a race against a more experienced rival, he must not give him more than two body lengths lead in the early stage of a middle distance race if he is to overtake him in the final sprint. If one desires to take the lead and stay out, he must be willing to pay the price. Some swimmers simply lack confidence in taking a lead, but are willing to swim along with the field and then challenge in the final sprint.

When two rivals are of equal ability, it may or may not be desirable to be out in front throughout the entire race. If one does relinquish the lead to an opponent of equal ability, it should not be greater than a body length and a half, if he expects to win. This is commonly called the danger line in racing tactics. Very frequently in such a close race, one relies upon the other to be carried along at an optimum stroke cadence, and keeps the leading rival near enough to sense quickly any change in tactics. Frequently a leading rival will go out at a terrific rate of speed with the idea in mind of causing his rival to press his stroke and throw him off his stroke rhythm and in this way out-maneuver him.

4. Passing an Opponent.—A middle distance swimmer who re-linquishes an early lead to his rival, may wish to challenge in the later stages of the race. He may attempt faster turns after the first half of the race and gradually build up the margin relinquished. Some swimmers like to sneak up and pass a less alert rival on a blind lap. These tactics may cause a less experienced swimmer no end of worry. Passing a swimmer is costly and he must be prepared to pay the price to stay ahead and meet a counterchallenge.

In the final stages of a race, if a margin must be closed, it should be closed gradually. The swimmer should close the margin early enough in the final stages of the race so that it is within the limits of accomplishment. If the opponent is tiring rapidly near the finish, then a final effort is made to overtake him. The swimmer must always be on the alert in going for the finish and use good judgment by swimming in good form and not making a "dog-fight" out of the finish. It is well to keep in mind that your rival may be tiring more rapidly than you are.

5. Meeting a Challenge.—The start may be considered as the first challenge in a middle distance race. When the field gets under way, the swimmer must decide if the speed of his opponents is approximating that of his own plan or whether it is too fast or too slow. He has the option of either electing or rejecting the challenge. He may desire to conserve his energy early in the race and then in the closing seconds of the race elect to challenge for the lead.

A challenge may occur at any stage of the race. One may be swimming at a very optimum rate of speed and may ignore passing tactics of an opponent. On the other hand, he may accept the challenge with the idea of breaking down excessive amounts of energy being spent by the challenger, and later reducing his stroke cadence. Quite frequently in a race a swimmer must decide quickly which is the wiser plan to follow, even though it does not fit into his predetermined race plan. In the last 50 yards of the race he should be ready to meet any challenge if he has hopes of winning the race.

Disastrous effects may be the direct result of accepting a challenge at a most inopportune time of a race, if the challengers interfere seriously with the effort distribution of the swimmer.

6. The Pace.—A swimmer should be thoroughly disciplined and schooled in the technique of pacing. Perhaps the ideal way to swim a middle distance race is to be able to distribute his rate of speed and effort in proportion to the distance covered. The swimmers who are breaking the records are swimming the first part of the race at nearly full speed and then gradually working into a steadiness of pace which is within the energy capacity of the swimmer.

A general plan is presented and recommended showing the beginner how energy may be distributed effectively for the middle distance swimming races (see Table II).

TABLE II

THIS TABLE SHOWS IDEAL SPLIT TIMES FOR VARIOUS RACING TIMES IN THE 220 YARDS CRAWL (25 YD. POOL)

ELAPSED DISTANCE YD.	ELAPSED TIME SEC.	SPLIT TIME SEC.	ELAPSED DISTANCE YD.	ELAPSED TIME SEC.	SPLIT TIME SEC.
25	11.3	11.3	25	13.0	13.0
50	24.7	13.4	50	28.1	15.1
75	39.0	14.3	75	44.1	16.0
100	53.4	14.4	100	1:00.2	16.1
125	1:08.3	14.9	125	1:16.7	16.5
150	1:23.3	15.0	150	1:33.3	16.6
175	1:38.5	15.2	175	1:50.1	16.8
200	1:53.7	15.2	200	2:07.0	16.9
220	2:05.0	11.3	220	2:20.0	13.0
25	11.9	11.9	25	13.5	13.5
50	25.9	14.0	50	29.1	15.6
.5	40.8	14.9	75	45.6	16.5
100	55.7	14.9	100	1:02.2	16.6
125	1:11.1	15.4	125	1:19.3	17.1
150	1:26.6	15.5	150	1:36.5	17.2
175	1:42.3	15.7	175	1:53.9	17.4
200	1:58.1	15.8	200	2:11.4	17.5
220	2:10.0	11.9	220	2:25.0	13.6
25	12.4	12.4	25	14.1	14.1
50	26.9	14.5	50	30.3	16.2
75	42.3	15.4	75	47.4	17.1
100	57.8	15.5	100	1:04.6	17.2
125	1:13.8	16.0	125	1:22.3	17.7
150	1:29.9	16.1	150	1:40.0	17.7
175	1:46.2	16.3	175	1:57.9	17.9
200	2:02.6	16.4	200	2:15.9	18.0
220	2:15.0	12.4	220	2:30.0	14.1

7. **Maintaining the Stroke Rhythm.**—To maintain and preserve a smooth, relaxed, and economical stroking cadence from the starting stages through the challenges and to the final stages of a race is a most commendable achievement in competition. If one is too easily excited under racing conditions so that the mind is diverted from the

stroke rhythm, he can hardly expect to maintain any stroke balance. Sometimes swimming near the path of another swimmer's feet causes one to lose hold of the disturbed water.

In the middle distances one should turn the head occasionally to both sides, for three reasons: first, to relax the neck and shoulder girdle muscles, second, to facilitate a respiration, and third, so that he can observe the position of his opponents. Care should be taken so that the body does not roll with this head movement.

CHAPTER V

THE DISTANCE CRAWL

A distance swimming stroke is built around the idea of getting a swimmer through the water with the least possible expenditure of energy. The stroke cadence is slow with efficiently well-timed, momentary rest intervals. It is a more or less coasting or free-wheeling type of stroke, once the swimmer is well under way. The distance crawl resembles the sprint crawl, excepting that the distance swimmer strokes with a minimum output of energy, yet maintaining effective speed. Relaxation is stressed and the stroke action is smooth. The distance crawl further differs from the sprint crawl in that the trunk angle is slightly flatter and takes on a stretched appearance; the arm action is less strenuous, and the strokes are longer and more deliberate; the height of the recovery arm is lower than in the sprints; the slide is delayed between the entry and catch, and breathing is deeper.

Characteristics of Distance Swimmers.—There is usually a wide range in size as to distance swimmers. The type more often advancing into the top-flight performers are tall and rangy, with well-developed endurance. Their muscles are usually long, rather than short and thick. They range in height from 5 feet 8 inches to 6 feet 2 inches. The weight range is from 150 pounds to 195 pounds.

Qualifications.—The first prerequisite that a candidate must possess for any type of competition, where endurance is a factor, is a good sound body. The physical condition is best obtained by the routine physical examination by the school department of health. If the health conditions are satisfactory, the next question the candidate should consider is, do I love to swim better than anything else, next to obtaining an education? He should then consider whether or not he is willing to "pay the price" exacted of him in the way of training for such strenuous exertion, as that demanded by the distance swimming events.

To withstand systematic rigorous training the candidate should have a strong heart. There have been studies made as to the actual size of the heart of swimmers. In nearly every case examined, the better type swimmer has a large heart. Since the heart is a muscle, it will naturally increase in size due to exercise, in the same manner as any muscle. This does not necessarily mean that it increases to the so-called "oversized heart." Individual hearts differ in size just as one nose or ear differs in shape and size. Whenever one is endowed at the outset with a large, strong heart, he seems to be at an advantage. If a distance swimmer desires to go far in competition, it is essential that he must either possess a strong heart or acquire one through training.

The distance swimmer must be of at least medium height, strong and durable, yet flexible and supple. He must be streamlined at the hips and legs. An individual with a pair of long, supple, or "rubbery" legs, usually makes a better distance or middle distance swimmer than a sprinter. This is an essential adaptation to distance swimming. The kick must be delivered with an even, smooth, and powerful continuous flow of propulsive force. Long feet and big hands are not necessarily essential. In some cases, they may be an aid. He must possess a good sense of rhythm in order to be able to make adjustments to either an increased or decreased cadence. He must be buoyant so that he will rely on the water to hold him up.

A winning complex is essential and a determination to extend and spend one's self is necessary. Courage to drive a tired body in the closing moments of a race to the finish wall, with a burst of speed, is an essential quality to cultivate.

Comparative Marks for the Distance Competition.—The longest distance for high school competition is 220 yards. For college, 440 yards in dual and league championships. The 1500 meter distance is raced only during the time of the National Collegiate Athletic Association Swimming Championship meet.

	WORLD'S RECORD	AMERICAN RECORD	INTERCOLLE-GIATE RECORD	HIGH SCHOOL RECORD
Twenty-yard course				
440 yards freestyle		4:37.0	4:46.4	4:52.0
Short course (25 yd. course)				
440 yards freestyle	4:40.8	4:40.8	4:42.5	4:45.7
1500 meters freestyle				
Long course (50 yd. and over)				
440 yards freestyle		4:46.0	5:05.3	
1500 meters freestyle	18:58.8		20:15.8	

The Technique of the Distance Crawl

1. **The Position of the Body.**—The body should ride high in the distance stroke, but not as high as in the sprint crawl. It should be stretched so that water does not flow over the back. The speed and distance to be covered are the criterion which regulate the riding angle of the swimmer; the greater the speed the greater the angle.

2. **Position of the Head and Neck.**—The head position is slightly lower with the water level, somewhere between the eyebrows and hairline. The neck should be somewhat relaxed, with the shoulder girdle loose but flat, and as nearly level as possible. The inexperienced swimmer usually permits the shoulder girdle to roll when swimming the distance crawl. This roll greatly increases water resistance.

3. **Position of the Hips.**—The hips ride near the surface and are maintained there by pressing down constantly on the hands and legs. Pressing down slightly with the extremities will cause the arms and legs to hold up the middle of the body.

4. **Position of the Legs.**—There is no departure in leg position from that already described in the sprint crawl. Long "rubbery" legs are an asset to a distance swimmer. The kick should be kept just under the surface for traction. Enough depth should be maintained to permit the water to wash down over the legs.

5. **The Leg Action.**—The technique of the distance flutter kick is, in principle, exactly the same as that discussed in the sprint kick. There is, however, a general difference in the width of stroke of the legs. This is due to the fact that the slower the speed, the wider becomes the leg stroke. The reason for this is that the legs must obtain traction in the water and when they kick less rapidly, less propulsive action is obtained. Therefore, wider action of the legs increases their pressure against the water and provides the traction. It is for this reason that "rubbery" legs are desirable for distance swimming.

The somewhat slower leg action in the distance stroke is compensated for by the arms. The slide of the arms between the entry and the catch is longer. Not only is a longer stride kick desirable in the distance stroke but also a longer slide of the arms is essential for conserving energy.

6. Transition From Slow (Early Season) to Faster (Later Season) Tempo.—During the early season conditioning of squads, distance swimmers as well as sprinters, usually take longer distances at very moderate speeds. It is through these longer swims that the sprinter must adjust his stroke rhythm and somewhat alter the arm slide and length of stride in the kick in order to cover the distance without having to stroke too fast. He does this by gradually drifting into a delayed arm slide, on the arm which has entered the water. He loafs on the anchored arm. Over a period of swimming in this cadence the leg stride has gradually widened without the swimmer being conscious of the gradual change.

There comes a time when the swimmer begins to work on starts and short sprints. He experiences difficulty with the rhythm and finds it hard to obtain purchase or "hold" of the water with either hands or legs. What is now commonly taking place is that he is reducing the slide of the arms and digging them in, the legs still kicking in the newly "grooved" stride. As a result, the legs have been more or less grooved to this longer phase kick and move at a slower rhythm than the arm stroke. Naturally, the first few times sprinting rhythm cadence is used the legs cannot readjust themselves to the rapidity of the arms, and the legs thus miss a beat or two and the kick becomes generally irregular in an attempt to keep up with the racing arms. This is a natural result of distance swimming and is not difficult to adjust. Many coaches will avoid this phase of conditioning procedure and not permit sprinters to swim distances continually. A week or ten days of orientation of special work on the "kicking board," working for a reduced stride and a more rapid cadence of the legs, will soon have the legs in a higher gear ratio to dovetail into the faster arm action. Thus the fault will be corrected.

This procedure is excellent training for a sprinter. It gives his legs greater effectiveness when the kick range is reduced to a narrower stride range. In the slower and wider leg stride range the angles of the legs are greater and the propelling surfaces of the legs become very effective. Then when the legs are "throttled" down with reduced angles, but with a more rapid cadence, the swimmer maintains an efficient leg action and derives greater propelling efficiency from his kick. This readjustment of the leg kick must also take place for the distance crawler, but not to the extent of great speed as that of the sprinter. Nevertheless, the distance swimmer, when in racing condition, does swim at a faster cadence than when training on the long distances in the early season and, therefore, must also pass through the step-up-gear-ratio of arms and legs.

7. **The Drag Kick.**—There are some distance swimmers who have a very ineffective leg action but a fast and powerful arm action. These swimmers will then rely upon a reduced leg stride, called the "drag" flutter kick. There is in this type of kick just enough hip and knee action to feather the legs with the legs held almost straight merely to give counterbalance to the arms. There will be just enough effort expended in the kick to maintain the body near the surface and every effort should be made to offer as little surface friction along the legs as possible. The water must slip smoothly under and past the legs.

Common Errors in Leg Action Technique.—Common errors in the distance crawl are most likely to occur in the leg action. Such errors are not due mainly to the leg action itself, but to some other phase of the stroke which is affecting efficient kick performance. One of the commonest of these is badly performed head turning mechanics in breathing.

A distance swimmer requires deep breathing in his race, and instead of using an independent head turning action in relation to his arm action, he usually falls into a slow rhythm coincident with the arm action. This action turns the head to the air and returns the head to the water too slowly. This causes the body to tilt and roll over to its opposite side, rolling the hips with it and, in turn, causing a lateral spread of the legs and an unbalanced kick. It is impossible to manipulate the legs in a vertical plane if the hip level is tilted at an angle.

The feet should not be fully extended or fully pigeon-toed continuously throughout the kick. This will keep the calf of the leg muscles and the plantar region of the foot muscles under a constant state of contraction and the leg will soon fatigue.

Swimmers often fail to remember that when swimming a sliding type of distance stroke, it is the function of the legs to press down forcefully on the down beat of the kick, in order to lift the hips and to relax the spine. The body must be maintained in a stretched and streamlined position.

8. **The Arm Action in the Distance Crawl.**—In order to slow the arm action and allow greater relaxation, the arm in the distance crawl is allowed to glide forward during the catch. However, to obtain the longer catch, the arm reaches out to enter at a very shallow angle and then slides into the catch. Then the elbow is bent more in order to shorten the arm lever so as to obtain greater driving power by driving the arm almost straight backward with some downward pressure. During the distance crawl, while the swimmer is using the sliding arm stroke, he relies upon a flat arc to propel his body forward. This gives the body efficient forward action from the drive as the elbow and wrist extend in a follow-through delivery. From the completion of this arm delivery, the elbow is then bent again and lifted above the surface, and the forearm is flung around to the reach and entry. Unless one has an efficient "rubbery" leg action kick behind a sliding arm stroke, the swimmer should reduce the slide.

(a) *The Reach.*—The reach may be made from either a high bent elbow or from a low bent elbow recovery. Both types are commonly followed in America at the present day.

In the high recovery, care should be taken not to let the forearm hang down vertically from the elbow, because then the hand is too close to the armpit during recovery. When the elbow extends for the reach, it usually enters wrongly because the hand over-reaches in nearly every case, and the elbow extends completely and the shoulder is dropped before the hand entry. The reach is made slightly slower than in the sprint type. However, it must not be too slow, otherwise the shoulder will roll down. Again in this type of stroke the shoulder must remain above the arm during the propulsive arc. The arm should not reach to its full extension above the surface. From the high elbow recovery, the arm comes down from above for the entry. In the low bent elbow recovery, the reach is very close to the surface and goes into the entry slightly sooner, usually with a press type of entry similar to the one described in the sprint stroke.

(b) *The Entry.*—The arm should be pressed lightly into the water and it should continue on under the surface. It should be constantly pressed at the wrist and hand, not the elbow and shoulder.

(c) *The Glide or Support.*—During the glide the pressure should be felt in the fingers. This causes the arm to glide downward slightly below the level of the shoulder which causes the body to rest on that arm but the shoulders and head are not permitted to lower. The water level at the head should remain constant throughout the entire slide. Throughout this slide the elbow should never be stretched or overextended. There should be a natural reach and elbow extension. The tip of the elbow should be pointing to the side, not downward during the slide. If the tip of the elbow is pointing downward, the elbow has been extended too far.

It is during the glide phase of this stroke that many swimmers want to push the shoulder joint forward after the elbow joint has completed its extension. For best leverage and body mechanics, the shoulder should not be pushed forward with the glide. The body glides on the arm from the drive of the other arm and from the constant flow of power delivered from the flutter kick.

If the arm is permitted to glide on, or just barely under the surface, it is too shallow and the entry has lost some of its propulsive effectiveness. The entry should be a propulsive phase of the stroke, even though minor in force to the major propulsive arc. The arm while sliding should move downward as the slide is prolonged. From the study of underwater movies, the actual depth below the surface by very proficient swimmers is approximately six to eight inches at the completion of the glide. From above the surface it appears very much shallower and has the appearance of from two to four inches in depth.

In the low bent elbow recovery, the entry is usually effected with a press entry and the arm slides considerably longer than from the drop from above, or from a high entry. The arms should never be smashed into the water in the slide and pull style of crawl.

There is a stroke entry beginning to take form in distance swimming effected from a high elbow recovery. It is performed by holding the elbow high at the time of entry and permitting the fingers to enter knife-like with the palm turned out, then flattening the hand and pressing onto it during the slide. This permits the elbow to remain high naturally on the entry and will not let the elbow drop during the extension into the water at the entry. This type of recovery and entry can also be performed by turning the hand upon the elbow before entry so that the hand is flattened to the surface and becomes propulsive during the entry.

(d) *The Catch.*—The catch is effected at the completion of the glide the same as described in the sprint type of stroke. The pull or catch initiates the movement in the hand, then the forearm and upper arm follow in rapid succession. The mechanics of the adjustment from pull or draw to push and drive takes place exactly the same way as it is performed in the sprint crawl. Some swimmers use a decided elbow bend, almost a "boomerang" position, while others use a slight bend in adjustment. Whenever a decided bend is used, in order to maintain good leverage and kinesiology in the movements, care should be taken not to let the hand move too far outside the line of the opposite shoulder. Otherwise the mechanical advantage of the pull and drive is lost.

(e) *The Pull and Push Drive.*—The pull, drive, and release are identical in mechanics to that of the sprint type of stroke. The essential difference in the release from that of the sprint type is that it occurs farther back. As a general rule it takes place slightly beyond the hip joint. A few swimmers will pull much farther. However, this is not advisable because the body will flatten out too much and lose its balance, the body sinking and rising with each arm stroke. It is also essential in the release to notice if each hand has the same length of drive to the point of the release so that balance is maintained.

(f) *The Recovery.*—The recovery of the arms may be accomplished as described in the sprint crawl arm recovery. Some swimmers employ a quick recovery, sometimes called a "flip" recovery, while others usually use a slightly slower recovery. Whatever form is used, the elbow, forearm, and hand should be definitely poised in its forward movement immediately when passing the side of the face. It should not be delayed until the point of entry. Such errors cause inefficient flips of the hand at the entry, or an unwinding wrist as the hand enters.

(g) *The Timing of One Arm With the Other Arm.*—A very simple and accurate timing method can be used for both the swimmer and the coach. The recovery arm is used as a guiding basis. When the recovery hand has reached a position midpoint between the tips of the fingers of the sliding or supporting arm and the top of the head, the sliding arm starts its catch and pull. The recovering arm should enter immediately so that the force delivered from the catch and pulling arm slides the body forward on the entering recovery arm. The pulling arm should start the catch and pull rapidly. The weight of the body must not be shifted onto the recovering arm as the catch and pull begins, but must be shifted when the recovery arm is in the water and is in a position to furnish support. It is this timing point that many swimmers miss. The speed derived from this type of stroke is in a large part due to this timing. The principle of arm-slide is present in every type of stroke in the water. One arm is always pulling while the other either is reaching or thrusting forward. One does derive a feeling of continuously sliding downhill, if the entire stroke is performed well.

One can see how this timing differs from the sprint type of stroke. There the recovery hand has reached a position just to the side of the ear or slightly behind it, while in the distance stroke it is much farther forward before the sliding arm goes into its pull.

(h) *The Timing Ratio of the Arms and Legs in Relation to Each Other.*—The same timing is used as described in the sprint crawl stroke, except that where an arm slide is used, a slightly longer kicking stride is necessary to coordinate with the arms.

9. **The Relation of the Head Turning for Breathing to Arm and Leg Action.**—There is little difference in the timing of the head other than has been discussed in the sprint crawl. Even though it is generally agreed among authorities that more time is allowed for the taking of air, because deeper breathing is essential in distance swimming, yet actually no less time is or should be consumed in going to the air and in coming away from it. However, many inexperienced swimmers will, because they are stroking slower, move the head slower to and away from the air. This will disturb the whole stroke rhythm as well as body balance.

The distance swimmer must learn to turn the face equally well to either side for air. Occasionally, by alternating the breathing side, the shoulder muscles gain rest and relaxation.

Common Errors in Head Action Technique.—A common error is either not turning the head fast enough to the point of inhaling, or recovering it back to dead center after air is obtained. This is usually due to a rigid neck. If fatigue sets in too early in a race, breathing should be checked to see if it is adequate and properly executed.

One should not retard the recovery arm as it approaches the point of entry. This fault permits the shoulder to lower and submerge before the hand enters. The hand must drop immediately into the water as it nears the point of entry.

10. **The Throw-Away-Lateral-Spin Turn for Distance Crawl (With Head Out for Breathing).**—This turn is used for distance swimming and was introduced into this country by the Japanese. Its important feature is its ease of performance. However, it is a bit too slow for speed events.

As the body coasts in to the wall it is turned slightly to the side as the under hand touches the wall. The finger tips are turned upward and the elbow is bent to permit the head to come in close to the wall. The tuck is started at this point and the body turns partly on its side and face. The head lifts out and away from the water and wall to get air. The head is turned for air in such a manner that the cheek is flat on the surface. The free hand sweeps down from the hips in front of the body and across the chest. The body is tilted nearly in a sitting position. The turn is actually end-over-end in a tucked position. As the body is thrown away from the wall to a point just beyond a vertical sitting position, the hand on the wall is taken off in one of two ways. In the first method, it is recovered under water to join the other hand in front of the face. In the other, the hand is driven away from the wall above the surface, elbow bent, and speared into the water with tremendous speed. The hand enters slightly in front of the head and face. The arm is pushed down and forward to join the other hand in front of the head. The shoulders and head plunge down with the arm and as the arms extend forward the legs drive into the wall for the push-out. The body is actually tilted on its side slightly at the time of the push-off. Extending the turning arm out hard under the water tends to flatten the body. The speed of execution of this turn depends largely upon the speed with which the turning arm is literally jerked away from the wall and plunged into the water. The turning arm continues to push forward to help right the body again to the push-out position. Some swimmers will remain on the side after the turn is made and push out on the side, then right themselves with the first pull. This is a retarding movement and should not be practiced. The righting of the body, face down, should be performed at the wall. It should be fully completed with the feet as they leave the wall. The push-out in this turn and the break into the surface is the same as in the sprint crawl.

A common error in the execution of a distance turn is that it is usually performed too slowly. This fault is usually due to the habit adopted in early season swimming of making all turns in the same tempo as the stroke rhythm. Turns in practice distance training should always be executed faster than the stroke cadence. Inexperienced swimmers rely upon the turn for rest and the experienced swimmer relies upon it to gain in speed and distance on a napping opponent. The slow turning swimmer must then swim faster to regain what he loses at the turn.

Some swimmers lift the head and body too high above the surface in getting air. The turn should be done quickly, and the inspiration should be executed rapidly.

In any turn the legs should be tucked simultaneously as the turning hand touches the wall. Some swimmers will execute a $\frac{1}{4}$-turn before tucking the legs. This is decidedly slow and should not be practiced.

11. The Finish.—Racing fundamentals for the finish of a distance event are the same as those described for the finish of the sprint crawl. A swimmer should swim through the last 20 per cent of a race with all the speed and effort that he possesses.

The Race.—All racing fundamentals discussed for the middle distance swimmer also apply to the distance swimmer. The longer the race the more carefully the swimmer must plan the distribution of his efforts.

For the benefit of the inexperienced swimmer an individual race plan table is presented (see Table III). By observing this composite pace of championship swimming, one can observe that, as the length of the race increases, there is a tendency to cover the entire distance at an even distribution of effort and stroke cadence. There is no abrupt acceleration or deceleration at any portion of the race. But deceleration gradually takes place after the first 150 yards are covered. This is because speed decreases as the distance increases due to fatigue.

There are some who believe that with a special pacing device a swimmer should be able to swim each length of the pool in proportional time from start to finish and in this way preserve energy and perform the entire distance vastly more economically. Experi-

TABLE III

THIS TABLE SHOWS IDEAL SPLIT TIMES FOR VARIOUS RACING TIMES IN THE 440 YARDS CRAWL (25 YD. POOL)

ELAPSED DISTANCE YD.	ELAPSED TIME SEC.	SPLIT TIME SEC.	ELAPSED DISTANCE YD.	ELAPSED TIME SEC.	SPLIT TIME SEC.
25	11.4	11.4	25	12.0	12.0
50	24.9	13.5	50	26.1	14.1
75	39.5	14.6	75	41.3	15.2
100	54.1	14.6	100	56.5	15.2
125	1:09.4	15.3	125	1:12.4	15.9
150	1:24.7	15.3	150	1:28.3	15.9
175	1:40.5	15.8	175	1:44.7	16.4
200	1:56.4	15.9	200	2:01.2	16.5
225	2:12.3	15.9	225	2:17.7	16.5
250	2:28.2	15.9	250	2:34.2	16.5
275	2:44.6	16.4	275	2:51.1	16.9
300	3:01.0	16.4	300	3:08.0	16.9
325	3:17.3	16.3	325	3:24.8	16.8
350	3:33.6	16.3	350	3:41.6	16.8
375	3:49.9	16.3	375	3:58.4	16.8
400	4:06.1	16.2	400	4:15.1	16.7
425	4:21.4	15.3	425	4:30.9	15.8
440	4:30.0	8.6	440	4:40.0	9.1
25	12.5	12.5	25	13.1	13.1
50	27.1	14.6	50	28.3	15.2
75	42.8	15.7	75	44.6	16.3
100	58.5	15.7	100	1:00.9	16.3
125	1:14.9	16.4	125	1:17.9	17.0
150	1:31.3	16.4	150	1:34.9	17.0
175	1:48.2	16.9	175	1:52.4	17.5
200	2:05.2	17.0	200	2:10.0	17.6
225	2:22.3	17.1	225	2:27.6	17.6
250	2:39.4	17.1	250	2:45.2	17.6
275	2:56.9	17.5	275	3:01.3	18.1
300	3:14.4	17.5	300	3:21.4	18.1
325	3:31.8	17.4	325	3:39.3	17.9
350	3:49.2	17.4	350	3:57.2	17.9
375	4:06.6	17.4	375	4:15.1	17.9
400	4:23.9	17.3	400	4:32.9	17.8
425	4:40.3	16.4	425	4:49.8	16.9
440	4:50.0	9.7	440	5:00.0	10.2
25	13.7	13.7	25	14.2	
50	29.5	15.8	50	30.5	
75	46.4	16.9	75	47.9	
100	1:03.3	16.9	100	1:05.3	
125	1:20.8	17.5	125	1:23.4	
150	1:38.3	17.5	150	1:41.5	
175	1:56.3	18.0	175	2:00.1	
200	2:14.4	18.1	200	2:18.8	
225	2:32.5	18.1	225	2:37.5	
250	2:50.6	18.1	250	2:56.2	
275	3:07.2	18.6	275	3:15.4	
300	3:27.8	18.6	300	3:34.6	

TABLE III—CONT'D

ELAPSED DISTANCE YD.	ELAPSED TIME SEC.	SPLIT TIME SEC.	ELAPSED DISTANCE YD.	ELAPSED TIME SEC.	SPLIT TIME SEC.
325	3:46.3	18.5	325	3:53.7	
350	4:04.8	18.5	350	4:12.8	
375	4:23.3	18.5	375	4:31.8	
400	4:41.7	18.4	400	4:50.7	
425	4:59.2	17.5	425	5:08.7	
440	5:10.0	10.8	440	5:20.0	

ments have shown this method of swimming to be unsatisfactory. The swimmer cannot swim slow enough at the start. Then, too, he finds difficulty in maintaining a uniform stroke cadence as the race progresses and fatigue sets in.

CHAPTER VI

RELAY RACING

Relay racing is that form of competition in which two or more men swim the same specified distance, one relieving the other at the end of the distance.

Relay racing is fun for most swimmers as well as spectators, because of its spirited competition. Each portion of the relay race is designated as a "leg." Points in relay racing run very much higher than in an individual race. For this reason relays become very spirited because of the number of points which may be won.

Types of Relay Races.—The types of relays in swimming are usually of two kinds; medley (including the three competitive styles of swimming), and the freestyle relays, which may be classified as sprint, and middle distance races, that is, for each individual portion of the race. The length of each "leg" is quite definitely standardized for high school, college, and Olympic competition. Other types or varying distances come under the heading of noteworthy relay performances. These types are as follows:

1. *High School*
    a. 150 yards medley (75-foot pools) (3 x 50)
       180 yards medley (60-foot pools) (3 x 60)
       (Three swimmers on each team, each to swim one-third the distance; first, back stroke; second, breast stroke; third, freestyle).
    b. 200 yards sprint freestyle relay (75-foot pools) (4 x 50)
       160 yards sprint freestyle relay (60-foot pools) (4 x 40)
       (Four swimmers, each to swim one-fourth the distance).

2. *College*
    a. 300 yards medley relay (3 x 100)
       (Three swimmers on each team, each to swim one-third the distance; first, back stroke; second, breast stroke; third, freestyle).
    b. 400 yards sprint freestyle relay (4 x 100)
       (Four men on each team, each to swim one-fourth the distance).

3. *Olympic*

    a. 800 meters freestyle relay (4 x 200)

      (Four men on each team, each to swim one-fourth the distance).

Comparative Marks for the Relay Competition.—Relays for both high school and college are of two divisions. The first is the medley relay, and second is the freestyle relay. The distance for high school is shortened from that of college competition, depending upon the length of course.

	WORLD'S RECORD	AMERICAN RECORD	INTERCOLLE- GIATE RECORD	HIGH SCHOOL RECORD
Twenty-yard Course				
160 yards relay freestyle		1:11.8[1]		1:15.6
400 yards relay freestyle		3:27.9	3:29.2	3:45.1
180 yards medley relay				1:40.7
300 yards medley relay		2:53.6	2:54.5	3:05.7
Short Course (25 yards)				
200 yards relay freestyle		1:33.5	1:36.3	1:36.3
400 yards relay freestyle	3:31.3	3:30.7	3:28.8	3:46.5
150 yards medley relay		1:19.6		1:22.4
300 yards medley relay		2:51.9	2:51.9	3:08.5
Long Course (50 yards or over)				
400 yards relay freestyle		3:38.7	3:37.6	
300 yards medley relay		3:04.6	3:04.5	

The Arrangement of a Relay Team.—When selecting members of a relay team and the order in which they swim, a coach must first consider a number of factors as to the qualifications of the candidates, before making a decision. A number of these factors are:

1. Who is a fast starter and calm under fire of competition?
2. Which one will swim best when behind?
3. Which swims best when in the lead?
4. Which is the weaker competitor?
5. Which lead off man will give the most stability to the team?
6. Which anchor man will give most confidence to the team?

Another question which must be answered is, should all men be selected on a tryout basis? That is, for the particular meet for which a tryout is held, should those who win be on your team, because they were fastest on the day of the tryout?

Some coaches will rely entirely upon tryouts. Others will wait until well along in the meet and see how certain individuals per-

---

[1]Noteworthy performance, not a record.

formed in earlier races and then nominate the men for the relay team. If a meet is close and depends upon the last relay event, some coaches will often select, at the last minute, a slightly slower man but one who has been "tried and true." This is selecting on a percentage basis and is considered an advisable procedure. One cannot take chances and experiment when the meet is close. A faster man may be an "in and outer," or an inexperienced man may fold up when the going gets "tough." After the men have been selected, the next question to be decided is, what order should they be placed in competition? We must now go back to the above questions as to personal characteristics and qualifications.

For the sake of simplicity, let us list the men in the order of their speed, as 1, 2, 3, and 4 respectively. The most commonly used order is 2, 3, 4, 1. This arrangement places the weaker man in the number 3 position with two good men in front of him and the fastest man behind him. This should give the weaker man confidence.

Another commonly used plan is 2, 4, 3, and 1. This places the fastest man at anchor and the second fastest in the lead-off position, with the weaker man in the number 2 position. This arrangement is made with the hope that the second fastest man will hold his own or hand over a lead to the weaker man. Should those two men lose the lead, there are still two good men left to make up lost yardage.

Another order of swimming the sprint relay, and one which is often used to confuse opponents, is to arrange the competition in the order 1, 2, 3, 4. The idea is to put the faster man out in front to get the lead and the number 2 man to further gain or at least hold the advantage, so that by the time the weaker "anchor" man comes up, he has been given a substantial advantage. In case things do not go well for him, he still has quite a margin. In each race, the team standing in the meet, and the opponents' possible lineup, should be the determining factors in arranging the team. If a line-up has been decided upon before meet time, a last minute change is likely to disturb the composure and confidence of the team.

The Technique of the Take-Off.—The swimming take-off in relay racing differs from those in track relay racing. In track, the competitor receives a baton from his predecessor within a limited zone. He then must carry this on and pass it to his succeeding teammate. Such passing cannot be accomplished in swimming relay racing.

In the swimming relay the preceding swimmer finishes his "leg" by touching the finish wall. Poised above this finish lane and wall is the succeeding teammate who takes off as soon as his teammate touches the wall. There is some latitude given the swimmer at the touch-off comparable to the zone advantage given a runner. The starting swimmer may be in motion, such as arm swing or body lean, but his feet must not leave the take-off wall until his teammate has touched it. In competition this is checked in two ways: (1) a "take-off judge is to station himself in such a position that he can place his finger on the foot of each swimmer (after the first one) and at the same time see the end of the pool, and he shall judge whether the swimmer leaves his position before the preceding swimmer touches the end." (2) The usual method is the honor system. The judge stations himself at the side of the finishing end of the pool and merely observes if the rule is not violated.

There are several methods by which a swimmer may judge when to start his wind-up for the take-off. The swimmer must use his own judgment when to begin preparation for his take-off. A safe method is for the swimmer to begin preparation for his take-off when the head of his teammate is approximately 3½ feet from the finish wall. When the teammate's head reaches this point, the starting swimmer can drive with tremendous force and still have his feet on his mark when the "leg" is finished. The finishing swimmer must practice driving in with the finishing hand in order to time it perfectly. The starting swimmer must observe and practice judging a distance of 3½ feet. He looks down at the swimmer below him from under his eye lashes, but must hold his head well up. If the head is held low he is likely to lose balance, or when he does dive out, he is likely to dive short.

In a shorter sprint where speed is greater, a 4-foot margin can be allowed and timed with the windup of the starter.

In breast stroke swimming in the medley relay, the freestyle may allow not more than 2½ feet from the head to the finish wall, since the speed of the incoming swimmer is slower.

CHAPTER VII

THE BACK CRAWL STROKE

This stroke is of more recent origin than that of its sire, the crawl. Since its origin in approximately 1912, its speed has been improved more than either the crawl or the breast stroke. A comparison of the fastest times recorded for the three strokes in 1912 with those of the present time is as follows:

	1912 100 yd. (sec.)	1941 100 yd. (sec.)	Difference in time (sec.)
Back Crawl	1:12.0	:58.8	:13.2
Crawl Stroke	:58.0	:51.0	:07.8
Breast Stroke	1:10.0	1:00.6	:10.6

When the back crawl first became known as the fastest means of swimming on the back, the technique of stroke mechanics varied widely among coaches and swimmers.

Some of the questions considered are: Should the arms be recovered straight or bent? Should they be placed in the water behind the head, straight back from the shoulder or outside a line with the shoulder? Should the arms be pulled deep or shallow? Should they be pulled straight or in a bent position? Should the head be carried in line with the body or held up facing the legs? Should the body roll more than in the crawl? Through a long process of trial and error, a general agreement has been reached as to the best style, so that we have but one style universally accepted. This style will be called the Kiefer style since it was introduced by him. Practically every existing world's back stroke record has been established by Adolph Kiefer.

One must bear in mind that, in swimming the back crawl style, the man is on his back and structural limitations at the shoulder joint prevent him from pulling the arms through the propulsive phases under the body as in the crawl. However, to partially offset this limitation, he is able to maintain his breathing apparatus above the surface which is a great advantage. The fact that the swimmer does not need to turn or lift his head out to the side or to the front for breathing air, as is the case with the crawl and breast strokes, makes this stroke one of the most mechanically balanced of all the competitive strokes. Because no head turning mechanics are required for breathing, resistance to water is minimized and as a result, this is the smoothest of any of the swimming strokes.

Physical Qualifications for the Back Crawl Swimmer.—Almost any one endowed with ability in water, and better than average strength can swim the back crawl reasonably well. However, those who have ambitions of reaching the top should possess a height of at least 5 feet 11 inches and a snakelike type of build. Along with this, they must be endowed with strength and endurance. The 150 yards back crawl is probably one of the most difficult races on the college swimming program. A fast flutter kick is essential for speed. There are many boys who have long "rubbery" legs, but they do not possess either the power or speed to drive them fast enough for either 100 yards or 150 yards to be top-flight swimmers. Many shorter built swimmers are endowed with extremely fast driving legs and powerful arms who make up for their lack of long legs and arms by their speed and endurance.

The back crawl swimmer moves his arms and legs at about the same cadence as the sprint swimmer and yet he must cover a distance which is beyond that of the sprint. His physiologic characteristics are, therefore, a combination of the sprint crawl and the middle distance swimmer.

He must be able to move his legs rapidly, he must have powerful arms and flexible shoulders, and he must also have a considerable amount of endurance. His sense of rhythm must be well developed.

Comparative Marks for the Back Stroke Competition.—The longest distance for high school boys competition in the back stroke is 100 yards. For college men it is 150 yards.

	WORLD'S RECORD	AMERICAN RECORD	INTERCOLLE- GIATE RECORD	HIGH SCHOOL RECORD
Twenty-yard Course				
100 yards back stroke		:57.6		:57.6
150 yards back stroke		1:33.0	1:33.0	
Short Course (25 yards)				
100 yards back stroke	:58.8	:57.8		:59.9
150 yards back stroke	1:32.7	1:32.7	1:34.2	
Long Course (50 yards or over)				
150 yards back stroke		1:37.2	1:41.6	

The Back Crawl Start.—The back crawl stroke start requires an entirely different technique than the crawl or the breast stroke. In most instances the back crawler is put to a disadvantage in competition because of the lack of a secure hand support. Some pools do not even have a scum rail at the starting end of the pool, but only a flat wall 18 inches above the surface and nothing on top of the wall but a smooth flat platform. This is a disadvantage which should be corrected. Some type of starting blocks should be made with a hand bar for the competitor to grasp (Fig. 4A). The bar can be constructed so that it is in line with the starting wall. A more advantageous start could be made with hand rests 18 inches above the surface. Adjustable foot rests upon which to place the feet should be constructed to prevent slipping and to give substantial support to the foot. With this equipment a more powerful start could be made and would enhance the flight through the air and give an advantage to the start similar to that of the other events.

1. **The Starting Position.**—If no starting rail is available, the hands grasp the scum rail about shoulder width or spread slightly wider than shoulders. The feet take a position beneath the hands parallel to each other and spread hip width. The toes are from 0 to 4 inches under the surface and are never spread farther than the width of the hips. The feet are placed firmly against the wall (Fig. 4A).

Another position of the feet is to take a walking stride stance with the toe of one foot placed about level with the heel of the other foot. Either of these two methods of foot placing and spacing is used.

The body must assume a closely bunched tuck with the hips placed close to the heels. The arms may be held either straight or slightly bent at the elbows.

If a hand rail is used, it should be grasped with the first two joints of the fingers, the heel of the hand resting close to the wall. At the signal to start, the hand throw can be executed faster with the quick extension of the wrist against the wall.

The above stance is assumed when the official starter gives the command, "take your marks." At the report of the gun, the body is catapulted backward as if the body were crouched upon a powerful compressed spring which was suddenly released (Fig. 4B).

2. **Leaving the Mark.**—The aim of the throw-away action in the back stroke start is to make a backward racing dive by projecting

Fig. 4.—A, B, C.

Fig. 4.—A series of ideal form showing the start positions for the back crawl start.   A. The preliminary stance.   B. The "set" position.   C. Leaving the mark.   D. Body entering the water.   E. The start of the stroke at the end of the glide under the surface.   F. The position of the body in coming to the surface.

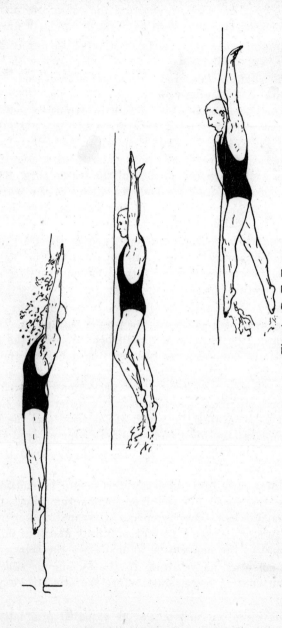

Fig. 4.—D, E, F.

the body out over the surface, entering the water and utilizing the momentum derived from the start in the glide under water.

The starting movement consists of driving the arms backward to a full arm extension above the head and in line with the spine. This arm movement is executed with tremendous speed. The head is driven backward simultaneously with the arms. The legs then begin extending at the knees and hips with explosive speed. When these joints are fully extended, then the ankles are extended. The final snap of the ankles gives added speed to the body. This should throw the body into a stretched position with back slightly arched and the hips well above the surface of the water (Fig. 4C). If no hand rail is provided and the body is sitting in the water at the start, the hips must be lifted out of the water, otherwise they will drag through the water causing a resistance.

The swimmer should grasp the hand rail in the starting stance, with the feet at the surface line. In this position the body can be driven far out above the surface with a very much faster start and a greater penetrating power into the water.

3. **The Entry.**—The position of the body is somewhat arched so as to gain a clean cut entry at the proper angle. As the hands enter the water, the head is held well back between the extended arms (Fig. 4D). The arms are fully stretched beyond the head, in line with the spine. The wrists should be held straight in line with the forearm. A common error is to hyperextend the wrists which causes the body to glide too deep into the water. The hands and arms should be separated the width of the head and the neck and face. The moment the head and shoulders have entered the water, the head should be raised in order to prevent the body from going too deep.

4. **The Glide.**—The glide under water should be continued to a point where the speed derived from momentum slows to a rate equalling that of the swimming speed. Overanxious sprinters have a tendency to start stroke action prematurely and thus do not take full advantage of the momentum gained from the start.

As the momentum is retarded to the swimming speed in the glide, the flutter kick begins just before the arm stroke action begins.

During the glide, air may either be expelled gradually or held until just prior to breaking through to the surface.

5. **Breath Control in the Back Stroke Start.**—When the arms are thrown back over the head, away from the starting wall, the chest region is lifted and expanded, causing air to rush into the lungs easily through a wide open mouth (Fig. 4C). The breath is held during entry and during most of the glide.

When one is lying on the back, under water, the opening from the nose into the throat is directly down. The body lying on its back under water causes considerable respiratory distress to the inexperienced back stroke swimmers, especially during the glide-out phase of the start and also at the push-out at the turn.

There are several ways to prevent this distress of water entering the throat by way of the nasal passage. One method is to curl the upper lip and press it up against the external nasal openings. This closes them entirely and prevents water entering the outer nasal and sinus regions. At the instant before swimming into the surface of the water and at the moment the nose has cleared the surface and the outer nostrils are free of water, the exhalation is started and the upper lip is removed. The mouth is then opened for an inspiration. A more conventional method is to expire air slowly through the nose continuously throughout the glide from the start and also throughout push-out from the turn. This method is most difficult to control by a beginner because while lying on the back there is created a tremendous pressure. This pressure causes the air held in the lungs to be forced out through the nose unchecked early in the glide. When the air has escaped in this manner, the inexperienced swimmer then finds himself just as helpless to prevent water entering the lungs through the nose before he comes to the surface.

6. **The Start of the Stroke Action.**—The arm stroke action begins while the body is still under the surface (Fig. 4E). The swimmer then comes up forward to the surface swimming.

While the first arm begins its pull under water, the other arm should remain firmly anchored under the surface and straight ahead in line with the body. Downward pressure on this arm is necessary to keep it under the water and prevent it from shooting out of the water. Maintaining the arm under the water streamlines the body and eliminates considerable resistance. The arm that is pulling should pull fast and hard. This first pulling arm should bend at the elbow to effect quick forward propulsion to the body, which is already moving fast from the start.

If the initial pulling arm is pulled in a straight-arm position, it will lead to two errors: first, it will push the body out of the water, instead of driving it straight ahead; second, the straight arm cannot pull through the water fast enough to maintain the speed. The body must come out of the glide swimming fast. The head should be raised as the first arm is pulled (Fig. 4F).

In the alternating type of initial arm action, the body slithers through the surface under continuous application of power. The body rides on a supporting arm which is alive and preparing itself to catch the water the moment the other arm releases the water. As the body is swimming out into the surface, the stroke continues with regular rhythm. The head has been raised to the proper carriage position in the next two or three arm strokes.

Back Crawl Stroke Technique.—Since the events in school, college, A.A.U., and Olympics are not longer than 150 yards, a sprint style of back crawl stroke swimming will be presented. The 150 yards is so nearly a sprint distance for most swimmers that it will be considered as a sprint event in this discussion. The style to be discussed can be easily modified for any distance because the mechanics can be adjusted to a slower rhythm without seriously disturbing the whole stroke. The swimmer seeks a lower floating level and strokes slower for the longer distances.

The arms perform in just reverse order to the crawl. The back stroke is more easily mastered than the crawl or breast stroke because it does not have the complex breathing skills to be mastered. The arms move in a regular cycle. The kick is similar in action to the six-beat crawl kick.

The arms are almost entirely straight throughout the entire stroke revolution. Once the stroke is mechanically mastered it seldom gets out of line. Sometimes a strong swimmer who is not highly endowed with motor skills makes a very fine back crawler.

1. **The Position of the Body in Swimming the Back Crawl.**—The body is held nearly in a horizontal position and is maintained as near the surface as possible, with the hips just low enough to keep the legs under the surface (Fig. 5A). The hips should not sag downward. The body is stretched. The chest and abdomen are

flattened so that the water slipping around from the side of the head and neck can wash smoothly over the shoulders and chest with as little resistance as possible. The back of the spine presents a slight convex position to the water. The back is curved just enough to cause the small of the back to conform to a continuous curved line from the hips to the shoulders. Stretching the body and relaxing the spine will place the body in this position.

(a) *Position of the Head.*—The head is carried in line with the body (Fig. 5B). The position of the head aids materially in forming the proper spinal curve. It also aids in balancing the body. The chin should be tucked close to the throat so that the eyes can easily see toward the feet. The back portion of the head below the ears should ride under the surface. The head in this position serves as a rudder. The position of the head in the water will vary somewhat with characteristics of the individual and the amount of speed generated. Usually the lower tips of the ears are at the water level.

The eyes, nose, and chin should be centered on the line of progression. Under no circumstances, except when glancing for the turn, should the chin move out of this alignment regardless of the movements of the shoulder girdle while stroking. In spite of a slight rolling of the body caused by the shoulder action of the arm stroke, the chin must remain centered and pressed down toward the throat. The body requires this stability of the head in order to maintain body alignment and balance during the stroke action.

(b) *The Position of the Neck.*—A long flexible neck is a definite aid to a back stroke swimmer because it offers a lesser amount of resistance to water than a short neck. In both the short- and the long-necked individuals, relaxation is essential. Unless the neck is relaxed the chin will not be able to remain fixed while the shoulder girdle is oscillating. However, if an individual has a long neck, then instead of having to hold the body in an angular position in order to elevate the head, he can hold the body in an almost horizontal line with the shoulders completely submerged (Fig. 5C). The neck is projected upward, with the chin tucked toward the throat and the back of the head presses into the water. In this position the water washes down smoothly over the entire length of the body.

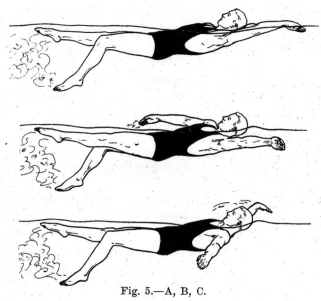

Fig. 5.—A, B, C.

Fig. 5.—A series of ideal form for the back crawl stroke showing the six leg beats and one revolution of the arm stroke. These figures also show the counterbalance of the arm and leg action and the position of the body in relation to the surface.

Fig. 5.—D, E, F.

(c) *Position of the Shoulder Girdle and Upper Spine.*—Ordinarily a swimmer who has a normal spine while walking will have the proper contour to his shoulder girdle and upper spine if he tucks his chin in and stretches the body and relaxes the spine and neck (Fig. 5A). In this position the cervical spines, from the shoulder to the base of the skull, will form a convex curve in line with the thoracic spines. A hunched back position would diminish power because the back muscles would be stretched and the pectorals would be shortened. The pectoralis major and coracobrachialis muscles are the chief pulling muscles in the back stroke. The assisting muscles are the terres major and the latissimus dorsi. The shoulder girdle muscles should be stretched daily to keep them supple and strong throughout the season. It must be remembered that the arms in the back crawl work in reverse gear. Therefore, if the pectorals are allowed to become shortened when the arms reach back for the entry, they will prohibit the arm from stretching backward and the body will have to roll over to accomplish a proper entry. The pectoral muscles should be stretched thoroughly so that there will be no resistance to the freedom of the arm action especially in the recovery and the entry where efficient muscular performance is absolutely essential to great swimming speed performance in back stroke swimming.

The major characteristic of swimming the Kiefer style of back crawl is in the method of recovery. The arms sweep back from release to entry in a low lateral swing. This style has two advantages over one which employs a vertical recovery. The advantages are: First, due to the structural limitation of the shoulder socket, if the arm is recovered vertically, the shoulder socket locks itself just as the arm is extended overhead and about to enter the water. With the shoulder girdle slightly bent upward like a sled runner, the forearm and hand really never get into the water unless the body is rolled over. The reason the shoulder joint locks is that the head of the humerus interferes with the coracohumeral and capsular ligament. The greater trochanter of the humerus also interferes by coming in contact with the acromion of the scapula which projects over the shoulder socket. However, if the arm is swung back low over the surface and placed into the water just outside the shoulder joint, with the palm down, the joint does not bind and lock itself; neither does the body need to roll over to accommodate the movement. It is because of this structural limitation of the shoulder socket that the low arm recovery is so much more advantageous than the vertical arm recovery.

The second advantage to this style is that the arm will not go into the water as deep as it usually does following a vertical recovery. However, by going deep, both the latissimus dorsi and the pectoralis major muscles are placed at a mechanical disadvantage. In the shallow pull both of these muscles pull with a very good mechanical advantage.

(d) *The Position of the Hips and Lower (Lumbar) Spine.*—A common tendency for back strokers is to permit the hips to sag downward. This is brought about by carrying the head too high and rounding the neck and shoulder spines too much. This is true in the crawl as well as the back crawl. This sag is eliminated by stretching the body while swimming. Not only should the body be stretched in order to lift the hips, but down pressure must be exerted on the two points of support; the arms as they enter and press, and the down beat of the kick. The pelvis is tilted forward to straighten a deep curvature of the lower back (Fig. 5C).

The hips do not have as much oscillation as in the crawl. There is, however, just enough undulating movement in the hips for counterbalance between the beats of the legs and the pelvis.

Lateral sway of the hips should be eliminated. This is usually caused by over-reaching in the arm entry.

2. **The Action of the Legs.**—As in the crawl, the six-beat kick is the most efficient and practical because of its natural counterbalance rhythm in stroke cadence.

There is little difference between the back crawl flutter kick and the crawl kick, as far as mechanics is concerned. The hip, knee, and ankle joints undulate the same way in either kick. There are, however, two essential differences. (Note diagram.[1]) First, the feet do not kick into or break through the surface. However, the legs lie just under the surface and at the completion of the up kick, the leg has straightened at the knee, but the knee and foot have not kicked through the surface. Underwater study of champions, including Kiefer, reveals the absence of air bubbles in the back crawl. This should explode the theory that air bubbles give added friction for the feet to get traction in the water. Air bubbles, if anything, increase

[1]Pictures of the kick from side view p. 122.

resistance rather than permit smooth water to wash down the legs. By the use of the underwater camera method, it is seen that the air bubbles pass backward at an angle and do not again come in contact with the other leg in either the down or up beat in the crawl flutter kick (note diagram 1).

The second significant difference between the two flutter kicks is that on completion of the up beat, the upper surface of the leg is on a straight line with the upper surface of the hips, abdomen, and chest.

In general, in the back flutter kick, the foot and toes bend inward in the up kick more so than in the down beat of the crawl kick. They do not remain in pigeon-toed position on the down beat. On the down beat the foot is fully extended.

In the up beat the knee bends and then quickly straightens to create a whip to the foot. During the bend of the knee, the inexperienced swimmer will very often bend or lift the knees too far and break the surface. This should be avoided. The water should be permitted to slip or wash down over the legs from the hips downward and not be retarded or resisted by poking the knee through the surface. To streamline the legs and avoid this knee lift, the legs should be stretched from the hips out. If the knee is lifting, the foot is not pressing against the water and is naturally ineffective. On the up stroke, the knee bends and does rise to the upper surface level of the body. When the knee straightens, the foot whips up so that at the completion of the knee extension the leg is in a straight line with the upper surface of the body.

The axis of action for this kick is in the hip joint as in the crawl. The initiating movement is in the thigh, driven by the power of the pelvis and thigh flexors and hip extensor muscles. Initiating the movement in the thigh creates an action in the foreleg and foot, giving them an appearance, when in motion, of waving fishtails. Power is transmitted downward through the legs by means of pressure at effective angles against the resistance of the water, giving this back flutter kick its propulsive force in water.

The most frequent errors are those of holding the head either too high or too far back. Holding the head high will round the back too much. Holding it too far back will flatten it. Lifting the hips and thighs above the surface of the water will cause too much surface friction and therefore slow the speed. Each individual should experiment with head level to find the best level for creating least resistance to forward speed. Anatomic characteristics make some differences among different individuals. Sometimes the legs are held too stiff and not relaxed to give free play to the joints. This is especially true in the action of the ankle.

3. **The Arm Technique and Mechanics of the Back Crawl.**—The movements of the arms in the back crawl differ from that of the crawl in mechanics as well as timing. However, arm and leg ratio is 1 to 6, the same as in the crawl stroke.

(a) *The Recovery of the Arms.*—When the hand has completed its drive at the side of the thigh and below the hip (Fig. 5D), the initiating movement in the recovery is started. The shoulder lifts slightly as the body weight is shifted over onto the opposite arm as it enters. The elbow of the recovering arm bends slightly as the arm is lifted out of the water (Fig. 5E). The wrist is turned so that the palm faces toward the surface. It droops slightly to permit it to relax and drain the water from the arm as the arm lifts out of the water. Bending the elbow slightly as the arm is lifted out of the water serves three essential purposes: first, it releases the tension of the arm flexor muscles and permits them to rest. Second, it permits the water to wash down the arm and drain off the finger tips as the arm is lifted out of the water, thus reducing an added weight and a curtain of water which is a retarding factor to speed. Third, the turning of the palm downward toward the water as it is recovered is facilitated by the rotation of the elbow as it is bent.

The moment the finger tips have cleared the surface, the elbow is extended rather quickly and the arm moves up just above the water's surface to the entry. The wrist can be slightly drooped during the recovery, but it must again be straightened in line with the forearm at the entry.

A common error is to bend the elbow during the recovery thereby causing the shoulder and elbow to enter the water before the hand and wrist enter. The arm is never above a 45° angle to the surface of the water during the recovery. If the arm is recovered much higher than this angle, the arm enters at a steep vertical angle which is likely to cause a faulty angle of pull under the surface.

(b) *The Entry.*—The entry should follow the recovery without any retardation. The movement of the arm is slightly accelerated just prior to the entry. On entering the water, the arm should be pressed into the water and should disappear immediately below the surface. This is the most important timing point in the arm action of the back crawl. There are far too many back crawlers who believe that their entire wrist, hand, and forearm are in the water at the entry when, actually, only the shoulder is submerged and half the forearm is projecting above the surface. In this position the wrist and forearm glide along the surface with the hand abducted down toward the entry, wrist joint locked, and palm vertical.

The correct hand entry is with the palm facing the surface (Fig. 5F). The wrist is slightly flexed at an angle of nearly 60°. The fingers are parallel with the line of the arm. The wrist should be straight, not abducted. The palm is now in a position to slide forward and into the water ahead of the shoulder, the same as in the crawl. The outer extremity of the arm, that is, the outer edge of the wrist, hand, and fingers, press into the water and give support to the whole body and prevent the shoulder from dropping below the hand. The hand should be pressed in quickly. When the hand approaches the entry position, it must get in before the shoulder. It should not be smashed, but quickly and smoothly pressed so that the arm will slide down to the catch and pull.

The hand should enter the water about 3 to 6 inches outside the shoulder line. The common error of the untrained swimmer is that he presses or smashes the arm immediately into the catch. The entry should be a quickened movement in order to keep the shoulder above the arm. If the movement is slow, the shoulder will ease down below the hand.

(c) *The Press-Slide.*—In the back crawl, as in the crawl, there is a definite press-slide phase (Fig. 5A). Even though brief, it is present in top sprinters, and it is there for a very definite purpose.

The hand and forearm press downward and slide forward to a very shallow depth in preparation for the catch. This is not deep as in the crawl, but barely an inch or two under the surface level. In this position the muscles which depress the arm have a good mechanical advantage. The shoulder is behind as well as above the arm in its drive. The palm is faced downward at an angle so that during the pressing phase, pressure is felt on the fingers.

During the entry and slide, the body should not roll into the arm. After the arm has entered, the body weight is inclined forward toward the arm, not laterally. This slight inclination toward the sliding arm also accommodates the opposite arm in lifting out of the water.

There is but little roll of the body in this type of back crawl. The fundamental movement occurs in a loose, flexible shoulder socket which gives the arm the freedom of action it requires. Tight shouldered individuals cannot swim this stroke until they loosen their shoulder girdle by using stretching exercises for the shoulder girdle muscles daily.

There are some authorities who believe that the arm should enter and "dig" or go immediately into the drive. There are some very good back crawlers who use such a type of stroke. However, it reverts back to the smash entry, and with a smash entry it is doubtful if a full cycle of six full measured kicks can be executed on one stroke revolution. Again, there are some coaches who advocate anchoring the arm into the water and watching the body go by. This is the sensation one has when the stroke is properly executed, but actually the arms are not anchored. They definitely drive through the water, even though it seems that the body goes by stationary arms.

(d) *The Catch, Pull and Push Drive.*—The catch, pull and push or drive phase of the back crawl will be considered as a whole, rather than broken down into its separate parts. In this stroke it is possible to pull the arm through to the release in either of two ways; straight or bent.

1. **With Straight Arm**.—There are really few back crawlers who keep the arm straight after they have been swimming for several years. In learning, it is best to start with a straight arm pull. Later, the skill of bending the elbow for the push phase can be learned. There are, however, many top swimmers using the straight arm pull. Kiefer is included. Any strong rugged boy can successfully use the straight arm pull all the way from the catch to the completion of the drive. If the arm is long, it requires powerful muscles to drive the arm through hard and fast. The straight arm back strokers usually develop a slow, lazy looking pull. In sprinting, the arms must move more rapidly through the water and the hand must grip the water and not permit it to slip. The longer armed boys who are less rugged would find a more productive speed stroke with the arm bent at the elbow. In this way, the lever arm is shortened which gives greater advantage to the muscles.

9

The catch in the straight arm pull is no different than for the bent arm pull. The hand must be alive and sensitive just preliminary to the catch. The fingers, hand, and wrist must not be fixed. They give and resist when pressure is applied against them. The first movement of the catch is in the fingers and the hand which curves and presses downward and backward with a quickened movement. The palm is faced outward and toward the feet as the pressure is increased in the pull (Fig. 5B and E). The arm pulls very shallow in this movement, approximately 2 to 4 inches under the surface, until the hand and arm reach a point directly out from the shoulder where the depth is increased to from 6 to 8 inches. From this point to the release the whole arm presses downward to the finish on a plane in line with the body and against the leg. The palm is faced rearward and completes its drive tight alongside the thigh.

2. **With Bent Arm.**—The catch is started with the hand and fingers the same as in the straight arm action. The pull is at a deeper angle and is slightly faster. Instead of stretching the arm out to its full length as in the straight arm, the arm length is gradually shortened as the pull progresses. A firm grip is maintained with the hand by bending the elbow down. When the arm and hand have reached a point just slightly ahead of the line with the shoulder, a mechanical adjustment takes place. The shoulder girdle is prepared for the transition from a pulling or drawing action to a pushing or driving action. During this transition the propulsive force is not weakened and no dead spot appears in the pull. On the contrary, during this phase the forearm muscles spring into action and begin a powerful forearm drive, followed by a continued contraction of the depressor muscles of the shoulder arm. As the forearm executes this drive, the elbow is bent downward and slightly forward and moves in advance of the wrist and hand. The action is similar to that of a baseball pitcher who is in the act of throwing with the arm poised overhead. The elbow is brought forward slightly ahead of the ball, but as the powerful forearm flexors come into play, the forearm and the hand give a final flip to the ball as it leaves the hand in the follow-through stages. The back stroke swimmers use the same arm action as the baseball pitcher in order to get speed to the drive. The swimmer's hand describes a letter "S." The swirls from the swimmer's hand drive can often be observed as he executes the fore-

arm drive. Although the hand does come very close to the surface in this stroke during the forearm whip, the hand in this movement should not break into the surface or pass through the surface water, or it will lose its hold against the water.

At the completion of this drive, the arm and hand finish at the side of the thigh as in the straight arm action. This type of propulsive arm drive should prove to be ideal for the long and weak-armed individuals. It is a movement that can move the arm with speed and force through the water in the propulsive phase. Sometimes swimmers are often unable to pull a straight arm through the water fast enough during the latter portion of the race when they are fatigued. The bent arm type of drive is then used to advantage.

(e) *The Release.*—The hand and fingers complete a whip or push from the wrist in the final stages of the drive of the arm in both the straight and the bent arm styles. The hands press the water directly backward toward the rear. At the same time that the upper arm and elbow are actually squeezing the water out from between the arm and body, the hand and wrist snap in an attempt to give a final push just before the arm has released its hold on the water. After the release, the arm lifts out immediately (Fig. 5D and E).

There are a great many coaches who advocate a feathering motion in the final stages of the drive. This is simply sculling with the hand. The idea is to give the arm a greater propulsive finish of its drive. Some back crawlers employ this sculling motion very skillfully. Whatever is gained in propulsive power is apt to be lost in the additional elapsed time it takes to complete the movement as the opposite arm must make up somewhere else the time lost in the stroke revolution. This delay usually takes place in the recovery or the glide.

There is another claim that this sculling of the hand is a supporting movement to the hips and that it holds them at the proper level. A hip sag can be eliminated by maintaining a constant stretch to the body with pressure placed on the arms during the entry and pull phase of the arms and slight emphasis placed on each down beat of the legs. This method gives sufficient support to maintain the hip elevation.

3. **The Timing of One Arm in Relation to the Other.**—In the back crawl stroke there is no independent movement of one arm from the

other. It is just like an elementary windmill action. One arm is always directly opposite from the other throughout the entire revolution of the arm stroke (Fig. 5C). Both arms should be even with the shoulder as one is recovering and the other pulling as they pass each other at the shoulder line. As the driving arm arrives at the side of the thigh, the recovery arm enters the water.

If the recovery arm is too slow, the drive of one arm is completed while the recovery hand of the other arm is still in the air. This is a very nice point in timing the back crawl, and when it is violated, the swimmer thus permits his shoulder to drop and the body to roll toward it.

Another serious error is to permit the arm to pause too long at the side of the body at the completion of the drive. This causes the body to lose momentum as the catch is made and the body moves along in a jerky manner. As one arm is completing the drive, the recovering arm must be entering the water (Fig. 5A and D), so that the body drives forward onto the arm entering. One must experience two sensations in swimming the back crawl. As the arm enters the water one must have the sensation of moving forward on it. Again when it pulls, one has the sensation of going past the hands.

Pulling the arms too deeply below the surface lessens muscular advantage as well as securing an ineffective purchase on the water with the arm and hand.

4. Timing the Arms and Legs.—Some back stroke swimmers rely upon the feel of smooth rhythm to judge their timing. Sometimes this method does not give accurate mechanical timing as there may be some part of the stroke deliberately delayed for which some other part must either mark time momentarily or gain time to offset the unbalanced movement.

The timing of the six-beat back crawl is illustrated in Fig. 5. The regular action of the legs is compared with the arm action in order to observe the timing of the arms and legs. A similar comparison was made in the discussion of the timing of the crawl stroke.

Beat 1.—As the left arm is extended and is pressing into the water, the right arm is releasing the water. The legs are fully open. The right leg is up and fully extended and the left leg is poised below, ready for the up kick. The count begins as the left arm goes into the pull and leg beat number one is executed. As the left arm presses into the water, makes the catch, and starts the pull, this downward action is counteracted by a similar downward thrust of the right leg.

As the right arm releases the water and is lifted for the recovery, the left leg is also raised upward which prevents a body roll (Fig. 5A).

Beat 2.—The left arm is pulling with a straight arm action. The right arm is out of the water and beginning the recovery. As the left arm pulls through and starts the push, it is counteracted by an upward thrust of the right leg.

As the right arm swings backward in undergoing the recovery phase, the left leg is driven downward in a natural balancing action (Fig. 5B).

Beat 3.—The left arm has completed the pull and is starting to push while the right arm is extended and completing the recovery, preparatory to the entry. The left leg is down and the right is up. Note how the entire body is stretched. As the left arm executes the push, it is pressing slightly downward in the water. The downward action of the right leg at the same time serves to balance this action.

As the right arm completes the recovery and is thrust backward to the entry, the left leg is driven upward which prevents the body from rolling to the right (Fig. 5C).

Beat 4.—Here the right arm is pressing into the water. The left arm is releasing the water. The right leg is down and the left is up. The downward action of the right arm as it presses, catches, and starts the pull is counteracted by a similar downward thrust of the left leg.

As the left arm releases the water in order to start the recovery, the right leg is also raised upward, thus giving balance to the body (Fig. 5D).

Beat 5.—The right arm has made the catch and is pulling. The left arm has lifted out of the water and is beginning the recovery. The right leg is up and the left is down. As the right arm is pulled through and starts the push, this movement is balanced by an upward thrust of the left leg. The backward swing of the left arm is compensated by a downward drive of the right leg (Fig. 5E).

Beat 6.—The right arm has completed the pull and has started to push. The left arm has completed the recovery and is starting to enter. The left leg is up and the right is down.

The action of the right arm as it presses slightly downward during the push is equalized by the downward action of the left leg.

As the left arm completes the recovery and is thrust backward to the entry, the right leg is driven upward which offsets the tendency for leftward rotation of the body (Fig. 5F).

The simplest way to check the timing is to observe that as the right arm presses in at the entry, the left leg is fully extended upward, and at the same time the left arm has completed its pull and is at the side of the thigh.

When this stroke is perfectly timed the back crawl is performed even smoother than the crawl because there is really nothing to disturb its working parts from a symmetric balance.

5. Breathing While Swimming the Back Crawl.—While swimming the back crawl, breathing is just about as elementary and simple as when walking. However, the traditional method of expiring through the nose and inhaling through the mouth is strictly adhered to. If one should inspire through the nose, one is almost certain of sniffing droplets of water into the throat and causing strangulation. The chance of breathing in through the nose in the back crawl is a chance a swimmer cannot afford to take. One splash of water into the nose may cause the loss of a race as well as some most distressing moments.

In former styles of back stroke recovery techniques, where the arms were recovered vertically, a curtain of water from the arm as it passed over the face caused considerable difficulty. With the present lateral arm recovery, this water hazard has been eliminated and breathing can now take place under almost normal conditions except when under water at the turn or start. The tension of the abdominal muscles in the back crawl during the up kick inhibits freedom of action of the diaphram in breathing for the untrained swimmer. A swimmer who trains daily and increases the daily load of work in proportion to conditioning these abdominal muscles eventually becomes very efficient and permits almost normal breathing, even during strenuous racing.

The number of breaths per length depends upon the individuals. For distances of 150 yards or more, breathing every stroke throughout the race is almost essential.

6. The Technique and Mechanics of Head Action in the Back Crawl Stroke.—The most stabilizing factor of the entire back crawl stroke is the head position. The head is fixed with the chin and nose remaining constantly on a central plane, while the body rotates about it on its longitudinal axis, even though the body oscillates slightly from side to side with each arm pull. In order to maintain the head fixed while the body oscillates during the stroke action, the head action must be isolated from that of the trunk. This is effected by maintaining a relaxed neck. By maintaining the head in a centered position, the body rides on an even keel and is prevented from rolling (Fig. 5E). It also prevents lateral sway which would move the body out of alignment. The head should lean in the same direction as the line of progression. The inspiration and expiration phases are carried on in a normal way. Inspiration takes place through a wide open mouth, with the lips curled out away from the teeth. Expiration should be through the nose to prevent strangulation and to maintain the nasal canals clear from water droplets.

7. **The Back Stroke Tumble Turn.**—The reach to the wall is made with a drive under water, just as the reaching inverted hand is about 12 to 16 inches from the wall. The head is lowered back with the arm. The hand dives to a depth of about 6 to 10 inches under the surface. The elbow bends, so head comes close to the wall (Fig. 6A). Air is taken just before the head is submerged. The free arm shoulder is slightly dropped. The body is brought into a very close tuck position, throwing the knees at an angle over the shoulder of the contact arm (Fig. 6B). As the knees come over, the body has already half turned around and is nearly flat on its back (Fig. 6C). By use of the contact arm on wall and a sculling motion of the free hand, palm inverted, the remaining half turn of the body is made while, at the same time, the feet plant themselves against the wall (Fig. 6D). The head should incline toward the angle of the knees which is in a partial oblique plane. This turn is not a somersault. The head in this turn is a guide and control to the entire turn, especially the placing of the feet on the wall. The body spins directly on its back while tucked. In the tuck, the knees should not gap apart. The body is now in push-off position. The arms are poised ready for the thrust; elbows flexed, palms up, one on either side of the head close to the ears, just over the shoulders. The chin is tucked down toward the throat (Fig. 6E). A vigorous drive of the legs is made while at the same time the arms are thrust out to full extension beyond the head for the coast to the surface (Fig. 6F).

This turn is often confused with the somersault turn. The body does not somersault, but merely permits the trunk and head to sub-

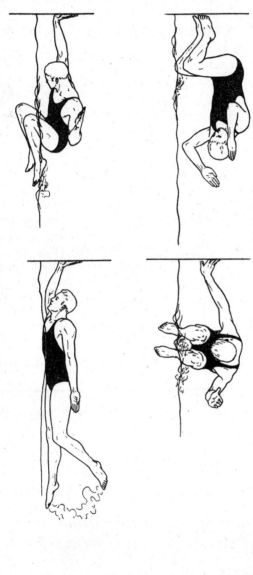

Fig. 6.—A, B, C, D.

Fig. 6.—A series of ideal form showing the back crawl stroke tumble turn. A. The touch at the wall. B. The tuck. C. The turn. D. The completed turn. E. The driving position. F. The glide after push-out.

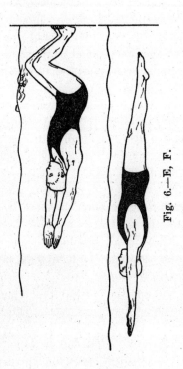

Fig. 6.—E, F.

merge with the trunk remaining in a horizontal plane throughout the entire turn. This turn is called the tumble turn. It is similar in general principles as the touch, tuck, spin, and push with head out as explained in the sprint crawl turn. This turn is the fastest of all the back stroke turns. Approaching the wall for the turn, speed is of utmost importance to flip the turn fast. Coasting to the wall slowly will result in a poorly executed turn.

8. **The Finish.**—A great many sprinting back crawlers make a serious mistake of turning the head to the side when pressed for a close finish. Instead of turning, they should press the head back into the water deeper in the last two or three arm strokes so that the approaching end can be seen over the forehead. This also gives a longer stretch to the body as well as permitting the touching arm to drive low over the shoulder to the finish wall or finish curtain. In this manner the swimmer can accurately judge the distance to the finish wall and fully extended arm reach can be thrust at the wall with tremendous speed. Many times this out-touches a slower touching rival. In this way the swimmer can gain at least a foot advantage in reach over an opponent who remains in swimming position. However, the head should not be lowered earlier than the last two or three arm strokes.

The touch on the finish wall should be made with the fingers inverted downward and the palm of hand flattened against the wall. This prevents injury to the finger tips.

The back stroker while in the natural swimming position is tempted to watch the other competitors in a race. This is wrong because it keeps his mind from concentrating on the number of strokes to the approaching finish. Not only that, but he is not centering the head on its longitudinal axis and will cause his body to flounder from side to side which loses speed for him when speed is most needed.

Another error often made in approaching the finish is to look for the finish wall over one shoulder. In doing so, the opposite arm will never take the full reach and the stroke is shortened and rhythm is lost right at the finish where driving speed is absolutely essential.

He should never fix the eyes on the finish wall over one shoulder as he approaches. This causes him to veer to the opposite side and the touching hand will reach the wall at an angle to the side of the wall. The head should be centered and lowered and the hand should reach directly back on line with the spine. This is the closest distance to the wall and gives him an advantage in reach with a fully extended arm in the head lowered position.

Seldom in an ordinary dual meet or even in the national championship meets are lane markers stretched over and above the center of each surface lane marked four feet from each end to give the back crawler warning for either the turn or the finish.

Many swimmers, therefore, rely upon markings on the ceiling when swimming in indoor pools. Roped markers should be stretched above the center of each lane for the back stroke races, for both indoor and outdoor races to aid in guiding backstroke competitors, or a warning rope stretched across each end of the pool 4 feet from the end walls. Surface lane markers should also be of a contrasting color about 10 feet from the end wall as a warning to the back stroker. End walls above the surface should also be of a contrasting color from the surface, so that they can be easily distinguished through the water-blurred eyes of a back stroker. A wall that is not easily distinguishable to water-blurred eyes often causes an optical illusion of the wall appearing either farther away or nearer than is actually the case. This causes the swimmer to reach for the finish or turn either too soon or too late, which may mean the loss of a closely and hard fought race.

Back strokers should be constantly trained to keep driving their legs as they are reaching for the finish. They often cease all stroke movements when reaching for the finish. This should never be tolerated by coaches in practice. While reaching for the wall and just inches short, the finishing arm should be held straight and on the surface as the legs drive him in.

As a general rule, if the reaching arm for the finish is less than 14 inches short of the finish, the arm should lie on the surface and the swimmer should rely upon the legs to drive him home to the finish. If the fully extended arm is farther than approximately 14 inches away from the finish line, the arm should be pulled through and the other arm driven into the finish wall.

Racing Fundamentals

1. **The Pace.**—The 100 yards back stroke can be grouped in the sprint event and for all purposes of training, the sprint type of training should be followed as discussed in the sprint crawl.

In the 150 yards event, a large amount of endurance combined with speed is essential in competition. The stroke cadence is just slightly slower than that used for the 100 yards. Usually the 100 yards elapsed time on the way to 150 yards, varies just from about one to two seconds. It is practically full sprinting effort. A great deal of sprinting, as well as distance endurance swimming, is necessary in training for this race. The standard table (see Table IV) for the 150 yards back stroke should be carefully studied and scrutinized in planning for competition. Both the sprint and middle distance technique of racing fundamentals should also be studied.

A common error of racing in this style is to look over to the side or over the shoulder to watch an opponent. This should be avoided and if done at all only occasionally; the head should again be centered after each glance. When one does glance to the side, the body rides off-keel and the opposite arm does not take its full reach. A back stroker should cultivate a sense of knowing where a rival is. For this reason, it is sometimes best to put the good back stroker in an outside lane where the weaker swimmer is not as apt to watch him as when he is in the inside lane next to a rival.

TABLE IV

THIS TABLE SHOWS IDEAL SPLIT TIMES FOR VARIOUS RACING TIMES IN THE 150 YARDS BACK CRAWL (25 YD. POOL)

ELAPSED DISTANCE YD.	ELAPSED TIME SEC.	SPLIT TIME SEC.	ELAPSED DISTANCE YD.	ELAPSED TIME SEC.	SPLIT TIME SEC.
25	12.3	12.3	25	14.7	14.7
50	26.7	14.4	50	31.6	16.9
75	42.0	15.3	75	49.4	17.8
100	57.5	15.5	100	1:07.4	18.0
125	1:13.7	16.2	125	1:26.2	18.8
150	1:30.0	16.3	150	1:45.0	18.8
25	13.1	13.1	25	15.5	15.5
50	28.3	15.2	50	33.3	17.8
75	44.5	16.2	75	51.9	18.6
100	1:00.8	16.3	100	1:10.7	18.8
125	1:17.9	17.1	125	1:30.3	19.6
150	1:35.0	17.1	150	1:50.0	19.7
25	13.9	13.9	25	16.4	16.4
50	29.9	16.0	50	35.0	18.6
75	46.9	17.0	75	54.5	19.5
100	1:04.1	17.2	100	1:14.1	19.6
125	1:22.0	17.9	125	1:34.5	20.4
150	1:40.0	18.0	150	1:55.0	20.5

CHAPTER VIII

THE BREAST STROKE

The breast stroke was the first of the competitive swimming strokes. However, in recent years the new styles of swimming this stroke have so revolutionized it that its original identity has been nearly lost. The stroke, with all of its newest additions, can now be classified into three divisions; two of these are legal for competition, but the newest has not as yet been accepted. These divisions are:

1. The conventional, or orthodox breast stroke.
2. The butterfly, or flying breast stroke.
3. The dolphin breast stroke. (The kick in this stroke is illegal for competitive breast stroke swimming at this time.)

Characteristics of Breast Stroke Swimmers.—It is difficult to say which type of body build is best suited for this stroke. One is able to find all sorts of body build among championship competitors. This may be due to the fact that the stroke can be readily adapted to any type of build. There is a method for the long, medium, or short contestant. In recent years, any one of these types has been able to go to the top in breast stroke swimming.

There is one definitely outstanding characteristic. That is, a candidate for breast stroke swimming must possess strength, durability, and a stout heart. The flying stroke especially requires a tremendous amount of energy, even for the 100 yards race.

The 200 yards event is a race long enough (with the use of the flying stroke) to demand special emphasis on endurance, since the problem in the race immediately becomes one of energy distribution. Since the flying stroke is a fatiguing one and is often interchanged with the less tiring conventional stroke in the course of a 200 yards race, it is very essential that the swimmer know how to spread his effort over the entire distance, not only in light of his own energy capacity, but also on the basis of the way in which the opponent distributes his energy.

Comparative Marks in Breast Stroke Competition.—The distance for high school competition is 100 yards, for college it is 200 yards.

	WORLD'S RECORD	AMERICAN RECORD	INTERCOLLE- GIATE RECORD	HIGH SCHOOL RECORD
Twenty-yard Course				
100 yards breast stroke		1:01.0		1:03.8
200 yards breast stroke		2:19.8	2:19.8	
Short Course (25 yd. course)				
100 yards breast stroke	1:00.6	1:00.6		1:03.9
200 yards breast stroke	2:22.0	2:22.0	2:22.0	
Long Course (50 yd. course or over)				
100 yards breast stroke		*	*	
200 yards breast stroke		2:27.5	2:29.2	

In the major colleges, 100 yards in the breast stroke are not considered as an individual event. Only in the 300 yards medley relay is the 100 yards event contested in college competition. Records made for the 100 yards in this relay event are not acceptable because a flying start is used.

The Techniques of the Breast Stroke Start

The various stances and techniques of the take-off described for the crawl stroke start also apply to the breast stroke start.

1. **The Line of Flight.**—There are some authorities who recommend a slightly higher line of flight than that used in the crawl. They recommend that the head be lower and the arms dipped for a deeper entry than that used for crawl stroke starts. Caution should be used in deviating too far from the traditional line of flight used for the crawl start, otherwise penetrating power is lost.

Another method of attaining a deeper glide is to adopt a slightly sharper downward angle of flight than is used in the crawl start. If the greater depth is not attained by the swimmer at the start, he would find difficulty in remaining under the surface of the water while attempting to swim several underwater strokes. The slightly sharper downward angle of flight is the most generally adopted method for the breast stroke start.

2. **The Entry.**—The entry in all respects, excepting that of the angle, is exactly as described for the crawl stroke as far as position of the arms, head, body, and legs is concerned. The angle of entry is slightly deeper than in the crawl start because of the fact that a longer swim under water is almost universally employed by all breast stroke swimmers at the start of a 200-yard race. In the shorter sprints where the butterfly stroke is to be used, some breast

---

*No records listed for this course.

stroke "flyers" will immediately come swimming to the surface on the first arm stroke after the entry. In this case the angle of entry as well as the line of flight through the air should be like that of the sprinting start used in the crawl stroke.

3. **The Glide Under Water.**—The body, whether the glide is shallow or deep, should be maintained in a straight position from finger tips to the toes. Preserving this body alignment at the point of entry and throughout the glide depends largely upon the action and position of the head. The head should be held low with the chin tucked in. This position will do a great deal to streamline the swimmer's body and will offer the least resistance while keeping the body at proper depth.

Since the breast stroke is the slowest of all the competitive strokes, it is essential to get all the speed advantage possible from the start. The body will glide with less resistance beneath the surface, than on the surface. Therefore, since the breast stroke is somewhat slower in speed as compared to that of the other competitive strokes the swimmer can make greater speed by remaining under water than by swimming the traditional stroke on the water's surface. The number of strokes to be used and the length of distance to be traveled under water depend upon several factors. First, the ability to glide; second, the ability to develop greater speed with the submerged stroke than one is able to do on the surface; third, the ability to repay the "oxygen debt" accumulated while swimming under water.

Swimmers differ as to physical contour and have different resistances to water. Some swimmers have low water resistance and literally slither through the water without any apparent slowing down during the glide after the start, after push-out from the turn, and the glide following a stroke. Others with higher resistance may drive a stroke just as powerfully but seem to drag down to a stop as if brakes were applied. A swimmer who has slow speed in the glide under water should be carefully checked with the watch to study accurately just where he should begin to swim, or where the starting momentum has subsided to a swimming speed, before starting his stroke. As the swimmer progresses under water, he should gradually bear upward, so that the angle is not too abrupt as he strokes to the surface. He should never lie deeper than two feet when the last stroke is taken before the break to the surface is made.

4. **The Underwater Stroke, Its Technique, Mechanics, and Timing.**—The underwater breast stroke differs in technique and

mechanics from that generally used on the surface. The essential difference between the underwater and the surface stroke is in the length of the arm pull. On the surface, the hands and arms are not pulled very far beyond the line of the shoulders in the traditional breast stroke. If they are pulled fully beyond the shoulders, the hands no longer can hold the body and head well up out of the water. This will cause the head to drop below the swimming level of the surface, and the swimmer will "bob" excessively. While under water this is not true. The arms can be pulled all the way back to the hips and still not disturb or alter body balance. This is definitely an aid to the propulsive force which is gained by the arms under the surface. The arm stroke under water has the possibility to develop motivating power equal to, or greater than, that developed by the legs. Some swimmers have been known to develop greater propulsive speed from both arms driven simultaneously to the hips than that gained from the leg kick. The effectiveness of this arm pull depends largely upon the technique used.

The technique and mechanics of this full arm pull may be executed generally in two ways: (1) The arms may be pulled by sweeping them laterally and holding the arms almost entirely straight. The arms should not be pulled downward and laterally because the downward press would push the body up toward the surface. On the lateral sweep of the arms, they should actually pull slightly below the line of the body, so that at the finish of the pull the hands are actually pressing upward which aids in pressing the shoulders and head downward and helps to maintain the body in its projected true course. The body, while submerged, usually tends to float upward due to buoyancy. The swimmer must acquire skill with the hands in order to maintain the proper plane of the palms throughout the arm drive and to cause the body to remain under the water in a straight line of progress. (2) The second method, which is more generally used, is to pull the arms with the elbows bent in a boomerang position. The upper arm is held almost in a horizontal line laterally with the shoulder, and the forearm is directed vertically downward and inward. In this movement, the hands start the action with a quick digging hold of the water and from there the arm drive is continued. The forearms press outward slightly and when they arrive almost in line with the shoulders, a transition takes place from a pull action to a terrific swift push or driving inward action to the hips. The arms finish alongside the hips, fully extended, with palms upward. Here the arms drift momentarily during a brief glide on the momentum gained from the powerful arm stroke. The arms should be permitted to drift in this position but not too tight to the body so that the water can wash and flow down the arms and sides of the body freely. If the arms are held too close to the body the water is pocketed between the arm and body and thus increases resistance. The arms should drag in line with the back. During this arm pull, the legs are held straight but relaxed and slightly spread so that the water freely washes down the legs without interference from between the legs. However, care should be taken not to spread the legs too far, otherwise a tail suction will occur behind the hips and the crotch. Approximately an inch spread of the legs is sufficient.

The legs remain straight while the arms start the recovery movement. In the recovery of the arms, the elbows are bent and the arms slide closely along the under sides of the body to a point under the chest or chin where both hands join palms down. This movement continues uninterrupted and the arms thrust forward to the fully extended gliding position.

The recovery of the legs begins just as the hands are about to join under the chest. The legs should recover in a fairly rapid movement with not too much of a drag or the timing point with that of the arm thrust is apt to be missed. The leg drive should be executed when the arms are not quite, but almost, fully extended in the forward thrust. The legs may thrust, sweep or whip, or squeeze, in their propulsive drive. At the completion of the leg drive the body again glides momentarily from the momentum gained from the leg drive. The leg drive, as well as the arm drive, in the underwater stroke is an individual unit of power in itself. However, if several strokes are to be taken underwater, the arms do not wait as long in the glide after the leg drive as do the legs after the arm drive. Some swimmers prefer the arm pull to begin almost immediately upon the completion of the leg drive, or as soon as the legs have closed from the kick.

Most swimmers swimming the 200-yard distance usually will remain under water for at least two or more strokes. Some top-flight swimmers will swim the starting length in a race in either a 20-yard or 25-yard course and not come up for air until the turn is executed. While in the sprinting distances of 100 yards where the butterfly will be used, just one arm stroke and no leg drive is recommended before

10

rising to the surface. This arm stroke drive will thrust the swimmer's shoulders well above the surface level so that he can easily come out flying the butterfly stroke. This is a very fast start, which is executed with a very shallow glide and gets the swimmer well under way above the surface. This type of starting break-through from the glide has two distinct advantages. One is that the average breast stroker can fly faster above the surface than he can swim underwater. The second advantage is that the swimmer can get air at once and has, therefore, less oxygen debt to repay. However, there is this point to consider on the other side of the question: To fly immediately uses up more energy than to remain under the water. Swimming under water requires less energy output even though an oxygen debt is built up by holding the breath longer while remaining under water. This is a factor depending upon the individual swimmer. The world's record was recently broken for 100 yards with the competitor remaining under water for nearly half of the distance, approximately 40 yards. However, this cannot be accomplished by the average swimmer or even the best swimmers without paying the price before the end of the race.

It is recommended that all breast stroke swimmers, especially high school boys, have a thorough medical examination before being permitted to compete in breast stroke swimming. Because, if so much of a race is swum under water, holding the breath and exerting oneself vigorously may be a strain upon the heart.

There are two essentials to bear in mind in breaking to the surface.

1. The proper depth of the body below the surface of the water. If too deep, the angle which the body must make to reach the surface in one stroke is too sharp and will decrease the forward speed, losing valuable distance. Additional loss of speed from rising at too abrupt an angle comes from expending forward motion when the body shoots above the swimming level. This deviation from good form will also force the legs too deep for good traction on the first kick.

2. The break to the surface should be initiated and effected by the kick, not the arm pull. This is accomplished in the following way: When the arms are thrust forward from under the chin, they should be directed at an efficient angle toward the surface. At the same time the head is raised and the legs drive the body upward. However, when the body arrives at the surface, it should be sliding forward, not upward. If the legs drive the body to the surface, the arms

are already placed in pulling position. This method prevents any break in forward motion which would cause the legs to lose traction. Too many distance swimmers err by pulling themselves to the surface with the arms. This shallow dive with immediate arm action should be used only in the sprinting races, as explained in the butterfly stroke. (See the Butterfly Breast Stroke Start, p. 164.)

The Technique of the Orthodox Breast Stroke

1. **The General Position of the Body.**—The position of the body in the breast stroke in the water does not differ essentially from that described in the crawl stroke. The body must be maintained in a streamlined stretch, but at the same time in a comfortably relaxed position. This is controlled principally by the position of the head. During the glide phase of the stroke the head should be held comfortably well up and maintained there (Fig. 7A). This is especially difficult for individuals who have short necks. The head in this position is in front of the center of weight of the body, and in this position will tend to balance the legs over the center of weight. This lever effect is believed to cause the body to slide down hill more effectively. The body itself, however, should not be carried too high, otherwise it will offer too much resistance, or it may even cause itself to slip backward during the execution of the stroke. A slight arch should be maintained with the body riding at a slight angle.

2. **Classification of Leg Kicks.**—Many attempts to improve and speed up the traditional breast stroke kick have been made in the past decade, in order to keep it abreast with the "flying" arms. Rather than relying upon the traditional kick which consists of a wide knee spread and wide whiplash of the legs, new methods have been devised. The knee spread has been narrowed and the heels have been lifted and the downward thrust has been executed in a circular motion. Many variations are used. A new kick, the "dolphin fishtail," was developed to be used with the butterfly arm stroke, in 1935.[1] This kick was ruled illegal, as it did not conform to the rules of the breast stroke kick. The basis for its illegality was simply that the soles of the feet did not engage the water on both up and down undulations and the kick was in the vertical and not the lateral plane. This kick was the basis for the development of the Kasley

---

[1] Armbruster, D. A.: "The Dolphin Breast Stroke," Journal of Health and Physical Education, April, 1935.

[2] See "Swimming," by Matt Mann and C. C. Fries, Breast Stroke Kick.

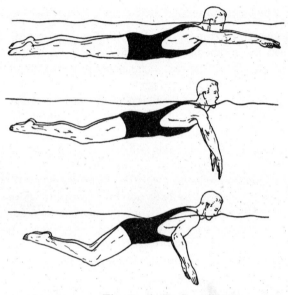

Fig. 7.—A, B, C.

Fig. 7.—A series of ideal form in the orthodox breast stroke. A. Showing the legs closing and the start of the arm pull. B. The mouth is lifting for air. C. Both arms and legs begin recovery at the completion of taking air. D. The hands are preparing for the forward thrust and the legs are preparing for the leg drive. E. The ideal timing position to start the leg drive in relation to the arm thrust forward. F. The arms in downhill coasting position and the legs completing the drive.

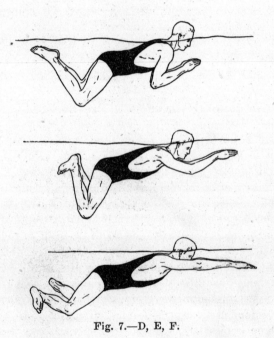

Fig. 7.—D, E, F.

kick.[2]   Thus, the "dolphin fishtail" was made to conform to the rules.   This has been a tremendous stride forward in the evolution of the modern breast stroke kick.

The variations of the kicks were naturally developed because of anatomic limitations of breast stroke swimmers.   Some swimmers are naturally crotch bound, which prevents a wide knee, or leg spread. Others are very flexible and supple and possess a wide lateral range of leg movement.   It was formerly believed that the wider the spread of the legs, the greater was the propulsive force which could be obtained because more water could be squeezed out from between the legs while completing the leg drive.   However, this theory was discredited when crotch-bound boys with a narrow knee and leg spread seemed to get as much, and in some cases more, propulsive drive from this narrow thrusting drive than others using the wide whipping drive.

Coaches now generally classify the kicks to be used according to the physical attributes of the individual.   That is, the height, strength, and build determine the general type of kick to be used.

The short-legged, rugged individual should rely upon the wide whiplash and squeeze type of kick.   The reason is that a short-legged individual has a better mechanical advantage in a wide lateral sweeping movement.   This lateral sweeping leg drive is a very mechanically weak position because one can only rely upon the adductor group of muscles, which are not a really powerful group of muscles, to sweep the legs together.   Some coaches have advocated rotating the legs outward by turning the feet out and up during the kick phase so that the swimmer could rely upon the hamstring extensor group of muscles to assist the adductor group.   A long broad foot on a short-legged individual gives him a decided advantage.   However, a long foot is seldom seen on a short leg.   The modern trend is away from the wide knee spread and toward the narrow knee spread because of a lessened resistance in spreading the knees.

The second classification is the long geared body type, which has long legs and long broad feet.   If this type of individual spreads his legs wide, the lever is too long and thus too weak.   The legs are drawn up toward the pelvis instead of spreading them and then a thrust, or screw type of kick, is made with the forelegs followed by the extension of the long feet.   This narrow knee spread and heel lift permit the long-geared boy to take advantage of a shorter mechanical lever; he is then able to execute the drive faster, more powerfully and more efficiently.

The third classification is for the medium height and build type of individual. This kick is a combination of the two types described above and has as a basis a modified and limited spread of the knees, so that a powerful thrust can be executed, combined with a snap or squeeze completing the drive of the legs. This type of kick is powerful and is most generally used by the average swimmer. All of the above kicks should be executed quickly and powerfully. The type of kicks used in the butterfly stroke will be described with that stroke.

(a) *The Traditional Kick.*—This kick may be used most efficiently by swimmers with short powerful legs. The kick is started from a moderate spread of the knees. Both legs are rotated outward so that the feet turn out and remain extended so that the soles of the feet almost face each other (Fig. 7C). The knees are spread wide and as the heels are drawn outward to a spread, they are drawn as closely as possible toward the hips (Fig. 7E). From this position, the feet may either be drawn out as far as possible or partially turned out and the toes flexed toward the knees, so that as the thrust is being made, the soles of the feet immediately engage the water (Fig. 7F). Just prior to the knees becoming fully extended, the thighs are driven and squeezed together. The feet extend fully during this whip phase. This movement, if accurately timed, gives a tremendous propulsive whiplash to the legs. The squeeze or snap of the legs should continue from the whiplash, so that the feet do not lose hold of the water. Too often in this kick, swimmers do not follow through in this squeeze movement, but instead permit the legs to drift together and therefore, the kick loses some of its effectiveness. The kick is performed with a thrust, whip, and squeeze. This is similar to the Kasley kick. As the legs close they should relax and drift slightly apart. There is a counteraction from the end of the down kick which gives the swimmer a feeling of lift of the legs to the surface.

(b) *The New Narrow Kick.*—This kick corrects for weak mechanical advantage in swimmers with long legs. Its action is to recover the knees with a narrow spread. The thighs are pressed down while the legs and heels are drawn just under the surface, toward the hips. The heels draw up to the outside of the hips. Here the toes and feet are turned outward and immediately go into a quick outward and inward circular thrust with the thighs snapping together just prior to the knees being fully extended. This entire kick is executed from a narrow knee spread. This type of kick not only corrects for the wide knee spread with a poor mechanical advantage, but also permits the legs to force the water back along the longitudinal axis of propulsion.

A variation in this kick in the propulsive phase or drive phase may be made. Instead of driving the legs and feet outward and inward in a circular motion, they are driven and directed downward and the thighs are driven backward and together just prior to the full extension of the knees. This gives the knees a rotation inward and upward movement, giving the foot a screw drive effect. The down drive, theoretically, gives greater resisting force against the foot. While in the backward inward snap of the thigh and knees, the powerful hamstring extensors spring into action to assist the thigh adductor group of muscles. This is also the type used for a fast orthodox sprinting stroke as well as for the butterfly stroke. This kick is not generally used, but will undoubtedly become one of the better types of kicks for the modern streamlined type of stroke. It is the next step to the dolphin stroke. Caution must be exercised in manipulating the feet on the downward thrust so that the toes are turned down and drawn toward the knees when the legs are "cocked," so that the soles of the feet engage the water on the downward action of the feet. This type of kick gives the leg action a vertical range of movement as well as a lateral range. This kick is very effective in propulsion especially, if the swimmer is endowed with a long, broad pair of feet and powerful legs.

(c) *The New Combined Narrow and Wide Kick.*—Swimmers with medium long legs will do best in maintaining a moderately narrow kick. The recovery of the legs is similar to the recovery in the short-legged individual, except that the feet and the knees are not turned out nearly as wide. The heels are drawn up very close toward the hips. From this point the feet are turned out and the outward circular thrust is made. The motion is a circumduction with the hip joint as the axis. The water is engaged at the start of the thrust with the inside of the foot as the knee begins to extend. Before the knees are fully extended, they execute an inward and backward snap, giving a whip to each leg, which gives tremendous propulsive power.

In all of the above three types of kicks, a common error is to draw the knees too far forward. The most effective results from the breast stroke kick are obtained by not flexing the thighs upon the pelvis farther than approximately a 45° angle with the spine. This limitation streamlines the thighs and causes the water to slide under the legs as they are drawn up with less resistance. Some swimmers are able to master such a technique and become very effective with the feet. However, few can master this technique in the orthodox type of stroke. In the butterfly stroke this type of kick is much easier to learn and a great many swimmers use it naturally.

The heels and feet should be drawn up as closely to the line of the hips as is anatomically possible. The feet there are able to engage the water nearer to the line of the hips. In this way, the feet are able to hold and push the water over a longer range, giving the legs a greater and longer area for propulsive resistance against the water during the leg drive. Too many swimmers are apt to kick the feet diagonally back, rather than pressing the feet directly out from the hips before the backward thrust is delivered.

The legs should not be dragged up in the recovery too slowly as has been formerly taught. There was a common notion that a slow recovery would cause less resistance. In the new type kicks, the legs are drawn up quite rapidly and immediately start the thrust.

3. **The Traditional Arm Stroke Action.**—The arms pull simultaneously in a lateral, downward, and backward movement. From an extended position in front of the face the arms are pulled to a point under the upper chest. Here the hands turn upon the wrists and join each other and are thrust forward to the starting position. The entire movement is a continuous uninterrupted movement. In the traditional arm stroke, the hands should never pull more than a few inches beyond the shoulder line. If the hands are pulled too far beyond the shoulder line, the support is taken from under the shoulders and head, and the body sinks, causing body balance to be destroyed. When the hands release pressure upon the water, they should relax.

(a) *The Press-Catch With Arms and Hands.*—The catch begins from the glide position (Fig. 7A). The arms are extended in front of the face at a depth of from four to six inches below the surface. The catch is initiated with the arms stretched forward, the finger tips and hands are turned downward, and the palms turn laterally. The wrists flex slightly in a quickened movement. At the same time, the shoulders lift in an attempt to get the shoulders over the forearms and behind the press and pull so that the water level at the face is not changed.

(b) *The Pull and Push.*—The pull is very similar to the crawl stroke pull except the movement in the breast stroke is made laterally as well as downward in a semi-circular movement. The path of both hands may best be described as drawing the upper half of an elongated letter O. The fingers should direct the path of the arms. The catch begins by a quick press and pull outward and downward of both hands and forearms. At the same time the shoulder blades rotate forward giving the arm tremendous mechanical advantage in the shoulder arm-push position while the arms are still well in front, but at eight to fifteen inches in depth. Both arms give lateral balance and support to each shoulder and the center of body weight is not altered. While both arms are pressing and pulling, the shoulders tend to be lifted out of the water (Fig. 7B). The lift should be minimized and converted into forward motion along the surface.

The pull phase of the breast stroke is of short duration, and really is a continuation of the press-and-catch. It is during the press-and-catch movement that the shoulders adjust themselves for the push phase. The press-and-catch draws and lifts the body. The movement must be a quick and forceful action of the hands and forearms. In order to perform this with skill, an active, flexible, strong wrist joint is absolutely essential.

The hand must have freedom of movement while in the water. During the press and pull phase the hand should be slightly flexed at the wrist, in order to hold the water against the arms. Some water is allowed to wash down the arm to give greater planing resistance against the arms. If the arms pull with the wrist set at a slight angle, a greater resistance is obtained by deflecting the water from the heel of the hand toward the finger tips. With the wrist cocked at a possible angle of twenty degrees, the wrist flexor muscles have a good mechanical advantage during the catch and pull phase. The wrist straightens as the shoulders move forward to get in front of the hands and arms. Although the swimmer does not actually anchor the arms in the water and then draw the body over them, they appear to do so. The swimmer should not be misled by this appearance and strive merely to set the arms in the water. He must actually pull and drive them through the water so that water will slip off the arm and form suction swirls behind the hands and arms which give traction with the water. With a quick movement of the hands at the catch, swirls form which give greater propulsive efficiency earlier in the stroke. The water pressure should be felt in the palm. The fingers should not be flattened to full extension, but to a very slight saucer shape. This gives greater strength to the fingers and is less fatiguing. During the catch and pull phase of the stroke, the arms should be spread downward, until the hands have reached a depth of from fourteen to sixteen inches. At this maximum depth the arms are still ahead of the shoulder line and maximum propulsive force has been attained.

There is a great deal of difference of opinion among coaches as to how the arms complete the push phase and the recovery. There are two generally recognized methods. In one, the elbows spread wide and the hands pull in under the elbow and toward the chest wall followed by an elbow squeeze toward the body. The other method is to pull the elbows back and toward the body with the hand and forearm following the elbow. Those favoring the first method rely chiefly upon the rotator muscles of the upper arm and the forearm flexors to assist the rotators in driving the forearm downward and inward. When the arms are on a line with the shoulders, the upper arm and elbow are then squeezed in to the under side of the chest wall. The hands follow, planing at an angle and pressing against the water.

Those coaches favoring the latter method advocate a flexed elbow leading the arm in a movement backward and inward to the under side of the upper chest wall. Here the pulling force is not from the weaker upper arm rotators but from the powerful arm depressors. In both movements, the elbows begin to flex early in the catch-pull phase of the stroke and increase in flexion as the drive continues through its maximum depth and to the completion of the arm stroke under the chest. The theory is advanced that in the wide spread elbow technique there is more arm surface area presented against the water and to offset the weakness of the muscles brought into action in the movement, the swimmer should train to strengthen these muscles.

The arm stroke is beginning to lose some of the orthodox wide lateral arm movement to a more downward movement to get the arms under the body. Speed in competitive swimming strokes being the chief objective, not only must the stroke be streamlined to overcome resistance to the water, but sheer horsepower must be developed.

(c) *The Release and Recovery.*—The pull phase in the breast stroke is actually completed when the hands have released backward pressure which occurs when the hands arrive at the upper chest wall. There are some coaches who advocate an earlier release while the hands are at their maximum width, and in line with the shoulders. In either case, this release is accomplished with a wrist whip and the hand rotates upon the wrist joint forcing the water to the rear. The hands are then relaxed and recovered to a point under the chest. This is a common method of release and recovery. A more skilled method is to continue the press of the hands at the end of the push toward a point near the chest, still pressing the water down and back and then releasing the pressure and cocking the wrists so that the fingers point forward from under the chin, palms down. While the movement is one of recovery, the hands actually do not release the pressure of the water while they complete the elongated letter O.

(d) *The Arm Thrust.*—The thrust is a continuation of the release and the recovery. There must be no separate motion of release, recovery, and thrust. It must be continuous. At the beginning of the thrust, the hands are aligned together under the chin, palms down and the elbows close to the sides of the chest (Fig. 7D). The thrust should be as streamlined as possible, with the least amount of resistance offered by the elbows and the shoulders. With some swimmers less resistance is obtained if the hands are separated from three to six inches during the thrust and glide. This depends upon the physical characteristics of the individual swimmer.

When the arms are being thrust forward, they should be moved rather quickly at an upward angle, but not thrust out of the surface or even close to it (Fig. 7E). When the arms are nearly fully extended, down pressure should be made upon the hands and forearms. They glide deeper and cause the body to slide downhill. The whole technique is as if an obstruction of a partially submerged log is lying across the path of the swimmer and he guides his hands up and over the submerged log and coasts down on the other side.

(e) *The Arms in Glide Position.*—The glide position of the arms may be made with the hands aligned together or they may remain apart (Fig. 7A). Under no condition should the arms become so relaxed that the elbows assume a slight bend and the hands and forearms do not press slightly to afford a planing surface to the upper part of the body. However, if the arms are permitted to spread, water will be carried along between the arms and against the head and cause considerable resistance to the forward gliding motion. The arms should remain comfortably straight, so that water washes down the arms in a straight path and passes on underneath the chest wall to the rear. At the end of the glide and just prior to the catch for the next stroke, the hands should be from three to six inches in depth.

4. **Timing the Arm Action to Synchronize With the Leg Kick Action in the Orthodox Breast Stroke.**—There are two types of timing to be used, depending upon whether a wide or narrow knee spread is being used.

(a) *The Timing of the Wide Knee-Spread Kick.*—The arms pull to the shoulders, then the legs recover (Fig. 7B). The arms recover to a point under the chin and go immediately into the thrust (Fig. 7D). While the arms are recovering, the legs are spreading and turning the feet out, poised for the leg drive. When the arms are almost fully extended in the thrust, the leg drive is made (Fig. 7E).

(b) *The Timing in the Narrow Knee-Spread Kick.*—The difference in timing in the narrow knee spread and the wide knee spread is that it does not take as long to recover the legs in the narrow spread as it does in the wide knee spread. Therefore, in order to coordinate with the arm stroke, the knees should not be recovered until the hands are recovered to the side of the chest wall. The drive of the legs is made at the same time in the arm thrust as in the wide knee spread. The legs lift up into the recovery very quickly and this movement can be executed while the arms move from the chest wall to the proper point in the arm thrust.

When a swimmer with a wide kick attempts to learn a kick with a narrow knee spread, he must readjust the timing of the recovery of the legs in relation to the arm recovery. Otherwise difficulty will be experienced in the timing of the stroke.

In both types of kicks, the arms should remain in the glide position until the legs have closed from the kick. Then the catch in the next stroke may be started immediately after the legs close, for a sprinting type of stroke. For longer distances, more time may be consumed in the glide position after the legs have closed, depending upon the individual's strength and condition.

In short races the swimmer uses a quick, narrow kick with a quick pull following the kick, almost entirely eliminating the traditional glide following the stroke. Top-flight breast strokers no longer depend upon a resting glide, but train and condition themselves to eliminate as much of the glide as possible in order to acquire great speed.

The "butterfly" stroke has really been responsible for bringing about the speeding up of the traditional stroke. Obviously, a competitor who cannot "fly" with the arms, cannot afford to glide far in a race with a good opponent who does "fly" well. He, therefore, naturally speeds up his stroke, not only by shortening the glide, but also by speeding up the execution of both arm and leg action. The kick spread of the knees is narrow so that the legs may execute the kick movement as fast as the arms execute the arm movement of the stroke. This quickened kick movement has geared-up the orthodox stroke to a higher speed level so that it may quite successfully compete against the "butterfly" stroke in the longer distances. This geared-up ratio tends to give the orthodox breast stroke an almost continuous propulsive action, rather than single units of power delivered at intervals in series. Usually one who uses a long glide will start the arm pull slowly as a means of gathering himself to deliver a powerful leg stroke. This slower gathering-up phase has been discarded and instead, more strokes per length of pool are used.

5. **The Timing of the Head Action in Breathing for the Conventional Breast Stroke.**—There are generally two types of timing of the head action used to synchronize and balance the arm and leg action.

1. The better method is to lift the head for air as the arms go into a stretch and press action and by the time the mouth has cleared the surface the arms go into the catch and pull. The head must be maintained high after air has been taken. This tends to ride the body high on the surface and prevents it from disappearing or bobbing up and down, thus reducing resistance.

2. The second method is delaying the head lift in the arm pull. The head is lifted for air after the arms have passed well back beyond the catch to about the point where the pull ends and the push begins. Unless one is skillful, this delayed head action causes the body to lift out of the water too high and to unbalance the arm and leg action. Considerable motion will be wasted. In the action of lifting the head for breathing, the level of the body should be kept

as nearly constant as possible. The body should remain in alignment with the level of the water and the forward plane of progress.

The head is not lifted backward, but the mouth is drawn forward to the air above the surface (Fig. 7B). When the eyes appear above the surface, they should focus on the surface in front of the mouth and be on guard for any choppy movement. The mouth is opened and, simultaneously with the opening, air should be gasped quickly. The mouth may be opened with the lower lip extended forward beyond the upper lip, curled out to ward off wavelets around the mouth on the surface. Another method of opening the mouth is to catch the tip of the tongue behind the lower front teeth and then "belly" the tongue forward into the mouth opening, leaving a narrow opening above the bulge of the tongue and the upper lip.

A most frequent and common error in lifting the head for air is to lever it backward out of the water, as if trying to press the ball of the head back between the shoulder blades. This faulty head movement is very detrimental to both forward progression and body balance. The head should be moved toward the line of progress, not against it.

Very often a swimmer will pull the arms too slowly during the press-catch-and-pull to accommodate the head lift in getting air. This slow arm action at the inception of the arm stroke retards accurate mechanical timing in stroke performance. In practice, a quick and independent head action should be stressed, especially in the longer distance workouts. The longer the distance of workout the more a fault is liable to be practiced.

Another common error is usually developed in slow long distance workouts. This is a "frozen" wrist joint. A wrist joint should be alive and flexible and at all times sensitive to the pressure of the water.

6. Coaching Methods and Techniques Used for Daily Practices.

(a) *For the Development of the Leg Action.*—Four methods are suggested to be used. One is Danish gymnastics for stretching the ankle ligaments and stretching the crotch muscles. Abdominal muscles should be strengthened as well as the back extensors by using free-hand body and leg lifting exercises and the use of wall weights. Second, the kicking board should be used early in the season and continued throughout the season with the load increased or decreased as the leg strength and skill develop. Some swimmers can perform the kick without the kicking board by holding the arms extended beyond the head. For other swimmers this position arches the back too much and therefore should not be practiced without the board. Breast strokers should also use a type of fast kicking movement by whipping the legs continuously without a pause at any point. This improves the leg flexibility. The third method is by using an elastic check rope and belt. This can be made from several bicycle inner tubes with a rope attached to a belt at the swimmer's waist and another rope attached to the other end which is fastened to a wall. The swimmer then kicks against this resistance. The fourth method is to practice the dolphin breast stroke kick which will aid in maintaining a limber supple back and rubbery legs. The hands should not flatten to a hyperextension of the fingers during the press and propulsive phase, nor should they be over-cupped. The fingers and the wrist joints should be slightly bent in flexion to give the finger, hand, and wrist flexor muscles a greater mechanical advantage, especially during the press, catch, and pull phase of the stroke. This position of the hand and arms also gives proper tonus to the arm muscles and thus delays fatigue as late as possible in the race.

Special attention should be given to keeping the neck relaxed. Tension on the neck muscles will cause early fatigue which will spread quickly to the other muscles of the shoulder girdle group.

(b) *For the Development of the Arm Action.*—Here again land drills may be used as a way of stretching shoulder joints and strengthening arm and shoulder muscles by use of weights and wall weights. The use of the elastic check rope and belt is perhaps the best method for conditioning the arms. The breast stroker should develop himself until he is sturdy and rugged.

7. The Breast Stroke Turn.

(a) *The Approach to the Wall.*—A swimmer must drive into a turn, not coast in slowly. Momentum gathered must be utilized to carry the body well up to the wall and for the tuck and turn. The swimmer should come into the wall with his hands about four to eight inches apart. The head is lowered just before the hands contact the wall. The hands are placed flat on the wall, with the fingers turned up and the fingers slightly projecting above the surface. The elbows bend until the head almost touches the wall.

(b) *The Tuck.*—The tuck of the legs is made simultaneously with the bending of the elbows. With a slight sideward pressure of the hands the hips are turned laterally.

(c) *The Turn.*—The head may either snap up for air or remain entirely under water as the turn is made. For sprinting events of fifty yards to one hundred yards, the head should remain under. For greater distances, the head should lift out and the mouth should be turned to the side to get air. The upper back should rise during the first half of the turn. If the turn is to the left, the left arm is jerked away from the wall and assists in the spin by a scooping motion across the chest. It then meets the other hand which has been on the wall and is now on its way forward. The body turns at a point slightly less than an arm's length away from the wall. When all these movements are timed perfectly, the body first rises slightly then sinks in rhythm for the push-off.

(d) *The Push-Off.*—The feet are set against the wall just as in the crawl push-off. The feet and knees are set at a hip width position against the wall. The knees are then snapped straight and the body is stiffened. Simultaneously with the drive of the legs against the wall, the hands, which have joined under the chin after assisting in the turn, are now thrust forward simultaneously with the push-off. The body is directed forward and slightly upward, the angle depending upon whether the swimmer desires to come to the surface immediately after gliding or desires to remain under for several strokes.

(e) *The Glide and Stroke.*—In the glide the body should remain absolutely straight from finger tips to extended toes. The back should not be arched. The head should be held low between the arms. The arms may be held together at the thumbs or separated, depending upon the individual. Legs also may be slightly separated or held together. Anything which causes resistance to forward progression should be minimized.

The number of strokes to take under water depends on the length of the course, the length of the race, and the distribution of energy over the distance of the race. Some swimmers very often remain under too long, some not long enough. Condition and the effectiveness of the stroke under water are also determining factors to be considered. A conservative system to follow as to the number of strokes under water is suggested in the following:

Sprint distances up to 100 yards.

Pull to the surface and

Kick when the surface is reached.

For distance events, 220 yards.

Pull under the water, kick, and guide to the surface with arm thrust, and then pull when the surface is reached.

There are some swimmers who would be able to pull and kick twice after every push-out in the distance events.

In sprinting distances the problem is not so acute because greater speed is maintained throughout the race, and if condition and stroke mechanics are right, the question of underwater strokes is not a problem because most swimmers can "fly" faster on top than swim orthodox under water. Most swimmers will do better to rise to the surface on the first arm pull and rely upon speed on the surface and not contend with repaying oxygen borrowed while under the surface. Some very skilled and thoroughly trained champions can stay under an entire length on the start and then a half length after each turn in a 25 yard pool. Some coaches instruct swimmers to remain under as long as they do not need air. When it is needed, come up swimming and get it. Sometimes this method is not to be commended. Even experienced swimmers will sometimes remain under too long and lose a race because of improper ventilation which results in early fatigue.

8. **The Finish.**—In general, the finish is no different from the approach to the wall in the turn. However, in a close finish when the swimmers' heads are even and it looks like a tie or dead heat, one swimmer may be going into the pull of another stroke, while the other swimmer is thrusting the arms forward in the recovery. The latter will appear to finish first. The one who is approximately an arm's length away from the finish at the end of the glide has the disadvantage because he cannot afford to coast in, even with the head low, since most of this momentum is already spent. He must, therefore, outwit his competitor and effect a quick catch of the hands and thrust for the finish without the kick. A full stroke would use up too much time and pull his head too close to the finish mark and arrive at the finish with the hand touch too late to win the race. In this situation, the swimmer should accurately measure the remaining distance to the

finish in terms of strokes with the head held high and the eyes having clear vision to the wall, so that when his body has arrived close enough to the wall, with the last arm thrust he hits the finish at full arm extension. The head should be held up even though air is not taken during the last two or three strokes. The swimmer should not turn the head to the side and watch his competitor as the finish is approaching. One should look straight ahead at the finish.

The Technique of the Butterfly Breast Stroke

The butterfly breast stroke has brought about a new era in competitive breast stroke swimming, except that they stroke and recover at the same time. In this stroke the arms perform in a manner similar to that of the crawl stroke. When a swimmer "flies" there is little resemblance to the original breast stroke. The legs retain the narrow lateral kick movement. Many minor and technical illegal uses of the arms and legs are being made with this modern stroke, yet few disqualifications are being made. This is due in part to the fact that there are usually too many swirls around the legs and arms, which are well under the surface and are not at all times visible.

Men swimmers enjoy swimming this stroke for several reasons. First, they can swim this stroke far faster than the orthodox stroke. Second, it permits a boy to use the strength in his arms and shoulders for propulsive force rather than having to depend to a large extent upon his kick.

Third, this stroke carries the swimmer high over the water where he is free to recover his arms above the surface with great rapidity.

Fourth, it creates a greater speed, and crawl strokers have no difficulty in learning it.

The above four factors are significant in attracting so many more boys to this modern stroke than was formerly true with the orthodox stroke.

There are many who contend that the stroke is too strenuous. The same thing was said of the crawl stroke when it first made its appearance. However, no one would venture such a statement today, not even in behalf of women. Movements are timed, levers are used properly, and more efficient training methods make this stroke easy for trained swimmers.

All of the above factors pertaining to narrow kicks and narrow arm pulls clearly signal a trend toward an even faster breast stroke, the dolphin stroke.[3] This kick eliminates all lateral movements but performs like the alternating flutter kick in the crawl, except that the legs move up and down together, in unison, like a "fishtail."

There is always the problem of transition from the traditional stroke to the flying stroke. In this connection a number of problems arise which will be discussed in the following pages.

1. **The Start.**—The technique and mechanics of the moving parts of the butterfly breast stroke start are no different from that presented for the crawl start (see Crawl Start, Chapter II).

The entry and glide technique also are the same as that described for the crawl start, and for the traditional breast stroke (see Breast Stroke Start-Glide).

The glide in the butterfly stroke will vary from that of the traditional glide only as to the number of orthodox strokes intended to be used under water.

As a general rule, the flying stroke being considerably faster than the orthodox stroke, fewer strokes should be taken under water. This necessitates a shallow dive as in the sprint crawl start. The swimmer comes out of the water "flying" on the very first arm pull if the race is short and sprinting speed is required, since more swimmers can "fly" faster on top of the water than swim under it. However, for distances of 200 yards or greater the number of strokes under water is increased in the starting glide. The number of underwater strokes in the longer distances depends upon the endurance of the individual. Some swimmers can go a full length of a 25-yard pool without embarrassment.

The world's record in the 1939 N.C.A.A. meet for the 200-yard race was made by swimming the first full length and a half under water and the latter part of the 200-yard race was finished "flying." Usually, swimmers in the 200-yard race come to the surface about one or two flying strokes short of the turn. These last strokes before the first turn are made in the orthodox type of stroke. The number of strokes to take under the surface depends upon the demands made upon each individual. Some swimmers can be trained to swim faster and farther under water than others.

The distance to be traveled under water in the glide to the point of the beginning of the first stroke depends upon the penetrating

---

[3]Armbruster, D. A., and Sieg, Jack: The Dolphin Breast Stroke, Journal of Health and Physical Education, April, 1935.

power derived from the start and the velocity maintained. The velocity maintained depends upon individual characteristics. Some men are more streamlined in physical contour and present less frictional resistance to the water. However, almost any swimmer should be out at least eighteen to twenty feet before beginning the first stroke. Stroking too early in the glide will slow down the speed of the stroke rather than increase its speed.

The only difference between the "flying" stroke and the orthodox stroke, as far as underwater swimming is concerned, is that the swimmer comes out of the surface flying on the very first arm stroke.

In order for the swimmer to perform this technique efficiently, the glide should be shallow. When the hands and arms spring into action, the arms should press and pull downward slightly wider than shoulder width and pulling toward each hip. The pull should be executed in such a way that as the body pops through the surface, it is in a forward movement, not upward, and the legs should lie shallow under the surface.

The break into the surface should be performed with the head held fairly low for at least one surface stroke before taking air. This should be done regardless of the number of strokes used under water. Forward swimming motion must be uninterrupted. This is an essential factor to remember in the start where great speed is desired.

Swimmers should avoid lowering the head unduly while swimming several strokes under water in order to maintain proper depth. Directional progression and depth should be controlled by the skillful use of the plane of the palm in the arm pull and the direction of thrust in the leg drive. The head should be in line with the spine.

The direction of the swimmer under water should be parallel with the surface and slightly upward early in the glide. Some swimmers attempt to swim downward constantly until the last stroke, and then rise upward. This is very inefficient, because the body would rise at too abrupt a vertical angle.

2. **The Leg Action in the "Butterfly" Breast Stroke.**—The type of kick, whether wide, narrow, or medium, depends upon the strength and skill of the swimmer's legs. A breast stroke swimmer who cannot "fly" easily with the arms, cannot afford to glide in a race beside a good opponent who does "fly" well. He, therefore, speeds up his stroke, not only by shortening the glide but also by speeding up the

execution of the stroke itself. The spread of the knees is narrowed considerably in order that the legs may execute the kick movement as fast as the arms execute the arm part of the stroke movement. This narrower knee spread with rotatory knee action gives the legs a very fast action kick with little or no pause of the legs after completion of the leg drive. The new narrowed quick leg kicks are faster in action but deliver less power. The whole idea of the butterfly stroke is to take the major drive of the stroke away from the legs and distribute it more equally with the arms. More strokes are delivered in the butterfly over a given distance than in the orthodox. The power in the leg drive is partially sacrificed by shifting it to a more powerful arm stroke, plus a more rapid cadence of strokes. The result is greater speed, even though somewhat more effort is expended. Breast stroke swimmers must train harder to withstand the wear and tear of swimming the butterfly over an entire race.

The legs really kick almost continuously without a pause for a glide after the completion of the kick. Instead of a glide the legs go immediately into the upswing recovery phase of the next kick. This is, of course, dependent upon the timing used between the arms and legs. This will be discussed later.

The kick is executed in the following manner. The legs lift while the knees spread moderately in the recovery (Fig. 8D). The heels are first drawn up toward the hips but are then moved outward instead of drawn directly toward the hips. The knees are slightly turned inward to accommodate the outward leg movement. The toes are turned slightly outward and downward and drawn toward the knees. This position places the lower leg in a vertical position above the knees (Fig. 8A). The idea is to engage the water with the feet as nearly on a line with the hips as is possible so that the water may be held with the legs and feet for a longer distance to the point of completion of the kick. The thrust is then driven outward and downward, and just before the knee has fully straightened on the downward kick, the upward drive is made. This gives a whiplike action to the distal end of the leg, the foot. On this up-kick the legs continue on to the next kick by bending the knees. The water is engaged on the outward-downward thrust with the soles of the feet which keeps the kick within the rules. To learn this kick best the dolphin kick should be practiced to obtain the continuous up and down action of the kick. Training methods can be employed by a kick rail or a kicking board. During use of kicking boards the face can be placed low in the water to look back underneath the body and observe one's own leg action.

3. The Arm Action in the "Butterfly" Breast Stroke.

(a) *The Entry.*—The entry of the arms should be at a point just inside the line of the shoulders with the arms naturally extended, relaxed, with the hand slightly bent down at the wrist (Fig. 8A). The hands and arms should press into the water rather than be smashed into the water. The hands enter about six to ten inches apart. Before the catch is made, the arms should prepare for the catch by stretching to a fairly deep position. While the hands are in the air during the recovery, the body has a tendency to sink. This sinking of the body can be reduced by a rapid recovery. Those swimmers who are less buoyant, especially, should stress the point of getting the arms into the entry as fast as possible without smashing them into the water. A skilled entry with the right amount of pressure on the forearms and hands will prevent the body from sinking as the entry is made.

(b) *The Press-Glide.*—Some coaches advocate a glide after the entry and before the catch is made. This glide is recommended for swimmers in a 200-yard distance or over and for very buoyant swimmers. Most swimmers sink too deep on the glide and lose the rhythm and balance. If a glide is taken the head should be held well up to carry the body high.

Without a glide, the swimmer goes into the catch as the legs close in the kick. In this faster cadence without the glide, the swimmer can ride more easily with the body higher, which is a distinct advantage in the performance of this "flying" stroke and so far as obtaining speed is concerned.

(c) *The Catch.*—The catch begins with a press as the shoulders lift slightly and begin to draw themselves over the hands along the level of the water. As the hands are well in the full catch, the elbows move slightly outward and just before the shoulders are over the hands (Fig. 8B), the scapula, as in the crawl arm action, shifts from a quick press to a push action. As this transaction takes place, the elbows turn in toward the chest wall as the arms drive back on a line

Fig. 8.—A series of ideal form showing the butterfly breast stroke. These figures also show the ideal position of the body in relation to the surface. A. The legs are shown cocked for the leg drive and the arms have entered and are ready for the arm drive. B. The legs are completing the drive and the arms are deep in the arm drive position. C. The body has been driven forward to take air as the arms lift in the recovery. D. The arms and legs are shown in the recovery positions.

Fig. 8.—A, B, C, D.

with either hip.   The path of this arm action with its changing directional line of drive can best be described by the hand forming an inverted letter S if one were to look down upon the stroke.   The hands first press outward, then inward and as the arms finish the stroke they again knife outward.   The lateral movement occurs during the first part of the arm pull.

There is an element of lift to the press and pull but this lift should be kept at a minimum.   Forward, not upward, motion of the body should be the objective.   This is based upon mechanically sound principles, giving advantageous leverage as well as efficient muscular action.   The principle is exactly the same as that applied in the crawl arm action.

(d) *The Release.*—After the hands push and drive backward from shoulder to hip, the hand releases the water just short of the hip joint (Fig. 8C) and knifes outward to the surface and goes into the recovery.   One should not pull too far in relation to the hips, otherwise the swimmer's body drops too deep and impedes arm recovery.   At the time of the release of the water and the armswing sideward, the elbows are slightly bent to relax the arm muscles and to drain the water off the arm.

(e) *The Recovery.*—This is a movement with which most "flying" swimmers have difficulty.   To assist this movement the body should be carried well up in the surface so that the back is well out of the water in order to free the arms for the recovery above the water.   This can be aided by a very powerful hand and wrist stroke inward, and downward pressure as the hand passes under the shoulders in completing the push or drive phase of the stroke.   This also gives the arms or elbows an outward and upward kick and easily lifts the arms above the surface.

Some individuals are limited and impeded structurally in either or both the shoulder joints as well as the shoulder blades.   Some individuals have broader shoulder blades than others and are limited in adduction of the scapula.   Sometimes enlarged body protuberances limit freedom of the shoulder joint action.   These are great handicaps to breast stroke swimmers who wish to butterfly.

The arms should recover in a low lateral sweeping movement above the surface, with rotation of the arm to accommodate the movement (Fig. 8D).   The body should be maintained high in the surface and it should not be permitted to sink while the arms recover. The arms are carried forward to a position opposite the shoulders with the elbows and the little fingers of each hand facing upward. The arms are held as relaxed as possible in this position. As the arms pass the shoulders, there is a rotation at the shoulder joint which accommodates the forward movement. The rotation continues until the palms are facing downward. In this position, the arms are in readiness for the entry. Sinking should be eliminated by pressing the hands into the water quickly, without smashing. Throughout the entire stroke the body should not rise and drop, commonly known as "bobbing." The body should progress over the surface at as nearly a constant level as possible, so that "bobbing" is held to a minimum. This will eliminate resistance and facilitate greater speed.

4. **Timing the Arm Action to Synchronize With the Leg Action in the Butterfly Breast Stroke.**—There are two methods of timing in this modern stroke. The difference lies in the type of kick. Those swimmers who have a very effective wide orthodox kick should start to recover the legs at the release. While the swimmer is using the continuous action-reaction narrow type of kick, he does not recover the legs until his arms are nearly opposite his shoulders in the recovery. The difference in timing between these kicks is due to the fact that the wider sweeping kick requires more time to execute than the narrower type.

The short, quick, narrow, powerful kick aids the arms materially in sustaining the body well up out of the water so that the arms can function by delivering tremendous forward motivating power. Then the drive of the legs should be delivered just as the arms press into the water and catch immediately for the next stroke. If a glide is desired, the arms merely pause for the glide following the entry.

5. **Timing the Arms With the Rotary Kick.**—

(a) As the arms press into the catch, the heels are close to the buttocks ready for the drive (Fig. 8A).

(b) The arms are finishing the catch and pull and commencing the push. The legs are extended behind and held straight backward, slightly separated, with the toes pointed backward (Fig. 8B).

(c) The arms are executing the release, elbows lifting for the recovery, and the legs are still stretched behind (Fig. 8C).

(d) The arms are being recovered and are approximately opposite the shoulders; the legs begin the rapid recovery (Fig. 8D).

(e) As the arms are entering the water, the legs are cocked ready for the drive.

(f) The legs drive and the arms follow with the pull almost simultaneously.

6. **Breathing and Its Timing in the Butterfly Stroke.**—The breathing technique in both the butterfly and orthodox strokes is practically the same, that is, inhaling through the mouth while pulling and exhaling in the water early in the recovery and glide. As the head is raised for air, at the start of the pull, the head does not need to be lifted nearly as high as in the conventional style, because the body rises much higher and the mouth can be faced down toward the water, taking advantage of the longer pull and relieving tension and strain on neck muscles. This permits the mouth to get air much more rapidly and the head can be slightly lowered permitting more freedom to the scapular movement over the upper back during the recovery. A very high carriage of the head at all times is advocated. Lowering the head after each breath would cause the body to "bob" up and down, causing too much friction and retarding speed.

For sprinting shorter distances, the swimmer may favor breathing on every other stroke, depending upon the individual and the demands made upon the swimmer as to lack of air.

7. **The "Flying" Breast Stroke Turn.**—There are very few differences in technique in the flying breast stroke turns from that used in the conventional type. In the approach one should time the strokes so that as the arms recover, they lunge into the wall above the surface with a lowered head. Then just in case that the throw of the arms was short, the momentum will drive the body forward into the wall. The turning mechanics are the same as in the conventional breast turn. When the turn is completed, if sprinting, the push-out should be shallow, if the swimmer does not intend to use underwater strokes. If underwater strokes are used, the recommended methods may be followed as used in the conventional technique.

8. **The Finish in the "Flying" Breast Stroke.**—For the finish the same principles apply as recommended in the finish of the traditional breast stroke.

A tired swimmer often lacks poise and good generalship near the finish when he is nearly "spent" by continuing to "fly." When

the arms feel heavy as lead and can no longer be used effectively,
he should revert to short, quick, orthodox arm sprinting strokes
and narrowed kicks to drive him to the finish.

Coaches should train swimmers to practice the finish approach
just as much as practicing starts and turns. There seems to be no
"rhyme or reason" to practicing starts and turns constantly, if the
swimmer is destined to lose in the last ten yards of the finish what
he gains by a good fast penetrating start and turns earlier in the race.

The Newest Dolphin Fishtail Breast Stroke

The dolphin fishtail breast stroke was developed at the University of Iowa in 1935.[4] This stroke is a further development,
and a step forward in speed, of the breast stroke. If changes
could be made on the arm and still stay within the scope of the
competitive breast stroke rules, then it would seem logical that
the legs could also be altered as long as the legs performed in
unison. The flying arms were powerful and created greater
speed, but the two movements, flying arms and orthodox breast
stroke kick, were not a good basic mechanical combination of movements. The kick was a retarding type of action compared to the
faster, more powerful action of the flying arms. Retarding factors in
the kick action had to be eliminated. A kick had to be developed
which eliminated a recovery phase as well as the tail suction behind
the legs.

The discovery of this stroke was merely an assembling into a perfectly timed combination of skills of arm and leg action which had
already been known for years. The kick was a simultaneous undulating action similar to a double "flutter" kick.

The dolphin breast stroke kick is fundamentally like that of the
crawl stroke, the only difference being that both arms and legs
move together in unison, while in the crawl, the same performance of
both arms and legs is executed in alternating movements. One may
further say that the "flying" arms in the breast stroke should not
be classified as a breast stroke but as a crawl-breast stroke, because
it is a combination of two styles of competitive swimming.

Breast stroke swimmers invariably use this dolphin kick in the
glide of the start and push-out from a turn. They use the short,

[4]Armbruster, D. A., and Sieg, Jack: The Dolphin Breast Stroke, Journal of
Health and Physical Education 6: 23 (April), 1935.

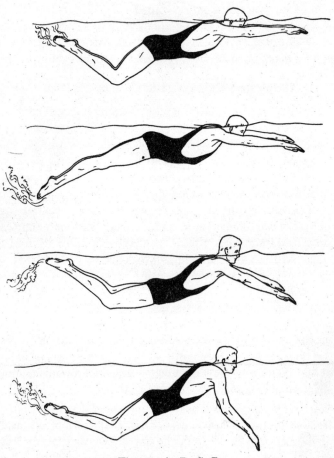

Fig. 9.—A, B, C, D.

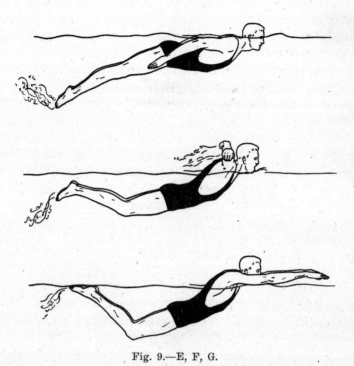

Fig. 9.—E, F, G.

Fig. 9.—A series of ideal form showing the dolphin fishtail breast stroke. These figures also show the ideal position of the body in relation to the surface. A. The legs have completed the up drive and are beginning to drive downward. The arms are in the gliding position. B. The legs complete the first down beat and the hips get an action-reaction upward. The arms press and spread into the downward catch. Note position of the entire body. C. The legs are beating upward to complete the first beat of the kick. The arms have completed the catch-and-pull and are beginning the push phase of the stroke. The head is kept in line with the body. D. The legs begin the second down beat while the arms are well in the push phase of the stroke. E. This figure illustrates the legs driving down through the axis of progression while the arms have released the water and begin the recovery. F. The arms are midway in the recovery and the legs begin the final upward beat in the stroke revolution. Note at this point air is being taken. Again note action-reaction of arms and legs. G. This diagram illustrates the arms about to complete the arm stroke revolution. The legs continue the up beat to complete the two-beat leg kick revolution. (See Fig. 9 A.)

quick, undulating dolphin action of the legs just as the arm catch is being made. It is a natural movement. It is very difficult for breast stroke swimmers to refrain from doing so. At present the kick is illegal for breast stroke competition. However, the stroke is included in this series of competitive strokes since it may become legal at some future date as a possible freestyle breast stroke.

Within a very few years, the International Rules Representatives will need to take steps and outline more specifically what shall be classified as a legal breast stroke under competitive conditions. At this writing news has reached America that the Japanese have already barred the "flying" breast stroke for future competition.

There is a strong sentiment among American coaches that the traditional breast stroke should be retained as a competitive event and that another event of freestyle breast stroke should be added.

The dolphin stroke is amazing in speed performance.[5] The kick itself produces greater speed than the alternating crawl-flutter. However, it seems on physical principles that this stroke never will develop the speed of the crawl stroke, even though the kick is faster. The dual arm action never will be as fast as the alternating arm action, because in the "butterfly" arm stroke there is a nonpropelling phase during the recovery. In the crawl movement one or both arms are always in the water propelling. This nonpropelling phase in the "butterfly" action would, therefore, seem to offset the increased speed derived from the dolphin kick. An alternating arm action with the dolphin fishtail kick does not synchronize naturally.

The Technique of the Dolphin Breast Stroke

This stroke is definitely dominated by the kick, resembling the tail movement of a flat-tailed dolphin.

1. **The Kick**.—The leg action is exactly like that of the flutter kick in the crawl. The feet have the same slant on the up beat as the crawl kick. The knees bend as the legs pass the central axis of body progression. At the end of the up stroke, the feet relax (Fig. 9 A to D). At the beginning of the down stroke the toes are turned inward, and the metatarsal part of the foot, together with the toes, is hyperextended. On the downward stroke of both legs, the knees are somewhat bent until almost the end of the down beat. The knees straighten

[5]Armbruster, D. A.: The New Dolphin Breast Stroke on Trial, Swimming Guide 1937, Am. Sports Publishing Co., New York, p. 52.

quickly, giving a tremendous whip to the feet. The up stroke is started with the legs straight until the legs reach the central axis of progression where the knees again bend in order to effect the propulsive action of a fishtail. As the legs weave up and down, they press backward against the water at an angle as the water washes down the legs. This action supplies the propulsive power of the kick.

The kick has several better and more efficient principles for delivering speed than does the alternating crawl flutter kick. First, there is less resistance at the thighs than in the crawl flutter or the traditional breast stroke kick. Second, there is less retarding resistance to forward motion than an alternating motion of the legs. Third, there is no waste return motion such as in the orthodox breast kick recovery. Fourth, there is no counter-propulsive reaction due to nonproductive motion in the direction of progress. For example, the frog-kick has a reciprocating jerk so that when one leg kicks backward the kick ends with a jerk due to the backward momentum of the feet.

In this kick, both legs and trunk weave up and down in the water, placing the axis of motion somewhere in the spine well up in the shoulder region. In the crawl flutter kick, the axis of motion is in the hip joints. In the dolphin kick, the whole body weaves as if made of rubber.

2. **The Arm Action.**—The technique and mechanics are identical with that of the "butterfly" breast stroke. The glide phase of the arms in this stroke can be either prolonged or diminished, depending upon the distance to be covered.

3. **Timing of the Arms and Legs.**—The best rhythm found for this stroke was two beats of the legs to one cycle of the arms. Since the kick dominates this stroke, the timing elements should be analyzed from their action. From a bent leg position and arms extended in a sliding position, the first timing movement begins (Fig. 9A).

The arms catch and press into the pull while the hips start the upward movement and the legs complete the downward beat (Fig. 9B). In Fig. 9C the arms are pulling while the legs are driving upward. Note the counteraction of both arms and legs in relation to the hip in Fig. 9B and C. In Fig. 9D the legs begin the second down beat, and the arms are entering the push phase. Note the pigeon-toed feet and the spread of the knees. In Fig. 9E the legs have completed the downward beat and the arms have released the water and are beginning to recover. Note how both the arms and legs are in line, as the arms have completed the drive. Fig. 9F shows the arms well above in the recovery, while the legs are beginning the second upward kick. Note that air is inspired in this phase of the stroke. Fig. 9G illustrates the legs completing the upward drive and the arms are entering the water. In Fig. 9A the arms have just entered and are sliding while the legs again arrive at the central plane of progression in the down beat and complete the stroke cycle. The whole body lies at a slightly greater angle in the water than in the butterfly. The undulating action of the legs and hips requires a greater depth of the body. This also changes the breathing principle to some extent.

4. **Timing of Breathing With the Arms.**—Since the body lies slightly deeper in the water it must be pulled forward and out by the pull of the arms. The down stroke of the legs causes the body to lift forward and out. During this movement the head is held down and no breath is taken until the arms are out of the water in the recovery. The air is taken when the arms are directly out to the sides from the shoulders in the recovery (Fig. 9F). It is logical to take air at this point because here the head is highest out of the water. The legs stroke down during this phase which makes it possible to have both arms and head out of the water at the same time. This is unorthodox to any other stroke excepting the crawl where only one arm is out when air is breathed.

5. **The Start, Turn, and Finish.**—The start, turn, and finish of the dolphin stroke have already been discussed in the butterfly breast stroke.

6. **Coaching and Teaching Procedures for the Dolphin Fishtail Breast Stroke.**—In order to learn the narrow spread leg-lifting type of kick for the dolphin breast stroke, some methods are recommended.

(a) First, the swimmer should learn the alternating flutter kick.

(b) The next step is to hold to the side of the tank and use the dolphin kick with the legs held together.

(c) Then go under the surface, trail the arms at the sides and do the dolphin kick.

(d) When the swimmer feels the movement, the up and down hip action should be minimized and the bend of the knees, as well as the whip at the completion of both down and up strokes, should be stressed.

(e) The legs can now be spread to about the width of the knee spread as in the butterfly breast stroke and the undulating action of the kick repeated.

(f) Gradually, as this undulating action takes place with the legs spread, a squeeze together of the legs can be stressed just as the legs are completing the downward whip, the squeeze can be emphasized on the continued up beat. Just as the legs are lifting for the up beat they can be spread out and the down beat is continued as described above.

(g) Gradually the ankles work properly and effectively so that the soles of the feet engage the water on both the up and down beats of the legs.

Kicking boards as well as elastic check ropes and belts can be effectively used as practice methods for acquiring efficiency in the movements. The elastic check rope and belt is an excellent method for practicing the arm action with the kick. This elastic rubber check rope can be made from used bicycle inner tubes.

Racing Fundamentals

Most athletes entering breast stroke competition should be able to swim the 100-yard distance using the butterfly style. The method for swimming this distance would thus be to swim only one or two strokes under water at the start and at the push-offs from the turns, rise to the surface and butterfly at a steady rhythm to the finish. Changing the rhythm of the butterfly to the orthodox and back to the butterfly is a costly procedure as a completely new pattern of the arm action and a completely new pattern of the timing of the arms and legs must be established for each type of stroke. The recovery arm action of the orthodox stroke is in the opposite direction of the action in the butterfly. Even the best swimmers require two or three strokes to find the new rhythm each time they change their stroke. The 100 yards race is too short to warrant such a loss of speed.

The inexperienced swimmer who cannot maintain a steady flying rhythm through 100 yards to the finish should extend the glide portion of his butterfly stroke at the fatigue portion of the race instead of reverting to the orthodox style. If a change in rhythm is to be instituted, this is best done at the turn.

The 200 yards breast stroke race is similar to the 220 yards crawl as far as pacing and distribution of energy are concerned. As but very few breast stroke swimmers can butterfly for 200 yards, the problem of when to swim butterfly and when to swim orthodox is raised.

The breast stroke competitors should aim to develop their flying stroke and their condition to such a level that they can fly the whole 200 yards distance. Until this level is achieved, the breast stroke swimmer must plan his race carefully in order to prevent himself from exceeding his energy capacity by attempting to butterfly too long.

1. **Race Plan.**—The swimmer's race plan must be well established before the competition takes place. A plan which has been used successfully by inexperienced breast stroke swimmers is as follows:

Elapsed distance	Style
25 yards	Butterfly
50 yards	Butterfly
75 yards	Butterfly
100 yards	Orthodox
125 yards	Orthodox
150 yards	Orthodox
175 yards	Butterfly
200 yards	Butterfly

A more experienced and better conditioned swimmer may be successful in using the following plan:

Elapsed distance	Style
25 yards	Butterfly
50 yards	Butterfly
75 yards	Butterfly
100 yards	Butterfly
125 yards	Orthodox
150 yards	Butterfly
175 yards	Orthodox
200 yards	Butterfly

The swimmer should then attempt to improve to the point where he can eliminate the orthodox at the seventh length, and finally eliminate the orthodox at the fifth length as well, so that he now covers the entire distance in the butterfly style.

By referring to Table V, the breast stroke swimmer can plan his race in accordance with the ideal split times throughout his race.

TABLE V

THIS TABLE SHOWS IDEAL SPLIT TIMES FOR VARIOUS RACING TIMES IN THE 200 YARDS BREAST STROKE (25 YD. POOL.)

ELAPSED DISTANCE YD.	ELAPSED TIME SEC.	SPLIT TIME SEC.	ELAPSED DISTANCE YD.	ELAPSED TIME SEC.	SPLIT TIME SEC.
25	12.5	12.5	25	13.7	13.7
50	28.0	15.5	50	30.4	16.7
75	44.7	16.7	75	48.3	17.9
100	1:01.6	16.9	100	1:06.4	18.1
125	1:19.7	18.1	125	1:25.8	19.4
150	1:13.9	18.2	150	1:45.3	19.5
175	1:56.4	18.5	175	2:05.1	19.8
200	2:15.0	18.6	200	2:25.0	19.9
25	13.1	13.1	25	14.4	14.4
50	29.2	16.1	50	31.8	17.4
75	46.5	17.3	75	50.3	18.5
100	1:04.0	17.5	100	1:09.0	18.7
125	1:22.8	18.8	125	1:29.0	20.0
150	1:41.7	18.9	150	1:49.1	20.1
175	2:00.8	19.1	175	2:09.5	20.4
200	2:20.0	19.2	200	2:30.0	20.5
25	15.0	15.0	25	16.2	16.2
50	33.0	18.0	50	35.4	19.2
75	52.3	19.3	75	55.9	20.5
100	1:11.8	19.5	100	1:16.6	20.7
125	1:32.4	20.6	125	1:38.5	21.9
150	1:53.1	20.7	150	2:00.5	22.0
175	2:14.0	20.9	175	2:22.7	22.2
200	2:35.0	21.0	200	2:45.0	22.3
25	15.6	15.6	25	16.9	16.9
50	34.2	18.6	50	36.8	19.9
75	54.1	19.9	75	57.9	21.1
100	1:14.2	20.1	100	1:19.2	21.3
125	1:35.5	21.3	125	1:41.7	22.5
150	1:56.9	21.4	150	2:04.3	22.6
175	2:19.4	21.5	175	2:27.1	22.8
200	2:40.0	21.6	200	2:50.0	22.9

CHAPTER IX

CONDITIONING

Conditioning is preparing the body for activity. It includes the building of health, strength, endurance, and speed. Training is the process of adjustment to the competitive situation and improvement in the skill in which the athlete is to perform.

A common occurrence in athletic literature is the erroneous use of the words conditioning and training synonymously. They are usually considered as being so closely allied in preparing an athlete for competition that no distinction is made between the terms. For example, as an athlete undergoes certain forms of physical movements in acquiring a skill, he is also by this exercise improving the quality of his muscles. Thus, while he is training he is also improving his condition.

From the coach's viewpoint in considering the preparation of an athlete for competition, the problem of conditioning and training presents a logical sequence. The body as a machine must be strong and be able to overcome the processes of fatigue to such an extent that the performance of the skill may not be hampered by the lack of these facilities.

Theoretically, a man can be in excellent condition and still not be trained in any skill. Also, on the other hand, he may be well trained to perform a specific skill but he may lack the physical capacity necessary to complete the performance or continue the performance for any length of time.

As an example, a boy may report to the coach at the swimming pool each day and there may receive the best education in swimming technique which the coach is able to give. As a result of this training, the boy is able to demonstrate a very highly skilled performance. His stroke mechanics are refined to the utmost degree. His timing of the stroke is perfect. However, on leaving the pool he violates good eating habits, and in the evenings he becomes toxic and gets inadequate nights of rest, thereby reducing his condition. After a period of such activity his performance in the pool becomes characteristic of a man who is well trained in technique but in poor condition. His stroke mechanics are still excellent and over a short distance and at a slow speed he gives all the outward appearances of a champion. But if he is asked to increase the speed, even for a short distance, he finds it difficult to do so. We can now say that the man is in poor condition and still is well trained. Conditioning the athlete for competition requires weeks and even months to achieve, but it can be destroyed within a very few days.

Although the processes of conditioning and training are carried on at the same time during a season, still each of the procedures may be considered separately. This chapter is devoted to measures which will improve the athlete's physical condition. The emphasis here will be on strength, endurance, and speed.

Speed, strength, and endurance can be improved by a carefully regulated program of conditioning procedures. These procedures include diet control, frequent and graded exercises, adequate rest, and observance of certain hygienic principles.

The coach usually imparts information concerning these procedures by the distribution of printed material, by posting a list of rules, and often by classroom sessions during the preseason meetings of the squad. The material pertaining to conditioning which appears in this chapter has been prepared in such a form that the coach can easily lift it from these pages and transfer it to his own rules for his swimmers.

Before reporting for a program of conditioning for swimming competition the swimmer should report for a thorough medical examination. This examination will bring to light any functional organic disorders.

1. **Diet.**—The first consideration will be that of the diet. As most swimming squads do not have the advantages of a training table, the most effective presentation of diet control will be in the form of a discussion of foods which are recommended and other foods which should be avoided. Food, the right kind and enough of it, is a factor involved in acquiring strength, endurance and alertness. Many athletes do not live at home to obtain an adequate diet for ordinary everyday purposes of living. These swimmers must, therefore, select their own food for an adequate balanced diet.

There are six essentials of nutrition: proteins, carbohydrates, fats, vitamins, minerals, and water. These are easily attainable by the individual through a properly chosen diet.

In terms of everyday food a proper diet consists, first, of milk and its by-products, fruit, vegetables, meat, fish, and eggs; then starches and sugars. A diet of this type is adequate for everyday living. In a normal person engaged in normal activity the six essentials will be satisfied without the addition of vitamin concentrates or other special foods. However, this general diet must be supplemented and altered to meet the exigencies of swimming, training, and competition. Fitness for swimming competition depends largely upon a proper diet.

During the season of training and competition the swimmer's daily energy consumption is increased over his everyday average. Large amounts of body heat are lost during submersion and exertion in the water; body substances are broken down faster, and a strain is thrown on the body processes. The food substances taken into the body must be increased to supply the necessary elements for promoting its growth and replacing its waste, and which yield energy for muscular work and heat, and for regulating body processes.

Foods may be classified according to function as follows:

1. Fuel foods or sources of energy
   a. Carbohydrates
      1. Sugars
      2. Starches
   b. Lipids
      1. Fats
      2. Lipoids
   c. Proteins
      1. Animal proteins
      2. Vegetable proteins

2. Body builders or tissue formers
   a. Proteins
   b. Lipids
   c. Mineral salts
   d. Water

3. Regulators of body processes
   a. Mineral salts
   b. Water
   c. Accessory food substances—vitamins

Of the six essential foodstuffs the carbohydrates are the most abundant and also the most economical source of energy. Most of the body energy is derived from the carbohydrates. Other foods are used, but these foods are ultimately in the carbohydrate form when used for body energy and for the maintenance of the proper environment of the cell.

Carbohydrates are derived almost entirely from the vegetable kingdom. They form the chief constituents of roots, tubers, and seeds. The most available sources of carbohydrates for human use are the cereal grains, potatoes, rice, tapioca, sugar (cane, beet, and maple), honey and sweet fruits. The only direct animal sources of the carbohydrates are liver (glycogen), milk (lactose), and blood (glucose).

The carbohydrates yield energy when burned in the body. That in excess of the body needs may be stored as glycogen, chiefly in the liver but also in the muscles and other organs. If greater quantity than can be burned and stored as glycogen is ingested it may be converted and stored as fat.

Sugars are soluble carbohydrates with more or a less sweet taste. We are most concerned with glucose (grape sugar), lactose (milk sugar), and sucrose (cane sugar).

Glucose occurs in nature as syrup; it is less sweet than cane sugar. Other sugars have to be changed to this form by digestion before the body can use them. Glucose is found throughout the vegetable kingdom, chiefly in fruit and plant juices. It is especially abundant in grapes; it may constitute 20 per cent of the weight in grapes. Glucose is a fuel food in a very readily absorbable form. It is an economical form of energy. If used for sweetening, large quantities must be employed.

Sucrose is chemically the same as cane sugar. Maple sugar has the same composition except for its impurities. Sucrose is derived from the sap or juices of a large variety of plants; from sugar cane, sugar beet, and maple tree. The common fruits and vegetables contain considerable amounts of this sugar. The solid product is obtained by evaporation and purification of the saps. The sucroses are valuable sources of energy. They must be used with discretion, however, for three reasons: (1) Large amounts of too highly concentrated solutions are irritating to the gastric mucosa. (2) These sugars ferment easily and are liable to fermentation in the stomach. (3) On account of the quickness of their absorption they may either satisfy the appetite before the needs of food have been met or they may blunt the appetite so that other foods necessary to insure adequacy of the diet may become distasteful. Dried fruits form a better source of food than pure sugars since they contain important mineral salts.

Lactose occurs in the milk of all mammals. It is less sweet and less soluble than cane sugar and does not easily ferment. On account of its mild flavor and because it is less irritating to the gastric mucosa, it is widely used in infant and invalid feeding. It forms a valuable source of fuel. Cow's milk contains about 4.8 per cent of lactose.

Starch is a white powder, insoluble in cold water, slightly soluble in boiling water or by dry heating at high temperatures or by certain digestive ferments. The first substances formed in the course of starch digestion are dextrins. These can be split into the disaccharides (maltose) which in turn will yield two molecules of glucose. Starch occurs widely in the vegetable kingdom. It is found in large amounts in seeds, roots, tubers, bulbs, and sometimes in the stems and seeds of plants. It constitutes one-half to three-fourths of the matter of the ordinary cereal grains and three-fourths of the solids of mature potatoes. Commercially, starches are obtained from wheat, corn, rice, potato, and tapioca.

Fats are almost as widely distributed in nature as are carbohydrates and constitute a more concentrated form of fuel for the supply of energy in nutrition. They form part of animal tissue and are contained in many plants.

The chief sources of fats in the diet are milk (cream and butter), olive oil, and other vegetable oils; meat fats, lard, bacon, salt pork, beef suet, and nuts. Less expensive forms of fat are found in the margarines which are made from fats as cocoanut, cottonseed, and corn oils. Oleomargarine is made from beef fat churned with milk. These fats have the same fuel value as butter but differ in their vitamin content.

Fat is the most concentrated kind of fuel, furnishing two and one-fourth times as much energy as the same weight of carbohydrate or protein. The most important function of fat is: (1) an energy supply; (2) protection to body organs against mechanical injury; (3) prevention of too rapid loss of body heat; and (4) its action as packing to support visceral organs, particularly the kidneys.

The fats tend to check secretion of gastric juice and retard motility of the stomach, thereby retarding the rate of digestion. The softer fats (butter) are digested more easily than the solid ones (suet). Heating fats to too high a temperature may decompose them and give products which are irritating to the lining membrane of the stomach. Foods fried in fat are coated with, or permeated by, it and are, therefore, less easily digested.

Lipoids are fatlike substances closely related both chemically and biologically to the fats, which occur widely in nature and are essential constituents of every living cell. The two most important of these lipoids are (1) lecithin and (2) cholesterol.

Lecithin occurs in considerable quantities in brain substance, blood corpuscles, and other nitrogenous tissues; it is present also in egg yolk. Lecithin is also found in plants, especially seeds.

Cholesterol is present in animal cells and in blood. There are considerable quantities in the brain and skin. It acquires antirachitic properties on irradiation. It is believed that light forms antirachitic vitamin D from cholesterol or ergosterol, another sterol, in the skin. It is present in cod-liver oil, egg yolk, and green vegetables.

The proteins supply both energy and body-building foods, i.e., certain parts of these substances are taken and build, with other substances obtained from other sources, into body tissues. Carbohydrate and fat have for their chief functions the furnishing of energy. The proteins form the only source of organic nitrogen, which is an indispensable constituent in animal and plant cells.

The proteins are found in nearly all solids of animal and vegetable organisms. Animal foods are richer in proteins than plant foods. Meat, fish, eggs, and milk furnish large amounts of proteins. They are found both in the whites and yolks of eggs. Legumes are the only plant foods which compare with the animal foods in their content of protein. Some of these are peas, beans, and peanuts. Certain nuts as almonds and pine nuts contain considerable protein.

Nitrogenous extractives are nitrogen-bearing substances found in muscle juices having little if any food value and are useful as stimulants to the flow of gastric juice. They give meats their flavor. These extracts of meat, such as beef tea and bouillon, are used widely in the diets of invalids or in healthy persons as a first course.

Cooking proteins at the higher temperatures tends to toughen them. Better results are obtained by cooking them for longer periods of time at lower temperatures because this renders them more tender.

Plain, wholesome, slow well-cooked foods are adequate for the swimmer. Each swimmer knows which foods agree with him and these he should select. He should eat slowly.

Mineral substances enter into body functions and structure. They are important elements in the diet. Mineral salts function in the following ways: (1) As bone constituents giving rigidity and relative permanence to skeletal structures. (2) As essential elements of the organic compounds which are chief solid constituents of soft tissues (muscles, blood cells, etc.). (3) As soluble salts held in solution in body fluids, giving these fluids their influence upon the elasticity and irritability of muscle and nerve, by supplying the material for the acidity or the alkalinity of the digestive juices and other secretions and yet maintaining the neutrality or alkalescence of the internal fluids as well as their osmotic pressure and solvent power.

Calcium and phosphorus are essential for hard bones and teeth. Iron is essential for building the red blood corpuscles. Calcium and phosphorus are the minerals most often inadequately supplied. Calcium occurs in milk, cheese, egg yolk, vegetables, and molasses. The calcium of milk is easily assimilated. Phosphorus is present in milk, cheese, egg yolk, whole grain cereals, vegetables, lean meat, and fish. Iron is present in liver, kidney, egg yolk, spinach and other green vegetables, potatoes, whole grains, fruits, and lean meats.

Sodium and chlorine are received as table salt. Sulfur is present in almost all protein foods and is adequately supplied in the diet, provided a variety of proteins are fed. Magnesium is adequately supplied in the ordinary foods as but little is needed.

Iodine is necessary for normal functioning of the thyroid gland. It is found almost solely in the ocean and, therefore, found largely in sea food, in table salt not too highly refined, and in water from regions near the sea coast; in plants and animals raised on a sea coast land which contains iodine. Little is known of the exact quantity of iodine in the foods.

The lack of any of the vitamins in the diet may give rise to a decline of physical efficiency long before outstanding or readily recognizable disease appears. Vitamin deficiency constitutes the principle "hidden hungers."

The people in some communities frequently have a diet which is deficient in nicotinic acid. The workers lean on their shovels, are discontented and sunk in apathy and despair. In other communities, thiamine is more commonly lacking in diets than is nicotinic acid. Many of these thiamine-deficients are nervous and apprehensive or irritable, tired and listless. Deficiency of vitamins of the B complex, including thiamine, nicotinic acid, and riboflavin, is due, in part, to the recent milling processes which remove the vitamin-containing portions of sugar and flour. Many people do not like brown bread. The new "enriched flour" and "enriched bread" has an increased content of thiamine, riboflavin, nicotinic acid, and iron.

Vitamin C is present in suboptimal amounts in many diets. Scurvy always has been a problem in Northern regions. The lack of vitamin C increases susceptibility to tuberculosis and other infections.

Uncertainty still surrounds the fat-soluble vitamins, vitamin A and vitamin D. Many diets are too low in vitamin A and lack of this vitamin provokes night blindness and lowers the integrity of epithelial structures, notably the cornea. The fish liver oils and butter fats are rich in vitamin A.

Vitamin D is obtained by the effect of sunlight on the sterols in the skin or by the ingestion of substances as fish liver oils or foods which have been suitably fortified. Vitamin D functions in the proper utilization of calcium and phosphorus.

Gelatin properly made is a wholesome food. It has special usefulness in adding variety to the diet when incorporated in nutritious soups or pleasant desserts which appeal to the appetite of many persons. The evidence available at the present time is insufficient to warrant the claim that the ingestion of gelatin increases physical endurance or is an aid in preventing fatigue.[1]

Whether the constant use of caffeine beverages is harmful, harmless, or merely indifferent is a debated question. There is fairly unanimous agreement that excessive amounts are definitely injurious. It is likewise agreed that athletes should drink milk. Because only limited amounts of liquids will be taken in a day, it is important that coffee, tea, and other beverages do not replace milk.

Approximately 60 per cent of the body is water. Water is constantly being eliminated by the skin, lungs, and kidneys. The loss is replaced conveniently by drinking water.

The daily water requirements for health cannot be defined with any degree of exactness, as activity, temperature and other conditions

[1] Accepted Foods and Their Nutritional Significance, American Medical Association, Chicago, 1937.

influence the demands. Sufficient water should be taken with meals and between meals to satisfy thirst. Glutting the body with water is not justified.

On trips away from home where only water of a questionable purity may be available, the use of good bottled waters is recommended. They serve as refreshing, pleasing drinking water with a maximum assurance of safety.

All foods except the simple mineral foods and water contain chemical energy available for use by the healthy body to support the many activities and life processes and incidentally to maintain temperature. This use of the term "energy" in defining the caloric or energy value of foods should not be confused with the popular usage signifying activity, vitality, strength, vigor, or endurance. These conditions depend on many factors, including freedom from disease, natural constitution, physical environment, training, habits, and others. Good nutritive condition, a necessity for health, requires far more than food energy only; all the nutritional essentials of a complete well-balanced diet, in adequate amounts, are demanded.

2. **The Swimmer's Daily Schedule of Living.**—The first cardinal principle for conditioning one's self for strenuous training is to have a regulated schedule for daily routine events. The student has a schedule of academic hours for every day in the week. He should also budget his study hours for every day in the week. Meals should be eaten at regular hours every day. He should set his bedtime and rising hour at a regular time. His training period is also arranged at a regular time each day of the week. Such a regulated schedule will keep the swimmer mentally and physically alert and healthy for a season of rugged competitive training.

3. **A Precontest Diet.**—There are, at present, excellent precontest menus[2] in the literature; therefore, menus will not be presented in this discussion. However, a brief discussion of the principles of precontest and postcontest diets will be presented.

(a) A reserve supply of energy. This can be provided by mixing one quart of orange juice with one-half pound of honey. Drink from three to five glasses, a glass each hour, starting six hours before the contest. A glass between events is excellent. This is just like high-test gasoline. It burns in a flash and creates immediate energy.

[2] See Menus, G. T. Bresnahan and W. W. Tuttle, in Track and Field Athletics, pp. 428.

(b) In a diet leading up to a contest, it is well to increase the alkali reserve by eating fruits and vegetables which will increase the potential alkalinity of the blood stream. This alkaline reserve will help to neutralize the acids which are produced by muscular activity and cause fatigue. (These fatigue acids have no relation to gastric acidity.)

(c) He should avoid such foods as heavy pastries and fried foods.

(d) Such foods which are of a questionable nature should be avoided. Beverages: Ice water, strong tea (weak green tea acceptable), coffee (except at breakfast), iced liquids.

Bread: Hot bread, biscuits, waffles, and pancakes.

Condiments: Chili sauce, meat spices, catsup, and any form of relishes as olives and pickles.

4. The Postcontest Diet.—Materials which have been used and excreted from his body during competition should be replaced between events and following the competition. Those replacements include the afore-mentioned glycogen and alkaline substances. Salts are also diminished by exercise and should be replaced.

Foods rich in protein are needed for tissue building and repair requirements.

5. Elimination.—The human body rids itself of waste materials, through defecation, urination, perspiration, and respiration. The swimmer need concern himself principally with the elimination of the fecal matter. Elimination should be regulated by a sufficient amount of roughage and other food materials to assure him adequate elimination. This elimination should occur at regulated periods of the day. The act itself is usually associated in the morning with rising and drinking a glass of warm water. Normally, the athlete should void fecal matter immediately following breakfast. The athlete should arise early enough to allow sufficient time, either before or after breakfast, to properly attend to this very important function of daily routine living. Too often a student rises late for an early class and delays his personal toilet. This is the forerunner of constipation.

Cathartics should not be taken unless prescribed by a physician to relieve a severe case of constipation. Usually it can be avoided by regular habits of defecation and by the careful selection of certain foods. If too much roughage is consumed to correct this condition, it may lead to other gastrointestinal disturbances.

6. **Rest.**—The youth who is attending high school or college and participating in athletics is usually a creature of extremes. He eats his meals hastily. He worries about his classwork and his standing on the team. He may have to work to pay his expenses at school. To these he may add inordinate social obligations.

The intensity of such activity taxes the resources of the nervous system to the extent that sleep offers the only sure means of recuperation.

The amount of sleep required by the athlete depends entirely on the individual; the determining factors being his age, daily activity, physical and mental development, and personal peculiarities. It is possible for an individual to obtain too much sleep. Temperance in sleeping is just as essential as temperance in eating and other habits of life.

A period of five hours of sound sleep is far more restful than a ten-hour span of semi-consciousness and tossing in bed. Absolute rest presupposes dreamless slumber. The result obtained is the desire to arise and be up and doing—a feeling that the capacity for work has never been greater. Excepting in cold weather, people sleeping out of doors or in amply ventilated rooms as a rule sleep deeply; hence, because of the quality, require less sleep. If a large number of blankets is required to keep warm, the weight of these will be a retarding factor in sleep. Normal and refreshing sleep is favored by moderate fatigue, reduction of sensory stimuli.

Swimmers should be taught a healthy sleep habit founded on the following principles:

(a) Arise at a regular hour, regardless of early morning fatigue.

(b) Stay awake all day.

(c) Determine the number of hours of sleep usually required to produce a feeling of absolute rest upon awakening. Calculate the hour of retirement accordingly. Establish the habit of retiring regularly at this hour.

(d) As you undress for bed, shed your worries with your clothes. Go to bed to relax, rest, and sleep.

(e) Have the sleeping room dark, well ventilated and as quiet as possible. If you cannot escape noise, make up your mind to become adjusted to it.

(f) If nervous excitation is marked or physical fatigue unusual, take a hot bath before retiring.

(g) It is of paramount importance that to become a great athlete, one must be and remain healthy.

7. Exercise.—Recent analyses of the factors which make for success in athletic performance have shown that strength is extremely important.

This is not surprising when the structure of the body is considered. The bones of the body are attached in such a way as to form levers which are moved by the muscles. The levers which are employed in sports, such as those of the arms and legs, are practically all of the type in which the muscle is attached quite near the end of the bone. The weight to be lifted is at the free end of the lever, and far from the muscle which is to move the weight.

While this arrangement may be very convenient for movements of speed in which little resistance is encountered, it puts the muscle at a great disadvantage where moving against resistance is concerned. To move against resistance, an extraordinarily large force is required in the form of muscular contraction.

For peak performance in swimming, the muscles, which are the sources of power, must be strong. As a rule the practice of the sport itself is not sufficient to develop the muscles to their greatest strength. The addition of strength-building exercises can be used to supplement this muscular development.

In many instances, swimmers reach a peak in their event that represents only the skill side of the activity. Further improvement is impeded by their limitations in strength. If they will increase their strength, they may extend their peaks considerably.[3]

The exercises used for conditioning and for the warm-up will vary with each individual.

The conditioning exercises should be easy to perform, require no special apparatus and should utilize the large muscles, as it is through the activity of these muscles that general physical condition is most improved. A program of this type increases:

(1) The size of the general musculature.
(2) Strength.
(3) Endurance, and
(4) Efficiency of performance.

[3]Morehouse, Laurence E.: The Physiology of Athletics (Strength), Scholastic Coach **10**: 1 (September), 25, 1940.

The warm-up exercises, used before practice and actual competition, have these immediate effects: (1) increase body temperature to that most favorable for muscular activity, (2) improve muscle tonus, (3) shorten the length of the relaxation period, (4) remove the effects of possible early contraction, and (5) decrease the chances of injury.[4]

One need only give the general Physical Fitness Index test to a general squad of growing boys to determine that some of them lack strength in many vital muscles. Some of these weak areas may be found in the forearms, wrists, hands, pectoral region, shoulder girdle, pelvis, spine erectors, lumbar region, abdomen, legs, and feet. The shoulder girdle and pelvis regions, especially, require rugged support and stability, giving sturdy anchorage against powerful arm and leg action. The soles of the feet require strength for starts and push-offs in turns. These should be strengthened by special exercises.

Some boys have muscles that are overdeveloped and shortened which require stretching to give them efficient suppleness and amplitude of efficiency. A stretched muscle is more efficient and responsive than an unstretched muscle. That is one reason why one should warm up before taking part in violent exercise. Muscles shorten under constant use. If the crawler or the flying breast stroker hopes to recover the arms above the water easily, and not pull against tight stretched muscles retarding these movements, he must give some attention to keeping the muscles stretched throughout the entire season. The hamstrings also shorten easily, hindering efficient freedom of action of the legs. To have supple, flexible, and undulating ankles, muscles which control this joint and those over the tarsal and metatarsal bones must be stretched constantly.

There is no longer any question or doubt as to the beneficial results to swimmers through relaxing and stretching shortened and tightened muscles.

The diving squad most certainly should include stretching exercises in its daily program of training. Divers must present a symmetric and well-postured body. Divers must emphasize the following areas: shoulder joints, spine, hamstrings, ankles, and toes. All joints of the body must have freedom of movement. The trunk

[4]Morehouse, L. E., and Baumgartner, A.: Conditioning and Warm-Up Exercises, Scholastic Coach 10: 8 (April), 28, 1941.

should flex upon the thighs deeply and easily. The back should be as if made of rubber, yet it should have strength.

Breast strokers should stretch the crotch muscles so there is no tension in the spread of the legs during the kick phase.

Back strokers should develop an especially loose shoulder joint so that arms can drop or press to the water easily on the entry phase of the stroke without a roll of the body to accommodate tight shoulder-arm muscles.

Benefits are derived from building up weak areas of the body through special exercises. By building up the secondary groups (synergistic group) the primary (or power groups) derive a reciprocal innervation from each other. This aids in balanced teamwork of the muscles of the body as a whole in their functional performance. A rugged, seasoned body is gradually developed. It prepares a great number of unused muscle fibers ready for instant use when needed later in the fatigue part of a race, in the late season.

These special exercises should never be undertaken when the body is cold. Warming up to a slight perspiration should first take place by jogging or running in place.

Special Exercises for Swimmers and Divers

A few exercises for the purpose of limbering, stretching, and strengthening the major muscles used in swimming are outlined below.

Exercise I.—Start the work with light exercises such as jogging or running in place, increasing the cadence of the run. While running, emphasize ankle rock. The foot or ankle should be fully extended before the big toe leaves the floor—in other words, depressing the toes as the foot is lifted while running. In making contact with the floor, again the toe should touch first with the ankle fully extended.

In stationary running, emphasize extension of the ankle causing a flexion of plantar muscles and the spring ligament. This is good strengthening work for the feet in starting, push-offs, in turns and springboard work. At the same time it serves to warm up the body. As running continues, have the squad increase the height of raising the knee in an upward movement until the knee is on a line with the pelvis or the hips.

When perspiration is starting to come to the surface, ease down the running to a jog—a walk—and stop. The muscles are now prepared for stretching.

Exercise II.—Stretching of the pectorals (major and minor)

Caracobrachiolis

Long and short head of biceps

Deltoid (anterior portion)

Rectus abdominus

Lifting entire anterior thoracic chest region, stretching the intercostal muscles aiding respiration.

The lengthening and stretching of the above muscles are accomplished by swinging vigorously over the head diagonally in the direct line and angle of the pectoralis major muscle. Start this movement from a cross-arm position in front of the hips. On the up swing, the palms are turned in. Press the arms back as far as possible without forward movement at sternum and hips.

Exercise III.—Rotating trunk on longitudinal axis.

Position: Stride stand. Arms extended at sides, shoulder level; palms down. While doing exercise, keep feet fixed flat on floor.

Benefits: Stretches intercostals—spine rotators—abdominals—hip rotators—hip and knee flexors and extensors. The legs adductor groups.

Relax muscles and turn body briskly as far as possible so that there is a strong resistance met at the end of range of movement.

Exercise IV.—Stretching and lengthening the hamstring or leg flexor group in back of legs. Bending down quickly in an attempt to touch toes. On the first attempt do not go all the way down; but each succeeding dip, bend lower and lower until finger tips touch toes—then try to touch whole palm on floor. Diver should stand on elevated object from 6 to 10 inches above floor and should easily bend over and touch floor with knees straight. Recover quickly and pause for relaxation between each succeeding dip.

Benefits derived—relaxing the hip girdle and allowing a greater freedom of movement between legs and pelvis in the various kicks of the strokes.

Exercise V.—(a) Ankle Stretching.

By sitting on the floor, cross right leg over left. With the left hand, grasp toes with palm along sole of foot. With right hand, grasp leg above ankle to steady the foot. Left hand now manipulates foot in a rotation motion. Pull on finger tips over top of toes when foot is in extension position, so that foot is extended to its fullest position. Repeat with left foot.

Benefits: This stretches ligaments and their muscles so that ankle has flexible ankle action. A swimmer must continue this exercise until his ankles are as loose as those of a scarecrow.

(b) Sit on heels and extend foot out along on floor, "Indian fashion." Then turn toes under and again sit back on heels to relieve tension on muscles in plantar region of the foot. Repeat this alternating exercise several times after first doing (a) in Exercise V.

Exercise VI.—(a) The Crab. (For divers only.)

This exercise stretches the abdominals, the spinus ligaments to permit the spine to bend as freely as rubber. Try walking forward and backward.

(b) Hand stand against wall to arch back but stretching body to its greatest and fullest extent.

Benefits: The spine is made more supple, limber and streamlined.

Exercise VII.—Shoulder girdle loosening and stretching performed in pairs.

Subject sits on floor, legs together, knees straight, toes pointed, trunk vertical and straight. Operator stands behind sitting subject and places one knee between shoulder blades and grasps subject's arms below elbows and slowly elevates them fore-upward and pulls them slowly back and lets them move side outward and down again for relaxation. During the movement, firm resistance is offered with knee against back. This is repeated slowly several times.

In the last two or three times, cross arms slowly behind the head.

Exercise VIII.—Stretching spine in thoracic region—extreme stretching for pectorals.

The use of the stall-bars is necessary.

Subject grasps round high above head, back to wall. Operator steps between subject and bars facing bars. Stand on lower round, hands on rounds shoulder height.

Place shoulders against subject's shoulders. Slowly push subject out and up until feet lift off of floor.

Use caution on this exercise.

Exercise IX.—Crotch stretch.

Breast strokers who are crotch-bound should stretch the adductor groups. This can be done by doing leg spreading exercises.

Special Body Building Exercises for Swimmers

Exercise I.—Trunk lifting.

Especially to strengthen the abdominals.

Performed in pairs.

Subject lies on floor (on back), arms at sides of body.

Operator places his hands on subject's feet to give support.

Subject now slowly rises from floor about 12 inches, holds it momentarily, and recovers to floor to relax. Repeat four to six times.

If abdominals quiver, the muscles are weak.

Increase number of exercises and hold longer before lowering to the floor in third and fourth weeks.

Exercise II.—Twisting small of back and spine rotators.

Subject lies on the edge of the pool, face down, so that hip joint comes directly over the edge of the pool.

Helper places hands over heels of subject and supports him.

Subject now raises trunk slowly up into deep arch, then lowers body as far as possible. Repeat several times. Then circumduct trunk several times to left and then to right.

This exercise is especially good for the development of all the back extensors.

Crawl swimmers should have strong extensors along spine and especially in lumbar region. It affords stability between pelvis girdle and the shoulder girdle.

Exercise III.—Running stationary.

Already used for stretching warm-up. Strengthens ankle ligaments and plantar region of foot.

Exercise IV.—Hand stand balancing and walking.

All swimmers should develop strong wrists. This exercise can be done in several ways.

Novice should lean legs against a wall from a hand stand. (Use caution on hard floors in learning.)

Helper can steady legs of subject.

Stretch body, keep knees straight, toes pointed. Especially recommended for divers.

Walking on hands.

Rubber sponge gripping exercises.

With helper, do a wheelbarrow.

Take a rinsing shower and report for water work.

8. **Trip Away From Home.**—When a traveling trip is made, regardless of the mode of transportation, competitors should make every effort to get themselves there in good condition. Athletes must be good travelers. If traveling by auto, a stop should be made every seventy-five miles and all men should get out and shake the legs loose. Positions in the car should be changed when again ready to travel. At the end of the journey, limbering-up exercises should be undertaken as soon on arrival as possible. Sitting in auto seats, as well as train seats, tends to flatten and pinch the buttocks (gluteus maximus) muscle and the hamstring muscles. These muscles should be exercised, through special exercises, and by kicking in the water, until they again function normally. This may require several work-out periods in the water. Swimming easily in the water several times is no more fatiguing to well-trained swimmers than walking several blocks for exercise. The swimming workouts do bring around those car or train-fatigued muscles to normal condition.

9. **The Weight Chart.**—At the beginning of school the swimmer should weigh and record his weight. From the preliminary, through the entire competition season, accurate recordings on a weight chart should be made at least two or three times a week. If a gradual drop in weight is noted, the coach should be informed. This may be a danger signal of overwork or it may be a forerunner of staleness. The weight chart, therefore, serves as a guide for the coach in prescribing the amount of work for each individual swimmer. Some swimmers will gain steadily and thrive on the work, at least so far as weight fluctuations may indicate. Fluctuations do occur, which are only normal, and should not necessarily be a disturbing factor to swimmer or coach.

During the competition season, as various swimmers on the squad begin to reach the peak of condition, a careful check on the weight chart should be maintained. If an excessive loss of weight is indicated a careful checkup is made. It is possible that a condition of "staleness" is taking place. There are a number of contributing factors to staleness. It may be due to overwork, worry, sleeplessness, illness, excessive fatigue, or loss of appetite. The athlete may become irritable, quarrelsome, and his whole attitude toward the event is changed. Sometimes a few days' rest away from the pool, prescribing outdoor hikes, is an excellent antidote. In moderate cases, merely decreasing the load of work will be sufficient. His diet should be checked by having him bring in a 3-day, 3 meals a day, menu. This can be studied for a possible vitamin deficiency, and corrections and suggestions given by the coach or school dietitian.

10. **Ultraviolet Ray Treatment.**—Student swimmers should seek the out-of-door work or activities during summer vacations as much as possible, especially in those climatic areas where winter indoor swimming is necessary. However, this does not mean that one should overexpose to the sun's rays. The skin of the swimmer should be nicely browned and sufficient rays absorbed to serve as a carry-over through the long indoor winter season. He should attempt to maintain this healthy brown color throughout the year by means of the violet ray.

Ultraviolet ray treatment should be started late in the fall and be continued daily. It is best to take it before the bath or work-out in the daily routine schedule. The violet rays react upon the oil in the skin. If these oils are washed off the body in the shower or in the pool, the sun rays have no beneficial effect upon the sterols in the epithelial structures, which is a source of the vitamin D.

11. **Massage.**—In this discussion, massage will be referred to only as a means of bettering the performance. Massaging as an aid to the repair of injured tissue will not be considered. That should be left to the physician or trainer.

Massage consists of kneading, rubbing, and thumping various parts of the body. In swimming its principal use is to loosen tightened muscles. It also affects the skin area, the subcutaneous tissues, superficial nerve endings, superficial cutaneous blood vessels, and superficial lymphatic ducts.

There is a difference of opinion among coaches as to its benefits. Some coaches prefer it as an aid to the warm-up in water before the competition. Others believe that the only way to loosen tightened muscles is to swim easily and relaxed until the tight muscles feel loose to the swimmer. The swimmer can best feel when he is warmed-up and loosened properly for his race.

A rubbing massage is restful and relaxing and gives a swimmer a feeling of well-being. For this reason, many coaches use it as an aid for its soothing and quieting effects upon a swimmer between events.

An oil ingredient is usually used to prevent irritation and friction to the skin areas. Oil is also used in massaging a swimmer with the purpose of lessening body surface friction to water in competition. Some swimmers normally have a very dry skin. Swimmers lose this oil in the skin during the winter months and the skin becomes very dry and chapped. An oil massage two or three times a week is very beneficial to a swimmer with a dry skin.

12. **The Common Cold and Its Prevention.**—Any sinusitis or any throat infection should be reported for proper treatment to the physician at the very earliest possible moment. A swimmer is a more susceptible creature to the common colds than perhaps any other athlete. He takes his training in the nude and with a wet body. This condition subjects his body to constantly changing temperatures during the course of an afternoon's training period. He comes from outdoors, undresses in the locker room, goes to the swimming pool, exercises, takes a shower and then goes into the pool. He comes out of the water and goes in again; and finally comes out to dry off and dress for the street. Each of the afore-mentioned changes has varying changes in degree of temperatures against his body temperature. The swimmer should, therefore, avoid draughts, or sitting on cold tiled floors. After the work-out he should thoroughly dry his body, hair, and ears before going out into the cold air. He should dress for the street adequately to meet changing weather conditions. In the Northern states generally, an epidemic of colds is brought on by the arrival of a cold wave.

If a swimmer has his health and condition seriously at heart, he will report a cold with the very first symptom of a sniffling nose. A cold then can usually be checked or cured. If it is permitted to go on without proper treatment for several days, little can be done for it except to let it run its course.

A common cold among squad members is a dreaded "nightmare" with a swimming coach throughout the season.

Many serious complications can arise, and proper care and treatment are a very serious problem. If it develops into influenza, it is very doubtful if that swimmer will again reach his peak of performance in less than six weeks, if at all for the entire season.

Young men who contract a common cold so often treat it altogether too lightly at the beginning which may give serious complications and later prove to be very disheartening to a boy who had been antici-pating keen competition for that season.

If proper preventive measures are adhered to throughout the sea-son, colds can be held to a minimum. Some of these are: (1) Per-sonal health habits of proper sleep, rest, and diet. (2) Dressing adequately for any weather condition, such as, dressing warm, keep-ing feet dry, wearing hat and keeping shirt collar buttoned. (3) wiping and rubbing one's self thoroughly dry, including the ears. If these simple rules of health are religiously adhered to, the common cold and its complications can be eliminated and vitamin concentrates would not be necessary for swimmers.

CHAPTER X

TRAINING

An athlete may have followed all the rules of diet, rest, and exercise and give evidence of being in top physical condition by being able to play a full game of football without undue fatigue. Yet, when he attempts to swim any distance, he tires within a few minutes.

The reason for this lies not in the factor of condition, but rather in that of training. The muscles of the football player and those of a swimmer may be equally strong, their blood equally capable of carrying away wastes, and their lungs equally adept in supplying oxygen and carrying away the carbon dioxide.

Still, athletes in such nearly identical states of physical condition will experience an earlier onset of fatigue in sports in which they are untrained and a prolonged onset of fatigue in sports in which they are trained.

Fatigue is due to the two factors: (1) accumulation of waste products of metabolism (fatigue toxins); and (2) depletion of energy-yielding foods. The onset of fatigue during exercise depends upon the rate and intensity of the work, and the frequency and duration of rest periods during the work.

The athlete trained for a certain sport prolongs the onset of fatigue by maintaining a certain degree of relaxation during participation. However, when he performs in another sport for which he has not trained, he endeavors to compensate for his lack of skill by tightening up in an effort to play harder. He thus reduces his rest periods to such a small extent that fatigue toxins accumulate faster than they can be removed, and food supplies are exhausted.

A common characteristic among champions is the extraordinary amount of relaxation which they maintain, even under stress of competition. The "natural" or "all-around" athlete possesses the same quality. He is able, through a proper balance of relaxation during work, to establish a steady state of activity in which the recovery mechanisms are able to maintain a muscular environment which is relatively free from toxins and is rich in food.

The athlete trained for swimming, executes his movements in a most economical manner. He has reached a high degree of neuro-muscular coordination. His working muscles can contract powerfully while the muscles which oppose them are nearly completely relaxed.

The nervous system is constructed in such a manner that when a muscle is stimulated to contract, the tonic stimulus to the antagonistic muscle is diminished and it relaxes. This phenomenon is known as "reciprocal innervation of antagonistic muscles."

During swimming, the movements are so executed that the muscles work alternately. The muscles which contract during a flexion thus become the antagonistic muscles during extension. Likewise, the extensors are the working muscles during extension and become the antagonistic muscles during flexion.

If the swimmer remains tense during performance and does not allow his antagonistic muscles to relax while his working muscles are contracting, he deprives his muscles of the rest periods they need for recovery and thus hastens the onset of fatigue. This is the paramount functional principle underlying efficient relaxation. This is why a swimmer must swim miles of distances to acquire it. Relaxation and proper muscular tonus are a natural result.

With a moderate amount of training, however, the football player will become adjusted to the water and will learn to swim for some distance with a minimum of accumulated fatigue. Likewise, the swimmer, through training, will learn to apply his energy more economically during a football scrimmage.

Training thus furnishes two refinements to performance. First, the movements become so timed that rest periods are allowed and, second, normal reciprocal innervation of antagonistic muscles is facilitated.[1]

The Training Season.—The training season which usually consumes eight months of a year is designed to improve the swimmer's level of skill in starting, in stroke mechanics, in the turns, in finishing, and to educate him as to pace and race efficiency. All of these factors are combined in one aim, namely, *to win swimming races.* Each item in training should contribute to this aim.

---

[1]Morehouse, Laurence E.: Physiology of Athletics (Training), Scholastic Coach **10:** 8 (April), 4, 1941.

In general, the season can be divided into four phases:

1. The precompetition period (2 months).
2. The dual-meet period (3 months).
3. The championship period (1 month).
4. The postcompetition period (2 months).

1. **Precompetition Period.**—This period starts at the first practice session and continues until about two weeks before the first scheduled meet. In most schools, the coach calls his squad together for the first formal meeting about the first of October. At this meeting certain phases of training and conditioning are discussed and the plans for the season are outlined. Although the squad is naturally divided into experienced and inexperienced athletes, the whole squad should be unified and spirit and morale should be fortified as this factor helps to win many races.

Most squads practice in the latter part of the afternoon after academic appointments are completed so that the swimmer can devote his entire concentration to his sport. The swimmer should try to leave his worries in his locker and enter the pool with a buoyant spirit and ready to enjoy himself in healthy recreation and pleasurable exertion. He meets his teammates in common bondage and feels that he belongs to a group which is interested in him and is seeking his interest in them.

The squad member should prepare to devote at least a full hour and a half to his daily practice so that he does not have to try to rush through his work and thereby eliminate the rest periods between the workout events. The swimmers should practice in the water every day and perform the strengthening and flexibility exercises along with the regular daily schedule of practice.

In places where the pool is small and the squad is large, the inexperienced swimmers should be assigned a separate practice time from the experienced men.

Even at this early stage of training, the coach should consider each man as an individual. He should discuss the separate problems of each man each day.

In general, the swimming workout for all men, including sprinters, during this period consists of distance swimming during which the coach attempts to iron out the faulty swimming mechanics and difficulties of breathing, body position, relaxation, timing, and balance. The effectiveness of this training is checked by noting the ease which the swimmers acquire and the increased distance they can achieve and sustain good form of stroke without undue fatigue. During this season the coach should accomplish the spade work for the entire season.

A general practice program around which the exercises and swimming workouts are planned for the entire season may be as follows:

Minutes	
5	Read notices and confer with coach.
3	Ultraviolet ray treatment.
5	Warm up exercises.
15	Limbering, stretching, and strengthening exercises.
5	Shower—two minutes tepid, and ½ minute cold.
10	Loosening swim.
5	Rest.
40	Water workout.
5	Shower—soap bath in tepid water.
93	Total

During the precompetition period a method which employs all strokes is used for all swimmers. Through practice of the crawl, back, and breast strokes the swimmer not only discovers which stroke is best suited to him, but his legs, arms, and body also acquire certain adjustments to the water which later aid and condition him in swimming any one stroke with greater ease and efficiency.

During the first three weeks the inexperienced group has a separate practice plan from that of the experienced group. From the fourth to the eighth week they follow the same plan.

During the first three weeks the emphasis is on bringing the distance swimming ability of the inexperienced swimmers up near the level of that of the experienced swimmers.

The fourth to sixth week both groups are working toward ease of swimming and elongation of distance. The sixth week, race efficiency is stressed.

Major corrections of stroke technique should be made in the early seasons rather than in the competition season. When making corrections, the coach should remain with the swimmer until the desired movement is accomplished. The swimmer should then attempt to duplicate, time and time again, the desired movement pattern until it is thoroughly mastered.

A. *Practice Schedules First Three Weeks of Precompetition Period.—*

(a) Inexperienced swimmers.

FIRST WEEK

Monday

    1. 6 lengths medley $\begin{cases} 2 \text{ crawl} \\ 2 \text{ breast} \\ 2 \text{ back crawl} \end{cases}$

    2. Rest 3 to 5 minutes

    3. Repeat Number 1

Tuesday

    1. Swim 6 lengths medley as above only treble the work with 8 to 10 minutes' rest between the last two.

Wednesday

    1. Repeat second day's work.

Thursday

    1. Swim 9 lengths $\begin{cases} 3 \text{ crawl} \\ 3 \text{ breast} \\ 3 \text{ back} \end{cases}$

    2. Rest 5 to 7 minutes.

    3. Repeat Number 1

Friday

    1. Repeat fourth day.

Saturday

    1. Swim 9 lengths medley $\begin{cases} 3 \text{ crawl} \\ 3 \text{ breast} \\ 3 \text{ back} \end{cases}$

    2. Rest 7 to 10 minutes.

    3. Repeat Number 1

    4. Rest 10 to 12 minutes

    5. Repeat Number 1

SECOND WEEK

Monday

    1. Repeat treble load of work of sixth day

Tuesday

    1. 12 lengths medley $\begin{cases} 4 \text{ crawl} \\ 4 \text{ breast} \\ 4 \text{ back} \end{cases}$

    2. Rest 5 to 7 minutes

    3. Repeat Number 1

Wednesday
1.   Repeat second day's work

Thursday
1.   Repeat second day's work

Friday
1.   Swim 12 lengths medley $\begin{cases} 4 \text{ crawl} \\ 4 \text{ breast} \\ 4 \text{ back} \end{cases}$
2.   Rest 5 to 7 minutes
3.   Repeat Number 1
4.   Kick 100 yards own style
5.   Rest 5 minutes
6.   Repeat Number 1

Saturday
1.   Swim 10 lengths—crawl
2.   Rest 5 minutes
3.   Swim 10 lengths—breast
4.   Rest 5 minutes
5.   Swim 10 lengths—back crawl

THIRD WEEK

Monday
1.   Swim medley $\begin{cases} 100 \text{ yd. crawl} \\ 100 \text{ yd. breast} \\ 100 \text{ yd. back} \end{cases}$
2.   Rest 3 to 5 minutes
3.   Kick own style 100 yards
4.   Rest 1 minute
5.   Swim Number 1

Tuesday
1.   Swim own style 200 yards
2.   Rest 3 minutes
3.   Swim medley 300 yards
4.   Rest 7 to 10 minutes
5.   Kick 100 yards own style
6.   Swim own style 200 yards

Wednesday
1.   Swim own style 200 yards
2.   Rest 2 minutes
3.   Kick 100 yards

4. Rest 1 minute
5. Swim 300 yards medley
6. Rest 5 to 8 minutes
7. Swim arms—drag legs, 100 yards
8. Swim 200 yards

Thursday

1. Swim continuously 500 yd. own style
2. Rest 7 to 10 minutes
3. Kick 200 yards (loosen leg muscles)
4. Practice turns
5. Swim 300 yards medley

Friday

1. Swim 200 yards
2. Kick 100 yards
3. Swim 200 yards
4. Kick 100 yards
5. Swim arms only 100 yards
6. Swim 200 yards (No rest between)

Saturday

1. Swim ½ mile continuously
2. Instruction on starting
3. Practice starts and turns
4. Fundamental skills in polo

(b) Experienced swimmers.

FIRST WEEK

Monday

1. Swim 300 yards medley $\begin{cases} 100 \text{ crawl} \\ 100 \text{ breast} \\ 100 \text{ back} \end{cases}$
2. Rest 5 to 7 minutes
3. Swim 300 yards medley

Tuesday

1. Swim 300 yards medley $\begin{cases} 100 \text{ crawl} \\ 100 \text{ breast} \\ 100 \text{ back} \end{cases}$
2. Rest 5 minutes
3. Kick 200 yards own style
4. Repeat Number 1

Wednesday
1. Repeat second day

Thursday
1. Repeat Number 1 Tuesday
2. Rest 3 minutes
3. Kick 300 yards own style
4. Swim 300 yards medley

Friday
1. Swim 300 yards own style
2. Kick 300 yards own style
3. Swim 300 yards own style

Saturday
1. Swim 300 yards medley
2. Rest 3 minutes
3. Swim 500 yards own style

SECOND WEEK

Monday
1. Swim 300 yards medley
2. Rest 3 minutes
3. Kick 300 yards own style
4. Swim 100 yards arms only own style
5. Swim 300 yards own style

Tuesday
1. Swim 400 yards own style
2. Rest 3 minutes
3. Kick 200 yards own style
4. Swim arms only 100 yards
5. Swim 400 yards own style

Wednesday
1. Swim 300 yards medley
2. Kick 200 yards own style
3. Swim 200 yards arms only
4. Practice turns
5. Swim 300 yards own style

Thursday
1. Repeat Wednesday's work

Friday
1. Repeat Wednesday's work

Saturday
1. Swim 400 yards own style
2. Rest 3 minutes
3. Kick 300 yards own style
4. Swim arms 200 yards own style
5. Swim 400 yards own style

THIRD WEEK

Monday
1. Swim 500 yards own style
2. Kick 300 yards own style
3. Swim 300 yards arms only
4. Swim 500 yards own style

Tuesday
1. Repeat Monday's work

Wednesday
1. Swim 300 yards medley
2. Kick 300 yards
3. Arms only 300 yards
4. Swim 300 yards own style

Thursday
1. Repeat Wednesday's work

Friday
1. Repeat Monday's work

Saturday
1. Swim 600 yards
2. Kick 400 yards
3. Arms 200 yards
4. Practice turns
5. Practice polo
6. Swim 300 yards

B. *Fourth Through Sixth Week of Precompetition Period (Both Groups).*—The daily plan of work for these two weeks is designed to mark time until the inexperienced group reaches the distance level of the experienced group. The load of work should consist of slow speed swimming, ranging between 880 and 1,000 yards. Speed should be slow enough so that swimmers do not break the good stroking mechanics and accurate timing of the movements.

The daily program can be varied in any number of distances, just so total yardage for the day is beyond the range of a half mile. Individual swimmers differ as to capacity to absorb this type of work and some can easily swim from 1,000 yards to a mile and a half.

The style of stroke can also be varied. The kicking and arm pulling should be increased for strengthening legs and arms in the water. The check-rope method can also be used to good advantage. There are many variations that can be used to keep the daily program interesting.

If the load of work has been exceptionally hard for some individuals on a certain day, the work for the following two days should be modified. Distance need not be shortened if speed is lessened. Sometimes the speed need not be modified, but the arrangement of the sequence of work can be altered, or slightly more rest can be given between each item of work on that day's program.

On at least one, or possibly two days, permit the swimmers to go through to the half mile without rest, either with one style of stroke or with all three with the kicking and arm pulling alternated between the swimming strokes.

At this stage of early season swimming an objective should be that of appreciation of distribution of effort over a distance. This is essential for learning pace later in the seventh and eighth weeks.

At the end of the precompetition period the swimmer should have acquired better breathing habits through relaxation, water strength should have been gained, hands and feet should be more sensitive and effective, and the entire body should be better adjusted to the water.

The squad is now ready for pacing patterns to be drilled daily. They have an appreciation of distance, but not as to time over a given distance. Up to this point little timing with the watch has been given. However, some authorities believe in timing the swimming at once during distance work, so that time as well as distance may be judged more accurately at an early period in the training.

The inexperienced swimmer should be encouraged constantly to extend and improve in his distance swimming, and to sustain a steady stroke cadence. This type of swimming tends to relax him and facilitate breathing habits.

C. *Seventh Week of Precompetition Periods.*—In swimming a distance at which a maximum speed cannot be maintained, the swimmer must attempt to distribute his effort in such a manner that he can cover the distance in his shortest possible time. When this proper energy distribution is accomplished, we may say that he has reached the highest degree of race efficiency.

The untrained swimmer invariably becomes excited during competition and swims the first portion of his race faster than he should. As a result, he tires quickly and is forced to reduce his velocity to such an extent that his swimming time for the event is very poor. Following proper and sufficiently long training, he develops a great ability to estimate his speed and his reserve strength and his efficiency is improved.

At the beginning of competition, a swimmer should work and build himself gradually into his first few races. In this way he can study the event and learn more of its strategy. The swimmer should be trained to be alert from the beginning to the end of his race. He should know all the rules pertaining to his event.

D. *Effects of Training.*—Training also produces a greater immunity to the exciting effect of competition[2] which causes the swimmer to swim the first part of his race faster than he should. The longer the race, the more attention the swimmer must give to the distribution of his energy. An observation of the summary of the finals of the Seventeenth Annual National Collegiate Swimming Championship[3] reveals that the variations in speed are less as the distances become longer. In other words, as the length of the race increases, there is a tendency for trained swimmers to cover the entire distance at a more even rate.

The strong desire for the inexperienced swimmer to take the lead at the start may be due to a transfer of training of track racing fundamentals. In the track races which are usually run without lanes around a curve, it is an advantage for a runner to obtain the lead and pole position by sprinting at the beginning of the race. He can then appreciably reduce the pace and force his opponents either to do likewise or run around him. This track race strategy does not apply to swimming as swimming races are always swum in lanes and the man in the lead does not block those behind him.

---

[2]Karpovich, Peter V.: Physiological and Psychological Dynamogenic Factors in Exercise, Arbeitsphysiologie 9: 6, 626-629, August, 1937.

[3]*National Collegiate Athletic Association Official Rules for Swimming, Fancy Diving and Water Polo.* American Sports Publishing Co., New York, 1941, pages 96-97.

Swimming a certain distance at a given time at a steady rate requires a little less work than swimming the same distance in the same time at an uneven rate according to Karpovich.[4] The work done in swimming may be expressed as Work = Force × Distance. It was found that the approximate force developed in swimming the crawl stroke may be calculated by the formula: Force = $0.65V^2$. Thus, Work = $0.65V^2$ × Distance, or $W = \dfrac{0.65d\ (d)^2}{t^2}$, where d = distance reckoned in feet traveled in a given t = time reckoned in seconds. To show the effect of a very slight variation in speed upon the work done in swimming 220 yards in 2:13.0, a comparison of two plans of distribution of effort is shown in Table VI.

TABLE VI

	DISTANCE (FEET)	TIME FOR EACH 150 FT. (SECONDS)	WORK DONE (FT. POUNDS)
Race Plan A (steady rate)			
	150	27.6	2,878.5
	150	31.0	2,281.7
	150	31.0	2,281.7
	150	31.0	2,281.7
	60	12.4	913.9
Totals	660	133.0	10,637.5
Race Plan B (unsteady rate)			
	150	26.5	3,169.0
	150	30.5	2,361.4
	150	31.7	2,183.1
	150	32.1	2,129.0
	60	12.2	943.3
Totals	660	133.0	10,885.8

The first 50 yards are covered in a shorter time in both plans because of a time advantage of about 3.4 seconds due to the start. The figure representing the time advantage due to the start. was calculated by comparing the time for the first 50 yards with that of the second 50 yards in the summary of the finals of the 100 yard freestyle race in the 1940 National Collegiate Swimming Championships. If it may be assumed that the entire 100 yards were swum at a maximum rate, then the shorter time required to swim the first 50

[4]Karpovich, Peter V.: Analysis of the Propelling Force in the Crawl Stroke, Supplement to the Research Quarterly 6: 2, 49-58, May, 1935.

yards may be attributed to the advantage gained at the start. The advantage ranged from 2.8 seconds to 4.0 seconds and averaged 3.4 seconds.

In Plan A, the swimmer assumed a steady rate of 50 yards in 31 seconds and maintained that rate throughout the race. The last 20 yards, swum in 12.4 seconds, are swum at the same rate as that in the preceding laps.

In Plan B, the swimmer sprinted for the first 100 yards, then reduced his velocity for the next 100 yards, and sprinted the last 20 yards to the finish.

The difference in the work required to swim Plan A (steady rate) and Plan B (unsteady rate) is 248.3 foot pounds. By utilizing the extra work done in swimming Plan B more efficiently, the swimmer could have considerably reduced his time for the 220 yard race.

In order to improve the untrained swimmer's ability to estimate his speed and reserve strength, a system of training in race efficiency was devised. This system involves the use of a pacing machine.

As the University of Iowa swimming pool is 150 by 60 feet, and practice and competition are held over the long (50 yard) course, the pacing machine is set so that the marker travels along the length of the pool. The marker is a small black flag attached to a continuous cord 288 feet in length. The cord is stretched over two 3-inch pulleys, one at each end of the pool. The pulleys are held in place by steel rods which are fastened to the ends of the pool and are of such a length that the pulleys are three feet from each end of the pool. This extension allows for the gain in velocity which the swimmer achieves at each turn. One pulley is operated by an electric motor and a device by which the speed of the driving wheel may be adjusted so that the marker can travel 144 feet at any desired interval, from 20 to 60 seconds' duration. The motor is $\frac{1}{4}$ horsepower and runs on a 110 volt, 60 cycle, 5 ampere, alternating current. The motor develops 1,750 revolutions per minute. The speed adjustment mechanism is a 12-inch cast aluminum disk which is held against the motor's driving wheel by a coiled spring. The motor's driving wheel is covered by a rubber tire and measures 2 inches in diameter. The motor is set on an adjustable platform which can be moved 6 inches backward or forward by means of a crank attached to a threaded rod screwed into two grooved pieces of metal, one attached to the motor's platform and the other to the fixed base. The velocity of the marker can thus be increased by moving the motor closer to the center of the aluminum disk and also can be slowed by moving the motor toward the outer edge of the disk.

During the early season of training the pacer is set so that the swimmer will swim one length in 50 seconds. (See Table VII.) Emphasis is made on swimming form, and condition is developed by long-distance swims (800 to 1,000 yards) at this rate.

As the swimmer improves his form the speed is increased gradually from day to day until it is noticed that he has difficulty in maintaining that rate for 500 yards. This difficulty usually occurs when the speed is lowered to 42 seconds for 50 yards, or 7 minutes for 500 yards. The pacer is then left at this rate until the swimmer improves his ability to swim 500 yards at this rate. Faults are being corrected and good form is still being stressed at this period.

After continued swimming with the pacer, the swimmer learns to judge his rate and needs to glance at the marker only once each 50 yards in order to check his velocity. A further check is made at this period by having him swim 500 yards without using the pacer and estimating his ability to swim 500 yards in 7 minutes.

When the swimmer is able to gauge his speed so that he is able to swim 500 yards in 7 minutes with an error of no greater than 10 seconds, then the speed of the pacer is again gradually increased and the fastest rate at which the swimmer can swim 440 yards is determined. In a like manner, each swimmer's best time for the 500 yards, 440 yards, 220 yards, 100 yards, and 50 yards freestyle, as well as the 200 yards and 100 yards breast stroke; and the 150 yards and 100 yards backstroke is determined. The coach can now advise each swimmer as to his best events and the swimmer can concentrate his efforts on these events.

The pacing machine is employed throughout the early season and the midseason to establish paces at lower levels than were first recorded during the preseason period. In many cases, swimmers achieve their fastest times while "racing" with the pacer.

E. *Eighth Week of Precompetition Period.*—By this time the swimmer has learned some concept of pace and can estimate to some degree his speed in the water. By increasing his swimming speed and maintaining a steady pace over shorter distances, he has some idea of the manner in which to cover a distance in the shortest possible time.

The rate at which champions swim successive laps of a middle distance or distance event, slows as each lap is undertaken. This gradual slowing is due, not to forgetfulness of pace, but to the accumulating effects of fatigue which tend to make the swimming strokes less effective as the distance is prolonged. This factor must be taken into account when planning a race.

The eighth week of the precompetition is devoted wholly to schooling in swimming the first 100 yards of a middle distance or distance

TABLE VII

THIS TABLE SHOWS THE TIME PER 50 YARDS WHICH IS NECESSARY TO SWIM A DISTANCE IN THE TOTAL TIME INDICATED

TIME PER 50 YARDS (SEC.)	100 YARDS TOTAL TIME	150 YARDS TOTAL TIME	200 YARDS TOTAL TIME	220 YARDS TOTAL TIME	440 YARDS TOTAL TIME	500 YARDS TOTAL TIME
50	1:40	2:30	3:20	3:40	7:20	8:20
49	1:38	2:27	3:16	3:36	7:11	8:10
48	1:36	2:24	3:12	3:31	7:02	8:00
47	1:34	2:21	3:08	3:27	6:54	7:50
46	1:32	2:18	3:04	3:22	6:45	7:40
45	1:30	2:15	3:00	3:18	6:36	7:30
44	1:28	2:12	2:56	3:14	6:27	7:20
43	1:26	2:09	2:52	3:09	6:18	7:10
42	1:24	2:06	2:48	3:05	6:09	7:00
41	1:22	2:03	2:44	3:00	6:01	6:50
40	1:20	2:00	2:40	2:56	5:52	6:40
39	1:18	1:57	2:36	2:51	5:43	6:30
38	1:16	1:54	2:32	2:47	5:34	6:20
37	1:14	1:51	2:28	2:42	5:26	6:10
36	1:12	1:48	2:24	2:38	5:17	6:00
35	1:10	1:45	2:20	2:34	5:08	5:50
34	1:08	1:42	2:16	2:29	4:59	5:40
33	1:06	1:39	2:12	2:25	4:51	5:30
32	1:04	1:36	2:08	2:21	4:42	5:20
31	1:02	1:33	2:04	2:15	4:33	5:10
30	:60	1:30	2:00	2:12	4:24	5:00
29	:58	1:27	1:56	2:07	4:15	4:50
28	:56	1:24	1:52	2:03	4:07	4:40
27	:54	1:21	1:48	1:59	3:58	4:30
26	:52	1:18	1:44	1:55	3:49	4:20
25	:50	1:15	1:40	1:52	3:40	4:10

race in either the crawl, back crawl or breast stroke in a certain set time. For example, a swimmer who can repeatedly swim the 100 yards in less than 1:05 seconds is asked to swim 100 yards in 1:10

seconds. At his first trial he will usually be surprised that he has swum the 100 yards in about 1:06 or 1:07 seconds. He is then told to swim the same distance in 1:12 seconds. This time he comes closer. The third trial at which he tries again for 1:10 seconds is usually within a second of that mark. He practices this distance at this time until he can remain within a 0.5 second error consistently. He is then asked to hit this 1:10 mark on the way to a 220 yards distance. After he has accomplished this, the time for 100 yards is lowered to 1:07 seconds and the swimmer repeats the procedure described above.

In all events over the 100 yards distance, the way the swimmer swims the first 100 yards is of great importance. The nature of the race after this point depends largely upon the energy he has expended during the first 100 yards. If he has allowed the excitement of the race to cause him to increase his swimming time for the first 100 yards beyond that which is a safe limit in his distribution of effort, only a partial amount of his finishing energy remains and he is hopelessly left floundering during the challenging moments of a race.

2. The Dual-Meet Period.

A. *The First Three Weeks.*—This phase of training introduces the factor of speed to the swimming workout. Until this period, the swimmers have been covering long distances in order to refine stroke mechanics, establish a perception of pace, and increase swimming efficiency.

The coach introduces the starting gun and increases the use of the stop watch for checking swimming time. Now, instead of individual work, the squad is drilled in groups.

At each practice, after limbering exercises and swims, the technique of starting is taught and a series of practice starts is given. After each start, the swimmers should continue across the pool, make a fast turn and push-off, and return to the starting edge. The time of the first width is noted and each swimmer is encouraged to lower the time.

The turns are made as fast as possible and after the first three days of this drill, the time for the two widths is noted. The importance of constant drill in the technique of making rapid and powerful starts and turns cannot be overemphasized.

Relay starting technique can be started at this time by practicing the touch-offs. All swimmers can participate in this practice in preparation for the medley and freestyle relay events.

Drills in pacing are continued throughout this week and each swimmer begins to concentrate upon the event in which he shows the most promise in relation to the rest of the squad. The squad is notified that time trials will be made on Saturday.

A careful record, complete with the split times of each man in each event, should be made during the time trials on Saturday. These are studied by the coach and each swimmer is advised as to his achievement and as to ways of improving his times.

B. *The Week Before the Week of the First Dual Meet.*—Drills in starts, relay take-offs, turns, and pacing are continued and frequent attempts to lower the swimming time for two and then three widths are made.

Either a freshman-varsity or an intersquad meet is scheduled for the Saturday of this week. Each succeeding day of practice an increasing effort is made to simulate actual meet conditions. On Saturday, officials are present and the meet schedule and organization is exactly like that of a regular dual meet. Spectators are invited and each event and its results are announced. By a careful observation of the behavior of each competitor the coach will gain a fairly accurate estimate of the racing ability of each squad member during competitive conditions.

The divers perform the dives they intend to use during the first dual meet. The dives are scored as in regular competition, and the coach makes notes on each dive and discusses the weakness of each diver after the meet.

The swimming time and the split times of each competitor are recorded for comparison with the previous performance.

C. *The Week of the First Dual Meet.*—On Monday the data and notes collected from each individual during last Saturday's competition are discussed with each member of the squad. Comparisons are drawn with the results recorded during the first time trials. Improvement or decline in performance is noted.

From these records the coach sets up a reasonable time which the swimmer should attain in his event for the dual meet this weekend. The remainder of the week is devoted to achieving consistency in attaining the set time.

D. *Fourth Through Twelfth Week of Dual-Meet Competition Period.*—During the intersquad or freshman-varsity and the early home meets, each swimmer on the team has competed in only one event and possibly the medley or the freestyle relay. At the meet before the first tough competition, the coach will select his best men and enter them in two events as well as the relay. This will increase the competitive ability of the members of the first team and get them in readiness for stiff competition. Proper methods of warm-up and recuperation are essential to insure that each man will be able to swim the three races at his near-maximum of ability.

Additional training of the members of the first team will be necessary as they must learn a race plan for each of three events so that in case they are used in all three, they will be able to do the best they possibly can.

If the swimmers have been well schooled in pace, this task will not be difficult. The procedure will be to decrease the time for the 100 yards distance so that the fastest time for the total distance can be achieved. This plan is devised for the back crawlers and the breast strokers as well as the middle distance swimmers.

The sprint swimmers should continually work on stroke techniques. They should also attempt to increase their speed by continuous work at a fast rate on the flutter board and by rapid flutter movements of the legs out of water. Remember, the well-timed whole crawl stroke can be no faster than the speed of the legs.

The breast strokers should study and practice their event so as to distribute their efforts best as to the number of strokes to be taken under water at the start and for each turn as the race progresses. They should also study and practice the number of pool lengths they should fly the stroke and how many to orthodox. Breast strokers must practice this constantly as the season progresses in order to improve skill of performance as well as effort distribution.

3. Championship Period.

E. *Two Weeks Before the League Championship Meet.*—During this period finer adjustments are made in technique and the swimmer's condition is watched closely. Special attention is given to the diet, rest, exercise, and hygienic habits of the swimmers. All swimmers who are eligible to compete in the championships should be nearing the peaks of their condition and performance.

In order to approximate the work which will have to be done at the championships if the swimmer is fortunate enough to proceed to the finals, time trials of the swimmer's events are repeated the number of times that are scheduled in the championships. This trial is given about 10 days before the championships so that the swimmer is given ample time to improve his condition after he recognizes what may be demanded of him.

The sprinters should swim three fast 100 yards with 20 minutes between each trial. The middle distance swimmers should swim two 220 yards with 30 minutes of rest between. The distance swimmers and back and breast strokers should also attempt this schedule with a 45-minute rest between trials.

Through weeks of continued training, throughout the entire season, relaxation is increased; efficiency, pace, and timing have also improved. The swimmer should experience sensations of power, speed, and relative freedom from fatigue. In other words, he has the sensation of power throbbing "under the hood." Breathing becomes effortless. All of the above swimming fundamentals coincide and the result is water-efficiency.

When the swimmer arrives at this stage of his training he is now in readiness for specialized training for his race. Starts become a daily event in his training for the purpose of improving faster reaction time. Timing and speed of performance of turns are emphasized. In the midseason of training, swimmers should not be permitted to make turns slowly. The turn rhythm should be independent from the stroke rhythm.

Postcompetition Period.—The first week of this period should be devoted to loosening up. All swimmers should swim every day.

At the end of the first week after the last meet, a time trial should be given to each man in his best event. It is frequently observed that the swimmer will turn in his best time of the entire season at this trial. Here is a good opportunity for the coach to demonstrate the effect of worry and overstrain of competition. The coach is beginning to do the spade work for the following season.

The remainder of the two months is usually devoted to life-saving, water safety, and water sports, such as water polo. Much of this time can also be given over to experimentation, and photographic and other forms of study of swimming technique. The swimmer should now ease down his training gradually, just as he gradually trained up.

CHAPTER XI

COMPETITIVE SPRINGBOARD DIVING

Introduction.—Diving was developed in Europe as an outgrowth of outdoor aerial acrobatics and tumbling. It became a competitive sport in England in 1905. Fundamentally diving consists of leaping from either a firm take-off or a spring take-off and alighting into the water, descending under the surface smoothly, either head or feet first.

Advanced and competitive springboard diving consists of performing intricate combinations of body movements in mid-air, between the take-off and the water, followed by an esthetic entry into the water. It is really a form of aerial acrobatics. The take-off is a very flexible springboard. The water serves merely to ease the shock of alighting, just as a net catches the trapeze acrobat. Needless to say, springboard diving is as spectacular as it is intricately difficult and is related more closely to acrobatics than to swimming. It offers a thrill and esthetic satisfaction to the performer as well as a pleasant experience.

Diving consists of projecting the human body high into the air and there performing a series of breathless, swift and gracefully controlled maneuvers, such as bending, twisting, somersaulting, moving one part of the body while anchoring in place another part. Then the body is suddenly righted and poised for a clean entry into the water. Springboard diving attracts and challenges the most courageous and stout-hearted youth. It provides an opportunity for youth to develop and cultivate a supple and graceful body, through skilled esthetic movements.

Some dives, when performed efficiently, cause the diver to move with the rhythm and tempo of "poetry in motion," especially such dives as the layout floating dives. Other dives such as twisters, rotators, and cut rotator dives, move and disappear as swift as lightning. Any dive, whether a layout, tuck, or twist, or whether slow or rapid in motion, must always have force, yet have the appearance of being performed with ease, comfort, and simplicity. When power and ease of performance are achieved, the dive is well balanced. When expertly timed and controlled the springboard dive is a thrilling acrobatic feat. It leads to confidence and poise in body control.

For an ambitious beginner who has hopes and aspirations of becoming a top-flight diver, it is absolutely necessary that he first master the elementary, basic, and fundamental jump dives before attempting the more intricate dives. Then, advancement will be easier and the advanced dives will be more easily mastered. Many inexperienced divers are satisfied as soon as they are able merely to perform a dive. One should not stop here, but make every effort to "dress-up" the dive by improved timing of the mechanics, even to the smallest detail, in order to give the dive personality.

If the movements, such as the lift from the board, are not well timed, the dive will appear unbalanced throughout its entire flight, as well as having the appearance of requiring great effort. Any dive, no matter how intricate, if well timed from the take-off to the entry, will have the appearance of being performed effortlessly.

Physical Qualifications.—The ideal diver usually possesses a body of slight and slender build. He is medium in height (5 feet 4 inches to 5 feet 9 inches) and weighs from 120 to 160 pounds. Slender hips, legs, and ankles are desirable qualities for competition diving.

A diver must possess an awareness of muscular movement or a kinesthetic sense of muscular control. In the performance of intricate dives he must be able to make one group of muscles perform one movement while another group must perform independent of the other group or groups. If a diver is aiming at the top, he must possess perseverance, courage, and patience. He must be willing to spend several seasons developing fundamental skills in the elementary dives to go far in competition.

Equipment.—Divers should be equipped with snugly fitting supporters. They should have two sets of suits or trunks; one for practice and another for competition. Sometimes a full suit which will cover physical bulges or excess curves is better adapted to the individual, thus giving the diver a more pleasing appearance. The diver must be neatly suited with a snug-fitted suit or trunk. The suit, however, should not be binding. The suit should be wool, not silk. Trunks should be some type of lastex to conform with the contour of the hips, when hips are either straight or tucked. See N. C. A. A. Rules for Regulation Spring Board Equipment. (Springboards, construction, care and maintenance of diving equipment, see The American Red Cross Swimming and Diving, pp. 250.)

Supplementary Exercises:

1. *Warming-up Exercises.*—To attain a pleasing physique on the springboard, one must be constantly striving to attain it, and when once achieved, to maintain it. Besides having a pleasing posture, the body must be supple. This can be attained through suitable stretching and bending exercises. A diver should try to achieve, as some coaches say, a "rubber back." Then, too, one should develop a certain amount of strength and power. If vital parts of the body appear weak, building-up exercises should be taken daily which are designed for their development.

Daily workouts should be started with warming-up exercises, such as stationary running. The exercise should be designed for three purposes:

(a) The warm-up. (Muscles should not be stretched until the body is well warmed up.)

(b) To strengthen the muscles in the sole of the foot as well as leg muscles. The "spring" at the take-off requires strong ligaments.

(c) To strengthen the ankle joint. Any exercise which requires the maintenance of the body weight by the sole of the foot, or which requires a ball-heel rock-over seems to develop the ankle "rock" technique which is used in dropping to the springboard.

2. *Stretching Exercises.*—After the warm-up the divers should join the squad for gymnastics which consist of stretching, twisting, and bending. Forward and backward rolls on the mats should be performed so as to warm-up the back muscles so that the diver is able to "bunch up" into a close tuck. The ankles and toes must also undergo stretching exercises so that they may be pointed in a straight line with the foreleg during the dive. (For exercises, see Danish stretching.) Divers should sit on the heels Indian fashion and lean backward so as to lengthen the ankle and the tarsal ligaments and muscles of the legs. This will aid in pointing the feet in a straight line with the legs.

The hip girdle requires special attention. The diver should bend forward from the hips, with the knees straight, attempting gradually to touch the floor with the hands. Another useful exercise is to press the head through between the legs from a leg spread. This stretches the hamstring muscles as well as the back muscles, thus aiding the diver in effecting a close bunched tuck, as well as to develop a deep "pike" position.

Many additional exercises can be practiced to develop suppleness, strength, poise, posture, and a sense of balance. Some of these are:

(a) Chin out of pool after each dive to develop the chest, shoulders, and arms.

(b) Leg and body lifting on face and back to strengthen abdominal and back extensor muscles.

(c) Stand and walk on hands.

(d) Walk slow and fast on a straight chalk line drawn on the floor as if balancing on tight wire.

(e) Stand with the back against a flat wall; heels, calves, hips, shoulders and head touching for a sense of posture alignment and correction. Mirrors are an aid. Check on proper tilt of pelvis as to amount of curvature in lumbar region (small of back). Tilt the pelvis back to straighten the spine. It should straighten so that just the thickness of a hand can be inserted between the spine and the wall.

(f) Divers should constantly practice poised positions so that an assumed poise on the board does not feel strange. While walking, the head should be carried well back, the chin and the chest out. Try to stretch in a relaxed manner while walking. Develop an easy, smooth gait.

(g) The crab walk is excellent for stretching and arching the spine.

The Fundamental Principles of Competitive Diving

As skill in diving depends upon the building of one skill upon another, the diver, whether beginner, novice, or skilled, should pay strict attention to each detail underlying diving performance. These basic skills are not easily learned simply by the process of smoothing out a complete performance, but can more simply be learned by starting from scratch and practicing each step until it is learned thoroughly. Through this process, the first skills become a part of the diver's reflex behavior as the succeeding, more difficult, skills are added to the performance.

It is exceedingly important, then, that each diver start his training at the level of skill at which he can perform each movement with continuous precision. As each succeeding step is taken, this same precision must be mastered before adding new skills.

15

If unbasic skills are first learned, the unlearning and relearning of new reflexes are time consuming and oftentimes very discouraging to the learner.

1. **Adjustment to the Springboard.**—When an inexperienced diver first walks out to the end of a springboard, he is confronted with a situation that is strange to him. His sense of balance and security is diminished until his visual relationships to near-by objects become adjusted and his equilibrium is re-established. He learns to calculate the distance to the water and objects about him become more familiar. He also learns to establish a better sense of balance by relying more upon his tactile sensations from the bottoms of his feet as well as the higher organs of equilibrium, the semicircular canals. As soon as this relationship is established, he learns to get the feel of the board by first slightly springing the board. He then gradually increases the movement until he finds just how much of a spring he can get and still keep his feet in contact with the board. By using the arms he maintains his balance, finds a rhythm of movement with the board, and increases the height of his spring. As soon as the diver can get into the rhythm of the board and can ride up and down with it without remaining tense, it may be said that he is beginning to be at home on the board.

As the springing is increased, the beginning diver soon finds that his feet leave the board after each lift. This has a tendency to throw the diver slightly backward off balance. By readjusting his body position to slight rises off the board, he soon learns to maintain his center of gravity over the balls of his feet which is the base of support during this action.

By gradually increasing the height of the lift and working in the action of the arms with the springing action of the ankles, knees, and hips, the diver soon finds that he can continue a series of fifteen to twenty springs well above the board without losing his balance and with an expenditure of but very little effort.

(a) *Technique of Springing the One-Meter or Three-Meter Board Facing the Water.*—While bouncing on the board, the body should be stretched upright with the eyes focusing on the tip of the board. The head should be held as high as possible while the tip of the board is being kept in sight.

As the body drops toward the board it is held straight. The ankles are extended and the toes are pointing toward the board. As the feet near the board they are slightly separated and are slightly flexed so that the toes and the balls of the feet will ease on to the board. As the foot comes in contact with the board the fall is broken, and the weight is distributed over the entire foot by letting the ankle flex gradually as first the toes and balls of the feet, then the heels, light on to the board.

The knees and hips also act as shock absorbers and prepare for the lift. They are slightly flexed as the body drops onto the board.

As the momentum and the weight of the body depress the board, the knees and hips flex slightly as they take up the landing shock. While the board is being depressed further, however, the knees and hips cease to give, and the full weight of the body settles onto the board. As the board approaches its fullest depression, the knees and hips begin to extend and drive against the board, pressing the board farther toward the water.

As the board recoils, the knees and hips continue to extend and propel the body upward. When the board has completed the recoil, the knees and hips have reached full extension and it is then that the ankles execute the final lift that sends the body soaring upward.

Just as the extended ankles and feet rock downward at the drop onto the board, they now rock upward to thrust the body into the air. The extension of the ankle and foot is vigorous and even the toes contribute to the snap upward as the feet finally leave the board.

The action of the arms must be turned into this whole springing movement. The arms serve to control body balance and also to supply a further force in the depression of the board.

In order to maintain balance, the arms describe fundamentally a vertical movement. If they are thrown backward or forward during the arm swing, body control is lost.

As the body is above the board ready to drop onto it, the arms are slowly moving into a position in preparation for the downward swing as the body descends. The arms are outstretched with the hands slightly more than shoulder width and just above head height. The palms are facing downward and somewhat forward and there is a comfortable flexion in the elbow joints.

The hands describe a slow outward motion, and as the body nears the board, the slow outward motion is converted into a rapid downward one and the hands reach the hips just as the board is being fully depressed.

The hands are forced downward to a position just alongside the rear of the hips and then are drawn forward and upward with the palms facing the hips. This sudden change in direction from downward to forward and upward transfers the downward momentum from the arms to the body. As the hands pass the hips, the downward extension of the legs against the board is made. The arms are lifting upward as the board is depressed to its fullest extent so that as the board starts upward the arms are nearly at shoulder level.

At this position the arms must be carefully controlled so that body balance will be maintained. The hands are elevated with the finger tips pointing upward and somewhat outward. As the hands reach shoulder height they are slowly pressed outward into the position again, poised for the downward drive. A common error is merely to swing the arms in circles.

While the body is in the air above the board, the legs are stretched in extension and the body is held erect. The hips must also be forward in line with the stretched body.

The head is inclined forward just far enough that the eyes can keep the front tip of the board in view of all times while the body is in the air during the descent. The moment the feet come in contact with the board the head is lifted and the eyes are directed forward. The eyes are focused on a point in front of the board at eye level during the entire ascent. As soon as the body again descends to the board, the eyes must find the tip of the board and hold it in focus until the feet actually come in contact with the board again.

(b) *Fundamental Techniques of the Front Approach, Hurdle, and Take-Off.*—After the diver has learned to spring the board in good form and has the ability to take twenty good springs without losing his balance, he is ready to learn the fundamental techniques of the front approach, hurdle, and take-off.

It is at this point that the various finer aspects of finished performance should be instituted so that as the diver repeats these polished movements they become natural to him.

The fingers and thumbs should be held straight and slightly squeezed together and the palms held flat from the moment the diver steps onto the board. The arms move smoothly and are kept under control by restricting their range of movement. The hands and arms are never thrown, but are either lifted or pressed into a position. Whenever the diver leaves the board, the toes are pointed and the

Fig. 10.—A series of ideal form showing the various types of springboard diving take-offs in preparation for executing the elementary jump dives as well as the standard springboard dives, from either 1 or 3 meter height. Also showing a series of ideal form of executing the various elementary jump dives. A. A series of ideal form for executing a standing take-off with the body facing the springboard. B. A series of ideal form for executing a standing take-off with the body facing the water. C. A series of ideal form for executing the three step run, hurdle, and take-off. D. The standing or running front jump dive, body straight. E. The standing or running front jump dive, pike position. F. The standing or running front jump dive, tuck position. G. The standing or running front jump dive with a one-half twist to the right. H. The standing or running front jump dive with one full twist to the right. I. The standing backward jump dive, body straight. J. The standing backward jump dive in the pike position. K. The standing backward jump dive in the tuck position. L. The standing backward jump dive with a one-half twist to the left. M. The standing backward jump dive with one full twist to the left. N. The forward running or standing semi-gainer jump dive, body straight.

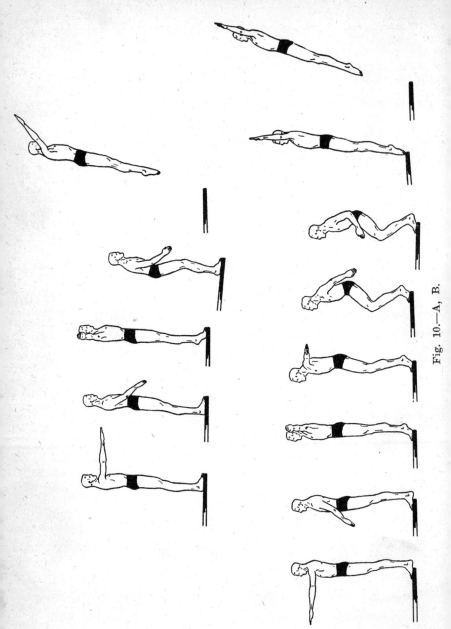

Fig. 10.—A, B.

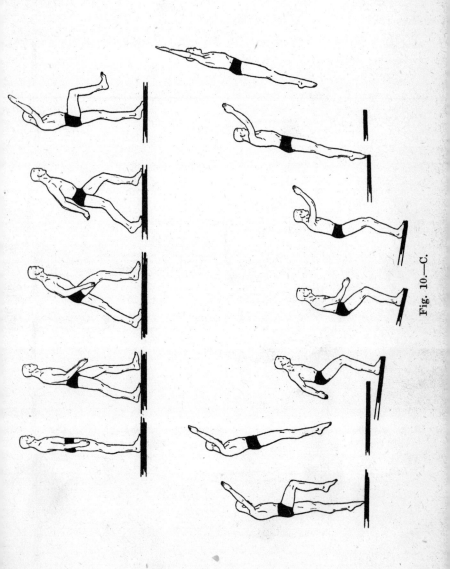

Fig. 10.—C.

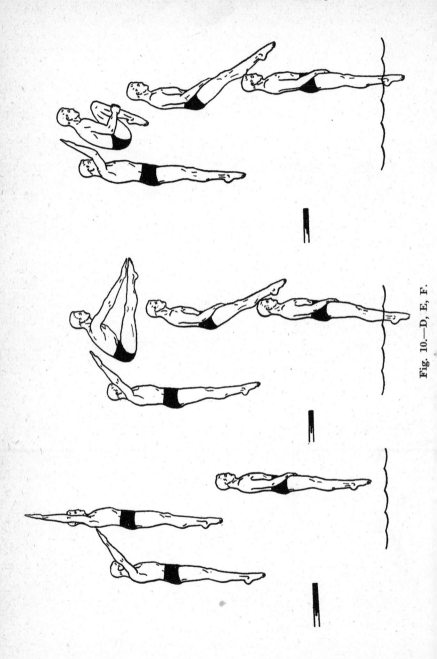

Fig. 10.—D, E, F.

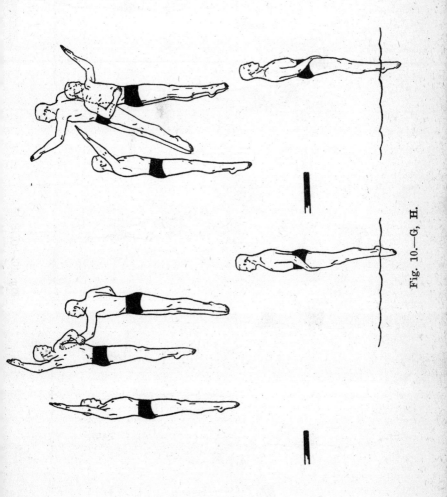

Fig. 10.—G, H.

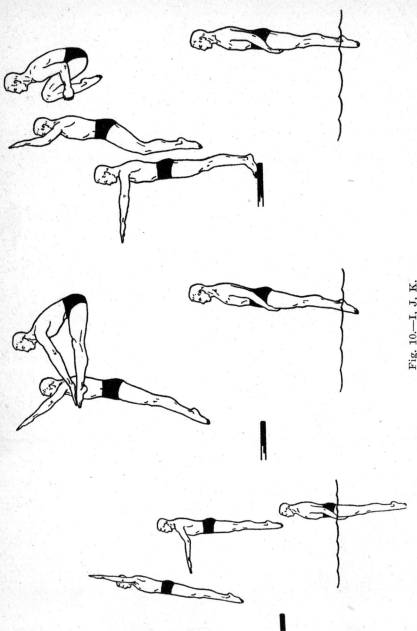

Fig. 10.—I, J, K.

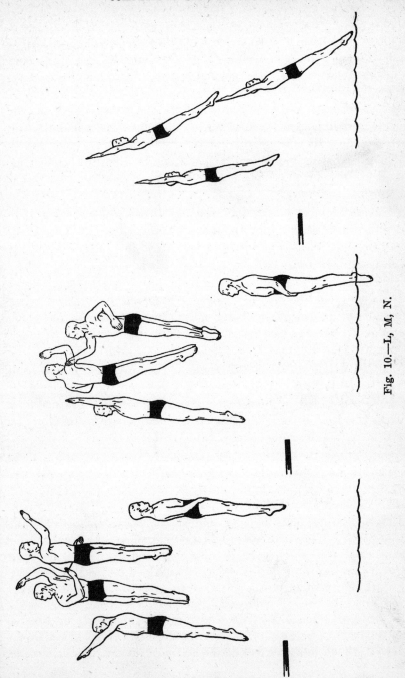

Fig. 10.—L, M, N.

ankles, knees, and hips are stretched in extension and held close together. The head is held in good position with the chin tucked in comfortably. The shoulders are held erect, and the chest is forward and the abdomen flat. The pelvis is carried forward so that an erect spinal posture is maintained. Divers should not rely alone upon their experience while on the board to adopt these positions, but instead should assume them as much as possible while walking, sitting, and standing during daily activities. If the diver has done this, he assumes the proper positions on the board in a natural manner and does not feel that these positions are strange. (See chapter on Special Exercises for Divers.)

By springing the board, the diver has become accustomed to allowing the board to lift him into the air, and he has also learned the fundamental movements of the arms, legs, and ankles during the spring of the board.

When executing a dive, only one spring is taken. In order to derive optimum lift from this spring, the manner in which the diver drops onto the end of the board must place the diver in the proper position to depress the board and obtain the lift from it. This elongated step into the spring is known as the hurdle (Fig. 10C).

2. **The Hurdle and Take-Off Angle.**—The hurdle is the base of all front running dives. If the hurdle is a poor one, the dive cannot be a good one. There are numerous basic techniques to be learned in an accurate hurdle in order to effect a true and powerful lift from the board into the dive to be performed.

On landing the hurdling foot (assume it to be the left) on the board, the body continues to move forward until the center of body weight is over the ball of the left foot. The left leg is slightly bent at the knee at the step into the hurdle. A powerful upward spring is given by extending the knee and powerfully extending the ankle (Fig. 10C). Simultaneously with this movement the right knee is lifted, and the toe is extended toward the board. The arms move forward and upward from slightly behind the hips. As the arms lift upward, the shoulder girdle is pulled up erect from a slight forward lean; the hips press forward until the body is straight. The head is forward just enough that the eyes may maintain focus on the end of the board. The right leg is then stretched downward alongside the other. All of these movements should have taken place before the body reaches the highest point in the hurdle. Both legs and body are now stretched straight down toward the tip of the board (Fig. 10C).

The hurdle leap must be accurately directed so that the body is at its highest point just behind the very end of the board. Here the body is prepared for the descent to the board. Too much power sometimes is attempted which causes the diver to crouch too deep during the approaching steps to the hurdle which causes loss of springing power as well as rhythm and timing. The result is a "wobbly" take-off. The diver should try a lower hurdle until he can relax into it and keep it under control. Then the hurdle should be as high as possible with no loss of balance. This is an important skill and requires weeks and weeks of practice. In the descent, the toes, ankles, legs, and the entire body must be vigorously stretched down toward the board. Check any over-forward lean with the shoulders in the drop or descent. There should be approximately a degree or two lean, just enough to have the center of weight of the body beyond the end of the board.

In the descent, the arms are delayed in their lateral descent just behind the hips until the weight of the body has dropped on to the board on the balls of the feet (Fig. 10C). Then, and only then, should the arms be driven down and suddenly caught or changed in direction, at the side of the hips, and then lifted upward. This delayed descent of the arms gives perfect timing with the board and with the take-off. Most divers get the arms down too soon and, therefore, derive ineffective timing of the take-off movement. The arm descent should be delayed because the board must be pressed down by the body weight, then the arms come down transferring their downward momentum to the body at the end of their swing to assist in giving greater downward bend to the board. The descent should not be forced. One can only drop as fast as gravity permits. Some beginning divers will flatten the feet several inches above the board and slightly bend the knees and then stomp the board for the take-off. This stomping should never be permitted. Most boards today are slow and flexible. They should not be stiff and quick. This type of board causes the diver to stomp which develops the dreaded shin splints. The body should drop to the board and settle onto it as lightly as a feather, without a sound when contact is made with the feet.

An important technique takes place as the balls of the feet land on the board. About an inch from the board in the descent, the toes lift toward the knees. The ankles remain extended so that balls of the feet can first contact the board. The balls of the feet must then never for an instant release downward pressure against the resistance of the board. This is performed by a tension in the leg muscles controlling the ankle joint and the plantar muscles in the sole of the foot. There is a slight flexion of the hips and knees which increases as the body is lowered onto the board. This places the legs in a position to depress the board farther by a forceful extension as the board reaches maximum depression. When the board has been fully depressed and begins to recoil, first the hips and knees, and finally the ankles, extend vigorously as if rising onto the toes to give still greater resistance to the upward rebound of the board. This technique executed in the feet and ankles gives tremendous lifting power to the body as well as giving the whole movement an appearance of ease of performance.

While practicing the hurdle, the diver should enter the water, feet first, at the completion of the take-off. This practice will drill the diver in the proper drop onto the board and the proper take-off angles and will not condition the diver to balk if a poor hurdle is made in regular competition. The attention at this point should be held to the hurdle alone. The techniques of the take-off, the flight through the air, and the entry will be learned later.

When the diver has reached the level of skill in the hurdle at which he has mastered the skillful body control and feels that he is acquiring a powerful lift from the board, he is then ready to learn the approach to the hurdle.

(a) *The Approach to the Hurdle.*—The approach to the hurdle consists of (1) mental and physical poise in the starting position, and (2) the run. The diver assumes his starting position at the far end of the board (Fig. 10C). He appears in better balance in relation to the board on the far end rather than somewhere between the two ends of the board, whether it is a 14 foot or 16 foot board. One can quite easily adjust the steps in the run to accommodate the longer stance.

The diver should assume an erect, active position. The head is held well back, chin in, and chest well up, but not extremely exaggerated. The abdomen is drawn in. The center of body weight is over the balls of the feet, not over the heels. The back is erect, the arms are at the sides, and the palms rest on the front side of the thighs. The legs and heels are held together, with the feet turned slightly outward. The eyes are focused on the far end of the board, without lowering the head to do so.

While in the starting position, the diver is concentrating upon the particular dive which he is going to perform. He should visualize his body going through the entire dive. While so visualizing, he should measure with the eyes, the height of his dive from the end of the board. The eyes are again lowered to the board and maintained there throughout the entire run and until he sees the feet placed on the board at the end of the hurdle. Before starting the run the diver should again shift his concentration to the start of the dive. He should take all the time he needs in the starting position to become ready for the dive. Before a large audience, a diver in the starting position is a human magnet for hundreds of pairs of eyes attracted toward him. As he becomes quietly and deeply engrossed in concentration of his announced dive, so too will the audience come to attention. This moment gives him inspiration. All outside stimuli about him are blocked out, and everything is centered in the performance of the dive. Throughout the stance, the diver should express confidence, strength, personality, and poise.

In competition, the diver should, in waiting for his turn, concentrate ahead to his next dive and practice behind the scenes some of its fundamental positions, such as tucking or arching the back. This aids the diver in making readiness for adjusting himself when on the board. If in previous dives his legs have a tendency to "buckle" when dropping onto the board, he should do knee bending exercises between dives to stretch and relax his muscles. He should keep himself warm while waiting for his next dive. A comb should be handy to keep his hair combed before stepping upon the board for his next dive.

(b) *The Run.*—The run must be smooth and forceful. A diver should not give the appearance of sneaking out. If he is too tense, he will usually shorten his normal steps and his hurdle will have to be a long one.

The run should consist of at least three steps before the hurdle. The length of board and the physical stature usually determine the number of steps. The run should not be too fast nor too slow. A more natural run is better for accuracy in dropping to the end of the board from the hurdle.

The length of the strides should be normal, jogging distance. The first step is slightly shorter than the others and each succeeding stride is slightly longer than the first. The first step of most divers is approximately 20 inches long. The hurdle take-off foot should reach a point approximately 2½ feet from the end of the board. The steps increase in distance as the speed of the run increases. Some divers try to put too much power into the step just prior to the hurdle, causing the step to over-reach and giving the body a crouched appearance.

In the three-step approach, start the first step with the foot from which you best take-off. Assuming it to be the left foot then, it is the left which also hits at the hurdle step (Fig. 10C).

In the four-step approach, start the first step with the foot opposite from the take-off foot so as to come out right at the hurdle step.

The run should be made with each foot placed directly under the center of weight of the body as if running out on a straight line. If placed on either side of the center line, it would cause the body to move from side to side with each step that would cause the body to drop to the opposite corner of the board at the end of the hurdle and lift the diver into the air at an angle that would be to one side of the board. It also causes twists of the body in the air if the diver attempts to lift straight out from the board from this position.

During the run the arms should coordinate in rhythm with the run (Fig. 10C). The arm swing should not be overexaggerated. The rhythmic run is best accomplished by swinging the arms slightly forward and backward from a hang in front of the hips. The main thing to keep in mind with the arm swing is to time it so that at the hurdle step both arms are ready to come forward from slightly behind the hips, with the hurdle take-off (Fig. 10C). In the three-step run, the arm swing is very simple. On the first step the arms swing in a slight arc forward. On the second step they swing backward, but not past the hips. On the third step the arms swing again in the same arc forward. On the hurdle step the arms swing backward and, as the body moves over the hurdle leg, the arms move forward and lift upward as the body leaps up high into the hurdle. Some divers will just let them swing easily from a shoulder hang, just merely attempting to coordinate the movement with the run as in walking. Then, at the hurdle step, they move behind the hips and swing forward with the leap. The arms should be held extended.

In the four-step run, the only variance from the three-step approach is that the arms move forward in a delayed manner on the first two steps and then swing back on the third step. This arm rhythm then continues the same as in the three-step approach. The delayed movement in the four-step approach in the first two steps is to time the arm swing in such a manner that the arms are in forward rhythm on the hurdle leap.

(c) *The Take-Off.*—As the lift from the board is executed, the arms lift into a reach, not a swinging movement. They continue on into a reaching, stretching movement (Fig. 10C). Just at what angle or how far the arms should reach depends upon the dive to be performed. This will be further discussed with each dive. However, when the board is depressed to its maximum bend, the diver times the arms to lift into a reaching stretch, beyond the head and in the intended line of flight of the body as it leaves the board. Too often the inexperienced divers swing the arms upward too abruptly or ahead of the recoil of the board and present an awkward, unbalanced position. Note in each dive the position of the hands and arms as the feet leave the board. The eyes should be steadily fixed upon the tip of the board until the feet drop onto it. The eyes then sight down the pool and again become momentarily fixed upon some object at diving height level.

The amount of lean when the body drops to the board in the hurdle also differs with each dive. In every forward dive there must be just enough lean so that the center of weight is just beyond the base of support when the feet are on the end of the board. One must distinguish between proper lean and the commonly known fault of falling forward. A plain front header and the backward dive is a half somersault and any somersault dive passes through a line of flight which is angular in motion. This angular motion can be obtained by merely having the body approximately one or two degrees off center. It might be said that there should be no forward movement at all once the desired degree of lean is obtained from the hurdle. Usually, angular forward motion continues once the diver has landed on the end of the board. This moving-lean will give a faulty take-off, reduce height and balance. The forward motion should be so slow, and the lean so slight that it can hardly be perceived. For example, place one end of a stick five feet long on the floor and perfectly balance it. Then move it just off its center of support. Notice that the early falling movement is so slow that it appears to be balanced. As gravity begins to act upon it the falling speed is accelerated.

16

With a diver, this falling fault usually starts in the descent of the hurdle if it has not been sufficiently counter-checked in the ascent of the hurdle. Through constant trials and practice, the diver acquires a sense of lean and just the exact amount of lean required during the ascent and descent of the hurdle necessary for the type of dive to be performed. He must, therefore, train to acquire different angles of lean at the take-off for dives requiring greater or less amount to obtain a desired line of flight. These body leans may possibly vary only from 1 to 10 degrees. One may readily note that to achieve such slight angles consistently requires accuracy in performance. Unless this fundamental is thoroughly learned, a diver can never hope to perform consistently in competition. It is the amount of lean that determines the distance a diver goes out from the board. A diver must then not "groove" himself to learn one angle of take-off for all dives, but he must be able to take-off at several different angles of varying degrees.

This flight will vary as the angle of take-off varies. Some dives require a flatter line of flight than others. The center of motion of the body describes the line of flight. In layout dives the center is just slightly above the hip joint. In pike dives the center of motion is not in the body but just outside and in front of the hips. In the tuck position the center of motion lies just outside of the body, in front of the hips between the abdomen and the thighs. An attempt is made to group these dives as to the amount of distance of entry from the end of the board. They are as follows:

1. Those farthest from the end of the board with a more or less flattened line of flight. The plain headers, all of the forward and backward somersault dives, whether tuck, pike, or straight. Also the somersault twisting dives, both forward and backward.

2. Those nearest the end of the board with a more vertical line of flight. Both forward and backward jackknifes. The cutaway group of dives. The jackknife dives with twists. All of the gainer dives including those with twists.

To practice for these angles the tip of a cane pole can be placed on the surface of the water at various distances from the end of the board and the diver attempts to enter at that point. Some coaches recommend diving into sand pits with marks on the sand at various distances. Some coaches prefer inflated tubes placed on the surface of the water and held there for a diver to dive through in practicing for the proper angle of take-off.

To practice and develop height in the hurdle some coaches erect a cross bar over the hurdle region of the board or holding a small stick in place. The bar can be raised to various heights as the diver improves the lift.

A most common error and tendency of most divers is that as the dives become more difficult to perform, the more hurried the hurdle and take-off become. Then too, there is a tendency to become more tense in the approach and hurdle, causing an inefficient take-off. Divers must remember to be properly relaxed in the approach of a difficult dive and perform the preliminary arm movement of the standing take-off slowly.

In the take-off, the hands, arms, head, and shoulder girdle should conform to the intended angle and line of flight of the body at the exact moment the body stretches off the board. The eyes then assist the body in the air by constantly spotting or focusing upon some object, to inform the diver as to his bearings and balance. The head of the diver should not move awkwardly out of body flight alignment for the purpose of focusing.

(d) *Height and Line of Flight.*—Height in diving is the vertical distance or the highest peak reached by the body's center of motion in the line of flight. The line of flight is the path described by the center of body weight from the take-off to the entry. To obtain optimum height in a dive, all essential movements to a good dive must be rhythmically timed and balanced from take-off to the entry. If this is attained, the body lifts effortlessly into the air. Wherever one observes a diver making tremendous effort to get height to a dive, it usually appears jerky in its motions and is usually unsymmetric in balance. Muscular power must be skillfully controlled. Height, then, is a natural result when the run and hurdle are well controlled and timed.

Some divers have a natural endowed gift of good springing muscles in the soles of the feet as well as in the legs. It is not practical for all divers to attain the same height in feet and inches, but each diver should utilize all of the potential lift from the board. When this force is transmitted through the central longitudinal axis of the body, the body will derive maximum height.

(e) *Entry.*—The point of entry of a dive should be at a point directly under the center of weight of the body, on a line with the descending flight of the body. From the surface, the line of flight should be projected directly down to the bottom of the pool. The diver's body should follow this projected line of flight to the bottom so that every part of his body will pass through the same opening in the surface of the water. In the foot entry dive, the pointed feet and legs must guide the body down this line so as to draw the shoulders and head into the hole without side, forward, or backward casts. Nearly every dive requires a different position of the spine, legs, head, and arms to effect a good entry.

In the plain header dive, the arms should be sharply closed several feet above the surface and held in line with the spine. This will give the diver time to adjust his shoulders and head and spot his entry directly under his center of weight. This also gives him time to check or countercheck an "over" or "short" dive. Some coaches recommend a stretch as the entry is made, while others advise relaxation for a sleek entry. This depends upon the build and suppleness of the diver. Certainly the body must be straight, slightly arched near the shoulder blades, with the body stretched both ways from this point. When a diver spots his entry in the descent, he should stretch and reach toward the bottom of the pool.

In header dives, there is considerable controversy among authorities as to whether the hands should be held together or spaced apart about head width. As a general rule with most types of divers, a smoother and less noisy entry is made when the hands are spaced about one to two inches apart, with arms held tightly against the head. It presents a more streamlined effect to the head and shoulders, just as in the glide of the racing start push-out after the turn, and in the breast stroke glide phase. However, some diving officials will penalize a diver for spacing hands in the entry. The rules state that the arms should be stretched beyond the head in a line with the body, the hands close together. It does not say held together, but close together, which infers a slight spread. It would be a question of interpretation as to whether one to two inches would be considered "close together."

In all foot entry dives such as the jackknife, cutaway, and gainer dives, the body should be held straight, without arch during the entry, in order to prevent splash or side casts. In these entries, the hollow of the spine should be relaxed and stretched, so that it can be straightened in the above dives. If the spine is held rigid, the hollow will appear. Tilting the pelvis backward will aid in eliminating this hollow curvature in the back.

In backward layout dives as well as gainer layout header dives a slight arch should be maintained during the entry. If the mechanics of the dive are correct and well timed and the dive is not short, the arch is straightened to a minimum. If short, or over, then the amount of arch varies from a deep arch to a straight line. Too much arch will never drive the diver to the bottom on a projected line with his line of flight, but will cause him to veer just under the surface and cause his feet to slap on the surface.

In the feet first entry dives the arms should be closed along the sides of the body with the palms of the hands curving nicely along and over the front of the thigh, just below the hips. This position is to prevent protruding elbows behind the line of the spine.

The knees and ankle joints should be straight.

In the front header dive, the head should not be lowered abruptly at the peak of the height for the entry, but just as it is entering the surface, and then not too abruptly. Neither should the head be ducked just a short distance above the water. If the head is to be lowered deep between the arms to save a short dive, it should be lowered slowly just below the peak of the dive so that it causes no abrupt movement, distracting from the smooth action of the dive. The head should not be lowered too deep between the arms if the mechanics of the dive are correct and well balanced. The back of the head should be well above the back line of the arms at the entry. The head in this position preserves the unbroken and continuous arch from the head down the curved line of the spine to the feet. In all header dives the arms, when extended above the head, should be in a straight line with the upper spine. If the arms are extended too far, the arch will be too great.

3. **The Mechanics and Technique for the Take-Off for Backward Dives.**—(Body Facing Board.) This take-off is executed without a run and the back faces the water at the end of the board where the stance is assumed (Fig. 10B).

(a) *The Approach.*—The diver steps on the board at the rear and assumes a momentary stance before executing the dive. In this position the diver must express confidence in his poise as well as be mentally alert for the dive he is about to perform.

The diver then walks briskly, yet poised, head and chest held high, and arms swinging naturally and alive as he takes natural moderately spaced strides to the end of the board. Some inexperienced divers make the error of walking out too slowly and showing a nonchalant attitude. The eyes may spot the end of the board as he walks out to it and the head should not be lowered. Upon reaching the end, he then transfers his eyes to a point on the far wall. The head does an about face pivoting quickly with his feet, and the eyes focus on the wall over the rear of the board at head height. Some divers focus on the board while in the back stance.

(b) *The Pivot Step.*—The pivot action of turning the back to the water may be performed in the following manner: The walk to the end of the board is timed in equal strides so that at the last step the left foot strides across the right foot and is placed near the end of the board and just ahead in line with the right foot and about three inches from the end of the board. The major weight of the body is placed on the rear foot, the body inclining slightly toward the board. The body pivots around to the right on the ball of the left foot and the ball of the right foot in an about face. The right foot then slides back along the side of the left foot and the feet are adjusted for the take-off. In this manner the least movement is made.

(c) *The Stance.*—The arms are placed shoulder height and shoulder width and straight as the pivot is made. The body must be straight and not arched. The curvature at the small of the back must be straightened by tilting the pelvis back. The center of body weight rests either in the balls of the feet, the toes, or the heels, depending upon the type of dive. The heels are level with the board. The body should never be stanced on a toe-rise.

If a stance is assumed for any of the cutaway dives or a back jack-knife, the body should assume more of an incline toward the board, with the center of body weight over the big toes. This slight incline accommodates a more efficient hip lift at the take-off. If in a backward dive or backward somersault, the center of body weight should be well back in the heels, even though the heels do not rest on the board.

(d) *The Take-Off Mechanics of Arms and Legs in Action.*—The arms are lowered slowly to the sides of the body so as not to disturb the center of weight which is balanced over the base of support. Throughout the entire preliminary arm action of take-off the center of weight must be maintained over the base of support, which may be toes, balls of feet, or heels, except on the final down and up swing. This is true for all backward dives. However, for all cutaway dives the weight must be maintained constant over the balls of the feet throughout the entire arm swing.

Continuing the arm swing upward, they lift rather than swing or drive upward, to either shoulder height or above shoulder level. No matter to what height the arms lift they must always move during the up phase of the arm swing in front of the spine or frontal plane, never behind it. If the arms are pressed back behind the spine on the upswing, the shoulders are pulled back, the chest is bulged forward, the lower spine arches, which causes the body to lose its balance over its base of support.

As the arms are lifting, the body is raised well up on its toes (Fig. 10B). The arms move up just strong enough to ease the weight of body off the end of the board. This will set the board in motion and in rhythm with the arms and legs for the remainder of the take-off. A deep breath is taken during this motion, through the mouth, and then the mouth is closed. The arms are lifted up and out laterally and held straight.

The preliminary and initial arm lift is the most important phase of the mechanics of the backward take-off, and the success of the dive depends upon the accuracy of its performance. Usually a diver drives the arms up too hard and fast which lifts the shoulder girdle up to the ears, causing the body to lift off the board (crow-hop), and then causing the body to lean backward prematurely at the angle of take-off. The arms when either raised or lowered should move laterally up and down, but in front of the spine or the frontal plane, and never behind it.

The final downswing of the arms is now executed as the legs are executing the down push, to press the board down as low as possible (Fig. 10B). In this action, the arms now really drive down as far as the hips with force where they suddenly change direction, further transmitting downward force while the arms begin the final upswing. The feet press down on the board as the heels lower again level to the board and the knees bend slightly, preparing themselves for the final push on the board. By a terrific and sudden extension of the knees and ankles, the arms lift and reach up into the line of flight

(Fig. 10B). While the arms swing down and the heels lower and the knees bend, the hips move back and down very slightly with the knee bend as if to sit down on a chair. However, the body or trunk must remain in a vertical line above the hips and not bend forward, or, so-called, bowing. (See Fig. 10A.) This movement does not give the body a "falling" appearance. It gives it, at the same time, true balance and the diver is able to keep the body under control on the take-off, as well as throughout the dive, while the eyes remain focused.

The movements for the standing take-off, body facing the water, are as those described for the take-off with the back of the body facing the water (Fig. 10A).

The Fundamental Jump Dives

The jump dives are devised not only for the beginner, but also for the experienced diver. The experienced diver should run through these skills and jumps at least once a week throughout the season.

The beginner should not attempt the advanced dives until he has learned these rudimentary skills of diving. Diving should then advance for him rapidly, because his technique is sound and basic.

In all of these jump dives it is a question of balance in the air. This the beginner should control right from the angle of take-off. When in the air he should rely upon the head and arms until such time as he can control the body quite accurately. When consistency in balance is developed, the arms are relied upon less and less and the head takes over in slight adjustments in mid-air. Finally, the diver relies upon the take-off to obtain the exact angle for each dive and rely upon this accuracy for body control in the air.

The jump dives should first be attempted from a standing take-off (Fig. 10A). The technique used in executing the standing take-off with the body facing the water is the same as that described for the take-off with the back facing the water (Fig. 10B).

The forward jump dives should first be performed by the beginner from the standing take-off. When he has adjusted himself to the feel of the movement of the arms and legs with the board he can proceed with the approaching run and hurdle as described in Fig. 10C.

1. **The Front Jump, Straight.**—As the body leaves the board, the arms reach upward about shoulder width. As the body reaches the

peak of the jump, the arms are stretched upward, fingers squeezed together, and the head and shoulders are pressed backward to keep the body well aligned. After the peak of the dive has been reached, the arms are flung downward so that the hands are placed in front of the thighs at the entry. The eyes are directed forward to a point on the wall in front of the board throughout the entire dive. At the entry, the toes stretch toward the bottom (Fig. 10D). On all foot entry dives, the toes should be flexed toward the knees after the feet are well under the surface to avoid injury to the toes on reaching the bottom.

2. **The Front Jump, Pike.**—The arms reach for the ceiling as in the front jump, straight. After the body has left the board, the legs should be lifted toward the hands. The flexion is in the hips as the thighs are lifted. The legs are kept extended, the ankles stretched, and the trunk and head held erect throughout the dive. The arms are lowered to the legs as the legs reach hip level in a horizontal plane. The ankles are brought up to touch the hands as the peak of the dive is reached. The diver should unpike immediately after the peak of the dive has been reached. The hands simply slide along the front of the legs to the entry position in the front of the thighs. This dive requires a considerable amount of body control in order to effect a vertical entry (Fig. 10E).

3. **The Front Jump, Tuck.**—This dive is easier to perform than the pike. The body is stretched momentarily as in the front jump, straight. After the body leaves the board the knees are brought up to the chest, knees and ankles held together and ankles extended. The hands grasp the lower legs and pull them in so that the heels are brought toward the buttocks in a tight tuck. The hips and knee joints must be relaxed.

As the diver comes into the peak of the dive he should hold his trunk firm and his head erect with the eyes directed forward. The tuck is held for a moment after he has passed the peak. As the legs are untucked, they shoot downward and slightly forward. They are then pressed downward and backward in line with the trunk. The hands slide down the legs and are held against the front of the thighs at the entry (Fig. 10F).

4. **The Front Jump, Half Twist.**—The arms are reached upward and the body is held in good alignment as it leaves the board. The

twist is started early and the pivot is made either to the left or to the right. If the twist is to be made to the right, the right arm remains elevated as the turning mechanics are executed with the left arm.

Swing the left arm downward across and close to the chest and push it upward past the opposite shoulder and slightly beyond head level. As the left arm passes in front of the right shoulder, the right arm is lowered with elbow bent and is pushed backward to square the shoulders. From this position the hands are brought to the front of the thighs and the legs are stretched downward for the entry.

The eyes are focused on a point on the front wall until the quarter turn to the right has been made and the right arm is being lowered. The head is then snapped to the right and a new focus is established at a point on the wall behind the board (Fig. 10G).

5. **The Front Jump, Full Twist.**—The full twist is simply an exaggerated movement of the half twist. As the left arm is shot across in front of the chest and upward to the right, it is pushed farther beyond the opposite shoulder. This movement executes the first half of the full twist. The right arm is then driven backward forcibly and serves to complete the second half of the full twist. The eyes are focused on the front wall on the swing of the left arm and the head is turned quickly and the eyes again focus on this wall as the right arm is brought downward. The main consideration to be made in performing this dive is to keep the body and head erect and to keep the legs from jacking too far (Fig. 10H).

The beginner should first practice the arm and head technique on the floor before attempting them from the springboard.

6. **The Backward Jump, Straight.**—As the body leaves the board, the arms lift with the hands passing closely in front of the face. The arms are stretched upward. As the body jumps upward and backward from the board, the head and body must be held erect. A falling take-off should be avoided. As the diver descends from the peak, the hands are lowered to the thighs and a vertical entry is made.

The eyes should remain focused on a spot on the wall approximately at eye level at the rear of the board. The eyes then aid the body to control itself during the dive (Fig. 10I).

7. **The Backward Jump, Pike.**—At the lift from the board in the take-off, the body leans slightly backward. The center of weight

is in heels which project beyond the board, as in Fig. 10B. As in the front jump, pike, the hands lift upward above and slightly in front of the head before the pike is made. The arms do not jerk to a stop, or they are not lifted to a full reach above the head as either of these actions would cause a transfer of momentum from the arms to the body and the body would be thrown out of alignment.

The diver should unpike immediately after the peak is reached. The legs should be held extended and the toes pointed. The hips should flex easily as the legs are lifted to the pike. The legs are horizontal when the pike is effected.

The entry should be made in the vertical position at a point from four to five feet from the tip of the board (Fig. 10J).

8. **The Backward Jump, Tuck.**—This dive is easier to perform than the front jump, tuck dive, due to the reduction of forward momentum. Here is a good opportunity to perfect the tuck motion because about all that is needed to be considered here is the tuck itself (Fig. 10K).

The reach is made before the tuck. At the peak of the dive the head is erect and the eyes are directed forward. The body is leaning slightly forward. The heels are held close to the buttocks, the knees and ankles closed tightly together. The toes are in full depression and the ankles extended.

Untuck soon after the peak is reached and attempt to gain a vertical entry with the body in good alignment, not arched.

9. **The Backward Jump, Half Twist.**—If adequate height is gained from the take-off, this dive is simple to perform. The diver simply jumps backward, executes the twist while holding the body straight and enters the water facing away from the board. Here is an opportunity for the diver to perfect the mechanics of a twist dive. The simplicity of the movements attending the dive allows near maximum concentration on the twist itself. Due to the small amount of momentum away from the front of the board, the body is easily held in good alignment.

The arm mechanics are the same as in the front jump, half twist. In this figure, however, the twist is to the left and the eyes are transferred from the rear wall to the front wall, as the left arm swings down and the elbow pushes backward (Fig. 10L).

10. **The Back Jump, Full Twist.**—Here again, as in the front jump, full twist, the twisting movements of each arm are exaggerated

half-twisting movements. The eyes are held on the rear wall as the right arm crosses the chest. The head is then turned quickly to the left and the eyes again focus on the rear wall as the left arm is swung downward and the elbow forced backward to square the shoulders for the entry.

Here is a dive that requires speed and ample height for its execution. The hands should be made to lift well upward before the twisting mechanics are performed in order to gain the desired adequate height and the well-aligned body position (Fig. 10M).

11. The Semi-Gainer Jump.—This dive is included in this series as it serves to orient the diver to movements in which the feet are swung forward. It will require large amounts of self-discipline and body control to achieve the skill required in this dive as the body should enter the water at a near horizontal angle.

At first, the dive is performed the same as the front jump and gradually the feet are swung forward a little farther at each trial until the body barely slips into the water at a sharp angle. When the diver reaches the level of skill at which he can hit this precarious angle four or five times in succession, he is ready to try the half gainer (Fig. 10N).

When the diver has mastered all of the jump dives he has learned all of the basic diving movements except the head first entry and the somersault movements. When these latter skills have been accomplished, the diver has in his repertoire all of the elements needed to perform any of the required and optional dives.

All dives are combinations of the forward or backward dive with either a somersault or a twist in one of the straight, pike, or the tuck positions. The announcement of the dive named "the half gainer, half twist, layout with forward one and one-half somersault, tuck" no longer sounds like an impossibility and the diver well drilled in the fundamental jump skills can picture the movements involved in this dive and, after some coaching and practice, can perform this dive himself.

The above-mentioned dive will not be a good one to present first, however. A better order of presentation will be used, namely, that of describing one group at a time. The first dive of each group is the fundamental movement and succeeding dives contain added movements which increase the complexity of the dive.

In learning the dives the most elementary of the dives in each of the groups should be learned first. As these are mastered, the succeedingly more difficult dives are attempted.

The following order may be used in learning all of the required and a few of the most elementary of the optional dives:

Order[1]	Group	
1	I	Header Forward, Straight
2	II	Backward Header, Straight
3	III	Isander (half gainer), Straight
4	IV	Backward Spring, Forward Dive, Pike
5	V	Half Twist Forward, Straight
6	I	Forward Somersault, Tuck
7	II	Backward Somersault, Tuck
8	III	Mollberg (full gainer), Tuck
9	IV	Backward Spring, One Somersault, Tuck
10	V	Full Twist Forward, Straight
11	I	1½ Somersault Forward, Tuck
12	II	1½ Somersault Backward, Tuck
13	III	Flying Mollberg (flying full gainer), Tuck
14	IV	Backward Spring, 1½ Somersault Forward, Tuck
15	V	Pike Dive with Full Twist Forward

Springboard Diving From the One- or Three-Meter Height

I. 1(a) **Header Forward, Straight.**—This dive is commonly known as the swan or plain front dive. It is, in reality, a one-half somersault. The difficulty of this dive lies in the large amount of body control required to maintain the body in a good alignment throughout the flight through the air. As the feet come in contact with the board at the end of the hurdle, the eyes are lifted from the board and are focused on the front wall. The face is held directly forward until after the peak of the dive has been reached. When the diver leaves the board the body should be stretched with the feet pressing forward. The hands are lifted from the hips and are spread out to a position straight from the shoulders with a slight angle forward. A line across the upper back should follow along the top of the arms when the body is in the layout position.

---

[1]See Table A. Intercollegiate Swimming Guide.
See Rules for Springboard Diving. Intercollegiate Swimming Guide.

Fig. 11.—A series of ideal form for executing the various forward somersault dives either standing or running from either the 1 or 3 meter heights selected from the standard table of springboard dives as listed in the N. C. A. A. and A. A. U. Rule Books. A. The header forward straight. B. The header forward (front jackknife). C. Somersault forward, body straight. D. Somersault forward, body in pike position. E. Somersault forward body in tuck position. F. Flying somersault forward body in tuck position. G. 1½ somersault forward body in pike position. H. 1½ somersault forward body in tuck position. I. Double somersault forward body in tuck position. J. 2½ somersault forward body in pike position. K. 2½ somersault forward body in tuck position.

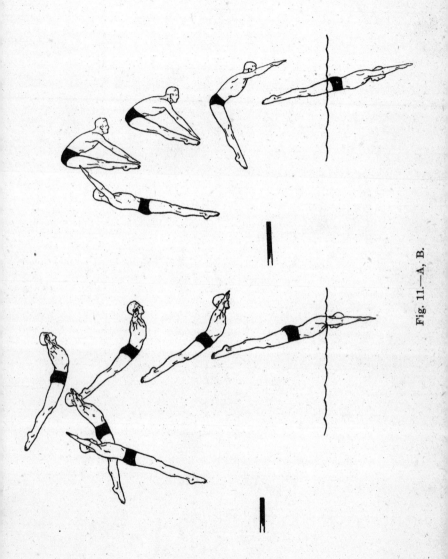

Fig. 11.—A, B.

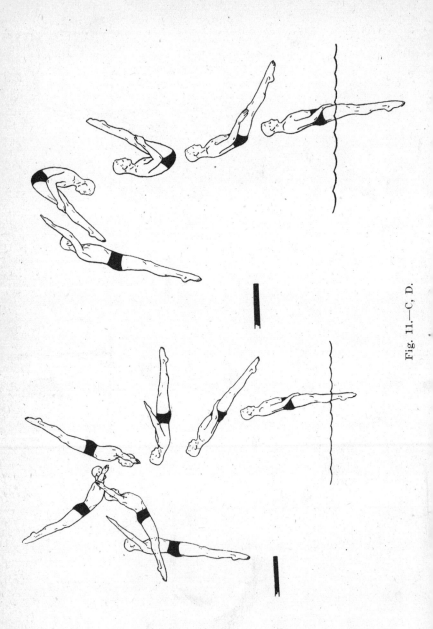

Fig. 11.—C, D.

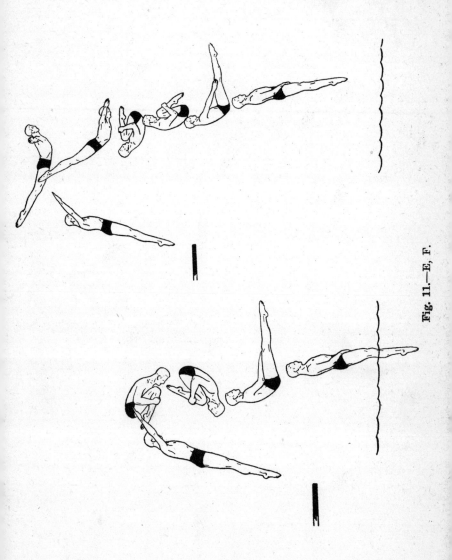

Fig. 11.—E, F.

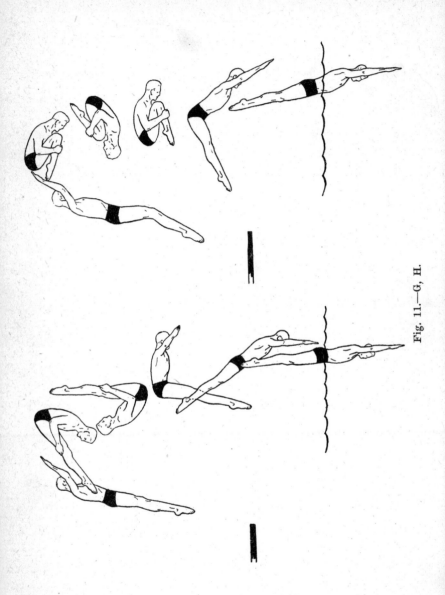

Fig. 11.—G, H.

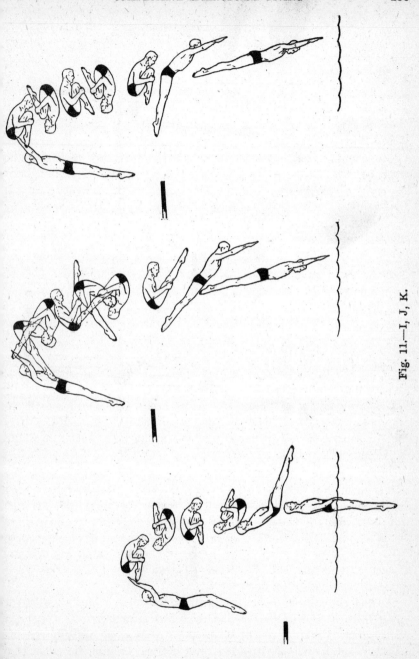

Fig. 11.—I, J, K.

The chest is pushed forward and a slight arch is formed in the lumbar or the small-of-back region. From the hips downward the body should be straight and legs held close together with the toes pointed backward.

As the peak of the dive is reached, the body rotates forward around its center of weight which is just above the hip joint. This rotation lifts the legs upward and levels the trunk so that the heels are just above the head level when the body is at its peak.

The rotation continues as the body falls from the peak and the head is slowly dropped between the arms as the eyes are shifted from the wall to the point of entry. The trunk is straightened and the hands are brought near together as the vertical entry is made. At the entry, the arms should be squeezed against the head and the hands are nearly touching.

The diver should reach for the bottom as he enters the water.

If the rotation at the peak has been too little or too great, a short or over cast of the legs can be prevented at the entry by lowering or raising the head.

A common fault in executing this dive is to bring the arms together too slowly and too near the surface of the water. The arms should be brought together quickly as the body has fallen to a level with the board. In the same dive from the high board, the arm spread may be held a trifle longer.

Another common error too frequently seen is the continuous backward movement of the arms in passing through the peak of the dive. This is caused by not accurately centering the body weight near the hip joints (Fig. 11A).

I. 1(b) **Header Forward, Pike**.—The take-off is made with the hands held close together in a modified reach. The pike is started at the end of the reach. The feet are pressed forward, the arms are depressed and the hips are lifted above the head as the body rises into the peak of the dive. The eyes are spotted well down the course of the pool. As the peak of the dive is reached the hands are brought in contact with the feet. The legs at this point are in a vertical position, with toes pointing downward.

As the body drops below the peak of the dive it has slightly rotated forward so that its position resembles an inverted V. The legs are then lifted slowly as the body starts to open up and the continued rotation of the body places it in a vertical position for the entry.

As the legs lift upward, the arms reach forward to a position along the sides of the head and the hands are held close together at the entry.

Common errors in executing this dive are: (1) The pike is not sharply formed in the hip joint, but takes place in the spine. (2) The legs are not pressed forward as the hips lift toward the peak of the dive. (3) In unpiking, the hands follow the legs back too far, giving the body too much rotation forward with the loss of entry control (Fig. 11B).

I. 2(a) **Forward Somersault, Straight.**—As the feet leave the board the legs are allowed to lift upward and backward and a more exaggerated arch is made than in the header forward. The arms reach upward at the take-off and are lowered into the spread position as the body nears the peak of the dive.

The body is rotating freely as a result of the upward action of the board against the feet. The legs or trunk do not work against this rotation but rather act to aid this rotation to continue.

The body is vertical with the feet uppermost at the peak of the dive. As the body falls from the peak and has rotated just beyond the vertical position, the chin is tucked inward and the head is thrust forward. The arms are then lowered sharply to a position with the hands on the thighs and the body is straightened and the legs press toward the water preparatory to the entry. The hands remain pressed against the front of the thighs as the vertical entry is made.

When the body is at a horizontal level, the head and shoulders are pressed backward to an erect position and the eyes commence to look for a spot on the surface of the water in front.

Pressing the head and shoulders backward before the entry keeps the body from being thrown forward and aids in straightening the entire body preparatory to the vertical entry. This dive is best performed from the three-meter springboard (Fig. 11C).

I. 2(b) **Forward Somersault, Pike.**—As the reach is made after the take-off, the hips are lifted up and over the peak of the dive and the shoulders and head are lowered with chin in as the body rotates forward. Instead of touching the toes as in the front jump, pike, the hands grasp the back of the knees and the elbows are held close to the hips. The hips are relaxed in order that the flexion can be deep. The legs are held extended and the toes pointed. The upper back is not rounded but held semierect. At the peak of the dive the trunk is nearly vertical with the head downward.

As the body falls from the peak of the dive and is in the V position, the trunk is held firm and the opening from the pike is started. The legs are pressed down and the head is pressed backward with chin in. The body should be nearly straight as it passes the level of the board. As the legs drop downward and the body straightens, the eyes focus at a point on the water well ahead of the point of entry as a vertical entry is made.

A common error in executing a pike somersault is to throw the trunk and head forward and downward under the hips. The pike is initiated in lifting the hips up and over the head. The radius of rotation becomes shorter which increases speed of angular rotation (Fig. 11D).

I. 2(c) **Forward Somersault, Tuck.**—The body leaves the board the same as in the forward somersault, pike. The rotation of the diver is facilitated by bringing the heels backward and upward toward the buttocks and bringing the chest forward and downward to the knees. The knees cannot be brought toward the chest in a sharp or forcible manner as such a movement would impede the forward rotation of the diver.

As the heels are pulled in toward the buttocks, the hips lift up and over the head and the head and the tips of the shoulders are brought forward. All joints of the body are relaxed to allow a full tuck.

Before the body reaches a vertical plane after it has fallen some distance from the peak of the dive, the legs are extended and the hands slide from the shins to a position against the front of the thighs. The eyes find the water and the body is straightened for a vertical feet first entry (Fig. 11E).

I. 3(c) **Flying Somersault, Forward, Tuck.**—This dive is more easily performed from the high board but is also a good dive from the low board if the diver obtains a sufficient amount of height from the spring.

The legs are lifted upward and backward as the feet leave the board and are continuously pressed upward and backward past the peak of the dive. The arms are stretched sideward and the body is well arched as in the header forward, straight.

When the body has fallen beyond the peak of the dive and the legs are in a 30° angle in front of the vertical, a fast tuck is made and released almost instantly. The radius of the body is shortened, which greatly increases the speed of rotation. All joints must relax to effect a close tuck. At the untuck the head and shoulders are forced backward as the legs are pressed downward so that the body is kept from tilting forward. The hands pass from the shins to the thighs as the body straightens for the vertical feet first entry (Fig. 11F).

I. 4(b) **One and One-Half Somersault, Forward, Pike.**—In this dive the diver should concentrate on his center of rotation which is in front of his hips when the body is piked. This dive is very similar to the forward somersault, pike, but the rotation is exaggerated by the continual pressure of the hips backward and the head and shoulders forward. The hips must be relaxed so that the pike can be deep.

While the body is descending from the peak, the opening should occur as the alignment of the head, trunk, and hips is horizontal to the surface and he can first see the water.

The legs are driven downward and backward and the trunk remains firm as the body straightens for the head first vertical entry. The arms move off the legs and are stretched downward toward the water and the head is brought between the arms as the entry is made (Fig. 11G).

I. 4(c) **One and One-Half Somersault, Forward, Tuck.**—This dive is very similar to the forward somersault, tuck, with the exception that an additional half forward rotation is made while the body is in the tuck position.

The tuck is entered at the end of the reach and the hips are lifted and the head and shoulders are depressed. The heels are brought sharply to the buttocks. The chin is tucked in and the back is rounded. The tuck starts to open when the body is horizontal on the one and one-fourth turn. The legs are extended and pressed backward as the hips are moved forward to straighten the body. This elongation of the longitudinal axis decreases the speed of rotation.

The arms reach for the point of entry and the body slides down the parabolic line of trajectory and into the water.

A common error in executing this dive is that after the tuck has been effected, the hips are given only an initial lift. The lift of the hips should be continuous around the center of rotation. Most beginners are apt to initiate the movement by pressing the head and shoulders around the center of rotation. If the rotation movement is started and continued in the hips the head and trunk will easily follow once the hips are lifted out of the way. This technique will also reduce the range of the radius of the entire rotation, thus increasing the speed of the rotation (Fig. 11H).

I. 6(c) **Double Somersault, Tuck.**—With the increased complexity of the dive, the diver is apt to stomp the board with the idea that this will give him an additional lift from it. The diver should not stomp the board but should drop onto it and make use of the rocking action of the ankles and the full spring of the board in order to get ample height. To obtain greater height, a higher hurdle should be effected so that gravity acting upon the body from this height, will increase the force exerted upon the board when the body lights onto it, thus bending it deeper. Naturally it follows, that the deeper the board is being depressed the greater the recoil, as well as imparting greater lifting force to the diver.

This dive is the same as the one and one-half somersault, forward, tuck, with a further one-half somersault added.

The tuck is opened as the body has reached the point of rotation at which it appears to be leaning backward in a chair with the legs tucked. The legs are thrust downward, not forward, and the toes are pointed so that as the feet strike the water they pierce the surface with a minimum of splash and sound.

The hands simply slide from the shins to the front of the thighs. An additional push with the forearms can be given to the opening of the thighs. The shoulders and head are pressed backward and the eyes spot the water at the opening (Fig. 11I).

I. 7(b) **Two and One-Half Somersault, Forward, Pike.**—This dive should be made from the three-meter board as an additional distance is required for two and one-half forward turns.

The pike and the somersaults are made in the same manner as that of the one and one-half somersault, forward, pike, except that more power is applied in the spin. The eyes should be lifted as the reach is made. This will help to prevent the diver from going into the somersaults before sufficient height is gained.

The chest must be beyond the 45° angle from the vertical before the opening is made. The arms must then be driven downward and the legs pushed backward. The hips must be straight before the entry.

As the diver increases the number of spins he may have the tendency to close the eyes. The eyes should be kept open at all times and he should learn to orient himself to his surroundings throughout the dive (Fig. 11J).

I. 7(c) **Two and One-Half Somersault, Forward, Tuck.**—The diver should be able to do the double somersault, forward, tuck from the low board before he goes to the three-meter board to attempt the two and one-half somersault, forward, tuck.

The only change that has to be made is that the movements must be more forceful.

The take-off should not be hurried and the tuck must not be started too soon. The body must relax for the tuck.

The opening is made as the trunk is beyond the horizontal after two and one-fourth turns have been made. The arms shoot downward and are continually stretched toward the bottom after the entry. This stretching movement gives support to the legs as they spring open.

The diver should concentrate upon his center of rotation during the somersaults and yet be alert for the instant the opening should take place (Fig. 11K).

II. 8(a) **Backward Header, Straight.**—Although the backward take-off dives are blind dives, they are easy to perform as the body is simply levered backward and additional movements are then made.

The backward header, straight, is performed similarly to the header forward, straight. As the body lifts from the board, the eyes are focused on the rear wall. The arms reach upward and slightly backward and are spread in line with the back of the spine. At the height of the lift and when the head is about at the peak of the dive, the head is stretched backward and the eyes commence to look for the water in the back of the diver.

During this head and arm action, the hips and legs should be lifted and the knees and ankles must be stretched. The arms are brought together when the body has dropped to a point opposite the board and the entry is made with the hands near together and the head between the arms (Fig. 12A).

II. 9(a) **Somersault Backward, Straight.**—This dive is similar to the backward header except that the head does not gain as much height and as the body is rotated backward the head continues pressing backward until the body is past the horizontal.

The hands are dropped forward from the arm spread position to the thighs as the horizontal is reached. The spine must be made supple in order to shorten the radius and get the required rotation at the peak of the dive (Fig. 12B).

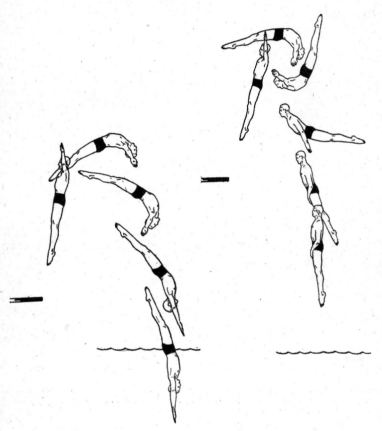

Fig. 12.—A, B.

Fig. 12.—A series of ideal form for executing the various dives selected from the backward somersault group of dives, performed from either the 1 or 3 meter heights. A. Backward header, body straight. B. Somersault backward, body straight. C. Somersault backward, tuck position. D. 1½ somersault backward, body straight. E. 1½ somersault backward, body in pike position. F. 1½ somersault backward, body in tuck position.

Fig. 12.—C, D.

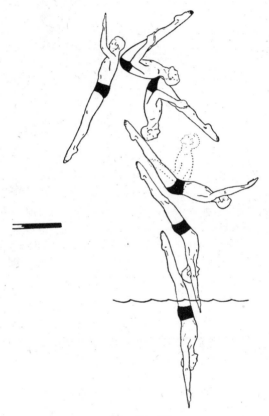

Fig. 12.—E.

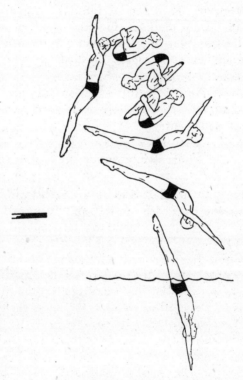

Fig. 12.—F.

II. 9(c) **Somersault Backward, Tuck.**—The tuck is made soon after the upward and backward reach so that the body is tucked at the peak of the dive. The tuck is made by lifting the knees to the chest and the hips follow behind this action to get the desired continuous rotation.

The head starts to pull backward at the peak and keeps pulling until the body is ready to straighten. During the turn the diver should concentrate on the center of rotation. Again as in the forward somersault group of dives, in order to effect speed and balance during the rotation, the diver must be constantly aware of the dominating angular movement of the hips.

When the chest is horizontal to the surface and well above the board, the legs are thrust to full extension and the toes are kept pointed. The head and shoulders are made erect so that the body is perfectly aligned at the entry.

As the body is opened, the eyes can focus on the board until the entry is made. The hands simply slide from the shins to the front of the thighs (Fig. 12C).

II. 11(a) **One and One-Half Somersault, Backward, Straight.**—As the body leaves the board, the initial pull backward is made with arms and head. The diver should not attempt to gain as much height in this dive as in the backward header, but should use this energy to accelerate his backward rotation. The back of the diver must be made supple in order to decrease the radius of the body movement so as to get the desired speed to the rotation at the peak of the dive. During this rotation the knees should be straightened as soon after the take-off as is possible.

As the peak is passed, the arms are thrown forward to a position in front of the thighs. This action imparts additional backward rotation to the body. The head is continually forced backward.

As the horizontal position is reached when one and one-fourth turns have been made, the arms are again thrust upward and backward and the reach for the water is made.

As the water is sighted the head is adjusted so that a vertical entry is made with arms stretched, legs extended, and toes pointed (Fig. 12D).

II. 11(b) **One and One-Half Somersault, Backward, Pike.**—After a moderate reach of the arms, at shoulder width, the legs are lifted and forced backward over the head and continually driven backward in the pike position. The chin is tucked in, the head is comfortably forward, and the back is rounded. When the body is piked, the head is stretched backward. The hands grasp the backs of the knees and pull the legs into a deep pike.

This pike position is held for a full somersault. When the body has made one and one-eighth turns and is in a V position, the opening of the pike is made and the body is straightened for the entry.

The legs remain nearly 30° in front of the vertical as the opening is made. The legs are held as if anchored in position as the body drops away from the pike for the straightening before the entry.

The eyes do not spot the water until the body is nearly straight. The arms are dropped down from the knees and reach for the water below the head (Fig. 12E).

II. 11(c) **One and One-Half Somersault, Backward, Tuck.**—This dive is done exactly as the pike with the exception that the knees are driven upward and backward toward the head and are continually driven backward as the hands grasp the shins in a tight tuck at the peak. The knees and hips are relaxed.

The rotation backward is continued by driving the head and knees backward simultaneously with the tuck. When the body has made one and one-fourth turns, the legs should be straightened and held in place while the trunk drops and the hands reach toward the water (Fig. 12F).

A common error in executing the opening of this dive is to throw away the arms, head, and trunk from the tucked legs. The opening should be initiated by snapping the knees straight with great speed and holding in place, and then the arms and head reach backward for the entry with a supple back.

III. 14(a) **Isander (Half Gainer), Straight.**—As the body drops onto the board preliminary to the take-off for this dive, the weight should remain over the toes and the diver should not shift his weight backward as his heels contact the board. As the board lifts the diver, his center of body weight (in the hips) should be shifted to a position just in front of the base of support (balls of feet), so that the body is easily projected forward and upward.

The hurdle and take-off should be thoroughly mastered in the semi-gainer jump dive before any of the gainer group of dives is attempted. As in the semi-gainer jump, the eyes should be directed forward until the end of the reach in all gainer dives.

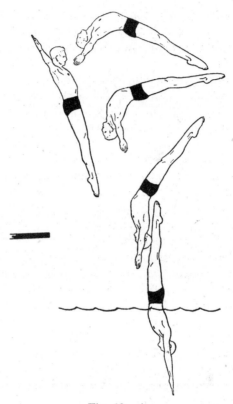

Fig. 13.—A.

Fig. 13.—A series of ideal form for executing various dives from the gainer group of dives, body facing water, from either the 1 or 3 meter height springboard. A. The Isander (half gainer) dive with the body straight. B. The Isander (half gainer) with the body in pike position. C. The Mollberg (full gainer) with the body held straight. D. The Mollberg (full gainer) with the body in a pike position. E. The Mollberg (full gainer) with the body in a tuck position. F. The flying Mollberg (flying full gainer) with the body in tuck position. G. 1½ Mollberg (1½ gainer), body in the tuck position.

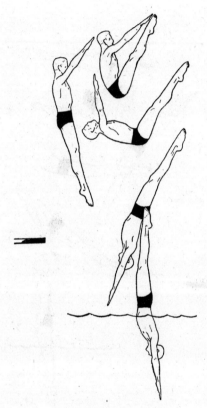

Fig. 13.—B.

Fig. 13.—C.

Fig. 13.—D.

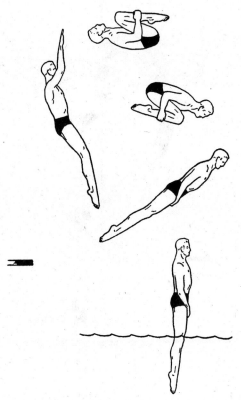

Fig. 13.—E.

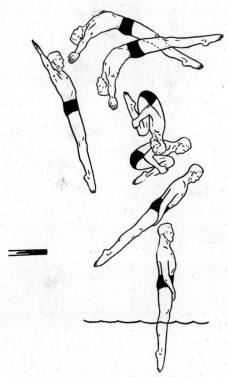

Fig. 13.—F.

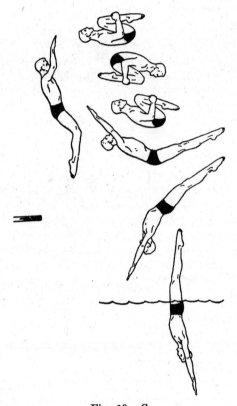

Fig. 13.—G.

In learning the dives in this group, the diver should jump out well away from the board until the mechanics and the body control are mastered. Then he may gradually move his dive nearer to the board.

The Isander, straight, is one of the most graceful of all the dives. It is, in its essentials, a backward dive from a forward take-off. The diver actually gains distance in a forward direction, thus, the name gainer which is given to it.

The arms lift to a spread position. At the end of the lift from the take-off, the head, arms, and shoulders are levered backward and the chest, hips, and legs are lifted as well as stretched. When the body reaches the horizontal at the peak, the legs remain lifted as if anchored as the backward rotation causes the head and shoulders to drop. The arms are closed and the head is brought between the arms at board level and the body is straightened as it drops into a vertical entry (Fig. 13A).

III. 14(b) **Isander (Half Gainer), Pike.**—This dive presents one of the most difficult yet one of the most beautiful movements of the body when expertly mastered and controlled. The alternating movements of isolating the trunk from the legs during the lift and just the reverse during the drop, is an esthetic achievement which requires a tremendous amount of practice to perform with finesse.

After the reach with the hands held close together, the trunk is held firm and the legs are lifted into the pike. The feet touch the hands and the body is in a V position at the peak of the dive.

The unpike is made by dropping the body away from the pike as the legs are held just beyond the vertical.

The trunk should be held relaxed as it falls away from the stretched legs and the arms are lowered to a position below the head for a vertical entry (Fig. 13B).

III. 15(a) **Mollberg (Full Gainer), Straight.**—At the take-off as the reach is made, the knees are relaxed and then straightened as a one-eighth backward turn has been completed. The trunk is not lifted into full height at the peak as additional force is needed to lift the legs and thrust the head, shoulders, and arms backward for the somersault.

The spine must be supple in order to decrease the radius as much as possible to facilitate the backward rotary movement.

As the body completes the three-quarter turn the arms are lowered to the front of the thighs and the body is straightened for the vertical entry (Fig. 13C).

III. 15(b) **Mollberg (Full Gainer), Pike.**—After the reach, the legs are brought upward and over the trunk and the hands grasp the backs of the knees. The hips are forced around the center of rotation. As the pike is made the head is moved backward.

The unpike is made as the body is in the inverted V position and has rotated past a one-half circle backward. The legs are forced downward and the head and shoulders are pressed backward as the toes reach for the feet first vertical entry (Fig. 13D).

III. 15(c) **Mollberg (Full Gainer), Tuck.**—After the body is stretched during the take-off, the knees are lifted as though they were to pass backward over the head. The hands are poised above the head preparatory to grasping the shins just before the peak is reached and the knees are pulled sharply into the chest. Simultaneously with the grasping of the shins the head is pressed backward.

After the body has rotated backward so that the trunk is approaching the horizontal and the eyes are spotting the water, the legs are shot outward toward the tip of the board. The feet are stretched toward the water, the head and shoulders are made erect, and the hands slide into position on the front of the thighs as a feet first vertical entry is made (Fig. 13E).

III. 16(c) **Flying Mollberg (Flying Full Gainer), Tuck.**—Perform the movements of the half gainer, straight, until the body is falling well away from the peak. The knees are brought to the chest and the hands pull the shins into a close tuck. This shortening of the radius of movement increases the speed of rotation considerably and the body must untuck immediately so that the legs can be swung downward and a vertical feet first entry can be made (Fig. 13F).

III. 17(c) **One and One-Half Mollberg (One and One-Half Gainer), Tuck.**—At the reach the arms are held about shoulder width and above the face so that they can be brought straight down to the shins when the tuck is made.

After the reach, the hips are lifted upward and the heels are brought to the buttocks. The knees are then lifted to the chest and the tuck is tightened by the pull of the hands against the shins. Relaxation during the tuck is stressed.

At the peak, the diver is fully tucked and the head is pulling backward as the body now spins faster due to the shortening of the radius. The tuck is held until a full backward rotation is completed and then the untuck is made. The arms reach backward and are stretched above the head for the entry. If the opening is made well above the level of the board, the diver will have sufficient time for a good stretch as the body is straightened before the entry (Fig. 13G).

A common error in executing this dive is during the opening. Beginners are apt to hold the legs tucked while opening the arms and trunk. The legs should initiate the opening movement with great speed and then be held in place, while the arms and head reach back for the entry with a supple back.

IV. 20(b) **Backward Spring, Forward Dive, Pike.**—While the body is poised over the end of the board, the center of weight is over the balls of the feet. During the preliminary arm movements of the take-off, the center of weight remains in this position.

At the lift from the board, the arms are raised to a moderate reach above the head and in front of the face. Palms are facing forward and slightly depressed.

At the end of the reach, the hips are flexed and raised and the arms are brought forward and downward and the hands touch the front of the feet at the peak. The hips have lifted above the head to the peak of the dive. The legs are vertical when the pike is effected. The eyes focus on the board at the peak of the dive, then shift to the water for the entry.

The body is held piked for a small rotation as it falls a short distance from the peak, and it is then unpiked quickly.

As the body drops to the vertical entry, the arms reach forward and stretch toward the bottom of the pool while the hips and legs are straightened in a well-controlled movement (Fig. 14A).

IV. 21(b) **Backward Spring, One Somersault Forward, Pike.**—After the take-off, the hands grasp the backs of the knees and the head and shoulders are driven forward around toward the lifting hips. The hips are continually spun around the center of rotation.

Just before the body reaches the vertical and is in a V position after nearly a full rotation forward, the eyes sight the board and the body is unpiked. The legs are swung downward and the head and shoulders are moved slightly backward to counteract further rotation forward as the body is straightened for a vertical feet first entry (Fig. 14B).

IV. 21(c) **Backward Spring, One Somersault Forward, Tuck.**—The heels are brought to the buttocks as the head is reached for-

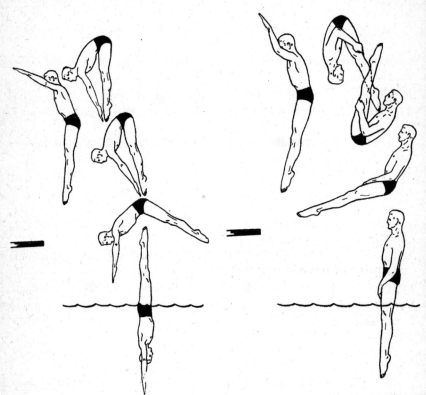

Fig. 14.—A, B.

Fig. 14.—A series of ideal form for executing various dives from the cutaway group of dives, with the body facing the board performed from either the 1 or 3 meter height springboard. A. Backward spring, forward dive (back jackknife) with the body in a pike position. B. Backward spring, one somersault forward with the body in pike position. C. Backward spring, one somersault forward with body in a tuck position. D. Backward spring, 1½ somersault forward with the body in a pike position. E. Backward spring, 1½ somersault forward with the body in a tuck position.

Fig. 14.—C, D.

Fig. 14.—E.

ward in the direction of the rotation. The hips are lifted as the peak is approached. The hands pull the legs into a tight tuck to speed the rotation forward.

As the body nearly completes a full rotation forward and is in a sitting position with the legs tucked, the eyes sight the board and the legs are untucked.

The legs are shot downward as the head and shoulders are held erect. The hands slide to the front of the thighs and the body is straightened for the feet first vertical entry (Fig. 14C).

IV. 23(b) **Backward Spring, One and One-Half Somersault Forward, Pike.**—When the diver has mastered the backward spring, one somersault forward, pike on the low board, he will find this one and one-half somersault dive an easy one to perform from the high board.

In this dive, the pike must be held much deeper and the opening is begun at board level when the body has rotated one and one-fourth forward turns and the chest is horizontal to the surface. The arms are stretched downward as the body is straightened for the head first vertical entry (Fig. 14D).

IV. 23(c) **Backward Spring, One and One-Half Somersault Forward, Tuck.**—The tuck is exaggerated in this dive so that a faster rotation can be derived. As the water is sighted after one and one-fourth forward turns have been made and the body is horizontal, the arms reach downward and the legs shoot backward and upward as the opening is made. The body is straightened as it enters the water at a vertical angle.

Common errors in executing this dive from the low board are: (1) Swinging the arms too vigorously during the take-off. This causes loss of balance, control, and height. (2) Falling away from the board at the take-off. (3) Throwing the hips away from the board instead of up above the head. The head and shoulders can then cut down and under the hips (Fig. 14E).

V. 25(a) **Half Twist Forward, Straight.**—Take-off as in the header forward. The arms are spread to a Y position as the body lifts into the reach. At the end of the reach, if the twist is to be made to the right, the left shoulder is lowered and the left arm is extended toward the point of entry. The eyes shift from the forward direction during the reach to sight along the right arm. The right shoulder is raised and the arm is pressed backward firmly. The

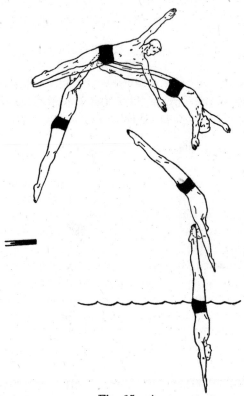

Fig. 15.—A.

Fig. 15.—A series of ideal form for executing various dives from the twisting group of dives, from either the 1 or 3 meter springboard. A. The one-half twist forward dive with the body held straight. B. The forward pike dive with a one-half twist. C. The full twist forward dive with the body held straight. D. The Isander (half gainer) with one-half twist body held straight. E. Backward 1½ somersault with one-half twist. (This dive can be performed in either straight, pike, or tuck.) F. The full twisting forward 1½ somersault. G. The one-half gainer, one-half twist layout with forward 1½ somersault, tuck position.

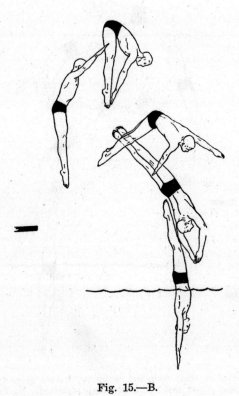

Fig. 15.—B.

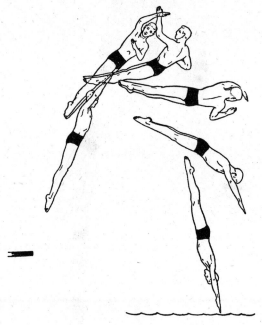

Fig. 15.—C,

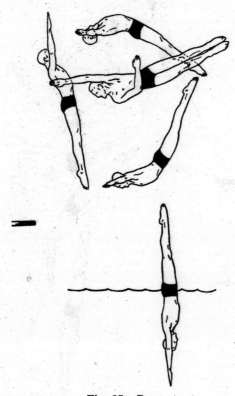

Fig. 15.—D.

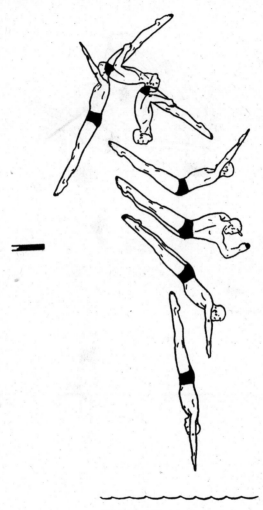

Fig. 15.—E.

Fig. 15.—F.

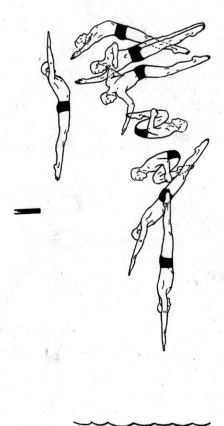

Fig. 15.—G.

arms move as though the hands were grasping and turning a large steering wheel counterclockwise. The legs constantly bear upward during the twist and the drop of the trunk.

The head should not resist the downward movement of the dive by pulling backward but should be allowed to follow the downward rotation movement. The eyes spot the point of entry until the body is beyond one-fourth turn and then the head is turned rapidly to a position as in the back dive.

The hands are closed slowly above the head, and the arms are pressed to the ears as the body is straightened for the head first vertical entry (Fig. 15A).

V. 25(b) **Pike Dive With Half Twist Forward.**—The body rises into the pike position at the peak as in the header forward, pike and the unpike is made just past the peak. When the diver is in the inverted V position as he unpikes, the arm on the twisting side is swung around and in front of the legs as the shoulder is depressed. The opposite shoulder is raised and the arm is borne backward. The hands steer the imaginary large wheel in the direction of the twist and the legs bear constantly upward.

At the entry the shoulders and hips should be on a parallel with the end of the board. The arms are stretched toward the bottom of the pool to align the body straight for the entry (Fig. 15B).

V. 27(a) **Full Twist Forward.**—As the diver rises into the peak, if the dive is toward the right, the left arm cuts in across the chest and bears upward. This movement lowers the left shoulder while the right shoulder is raised by partially extending the arm. The right arm is lowered and the elbow is driven backward. The eyes remain spotted on the water during the first half turn. The legs bear upward during the whole movement. The half twist has been made during the ascent to the peak and the diver is now in a horizontal position.

The head is now turned sharply to the right as the right elbow drives backward and the eyes spot the water at the point of entry. The left arm is thrust across the body as the head is turned. The left arm is then extended toward the point of entry and the right arm joins the left in stretching toward the vertical entry. This stretching action should be emphasized in this dive as it squares the body so that the hips and shoulders are straightened at the entry.

All movements in this dive should center around the longitudinal axis of the diver. Movements of the shoulders must be loose so as to avoid any lateral action caused by strained movements of the arms.

A common error in performing this dive is a failure to bear the legs upward during the twisting movements (Fig. 15C).

V. 31(a) **Isander (Half Gainer) With One and One-Half Twist.**— The lift from the take-off is made as in the half gainer, straight. As the body reaches the near-horizontal level at the peak of the dive with the arms well spread, the right arm is thrown across the chest if the twist is to the right. The head is turned to the right and the eyes sight the point of entry. The left shoulder is raised as the left arm is stretched upward in line with the longitudinal axis of the body. The legs bear upward throughout. These movements occur simultaneously and there is no hesitation once they are started.

After slightly more than one-fourth turn has been made, the left arm is brought downward alongside the right arm. The shoulders and hips are squared for the vertical head first entry by stretching the entire body and reaching for the bottom of the pool.

The arm mechanics in executing the twisting movements of this dive deviate from those described in other twisting dives. The deviation from the standard technique is used for the primary purpose of showing another standard method of arm technique in executing a twisting movement. The arm technique described above conforms to the law of action-reaction. As the arm swings straight across the abdomen, the body rolls toward the same side but in the opposite direction from that which the arm is moving (Fig. 15D).

V. 35(b) **Half Twisting One and One-Half Somersault Backward, Pike.**—The dive is identical with the one and one-half somersault, backward, pike with the addition of the one-half twist as a somersault is completed.

When one somersault is completed the trunk is vertical and the body is piked. As the twist to the right is made, the legs are held in place and stretched outward, and the left arm shoots across the front of the chest. The head is turning to the right and the eyes spot the point of entry. The right arm is pulled downward, and the elbow is driven backward simultaneous with the head movement.

The left arm is reached for the point of entry and the right arm joins it. The legs are anchored in an elevated position and are twisted with the body as it falls away.

The arms are stretched downward to square the hips and shoulders and a vertical head first entry is made (Fig. 15E).

V. 36 **Full Twisting Forward One and One-Half Somersault.**— The arms reach upward and are brought downward to an open pike after the take-off has been made. The trunk completes a one-half somersault.

The twist is started to the left by driving the right arm across the chest. The body pivots in the head-down pike position and the legs swing around the center of rotation from the rear to the front.

The right arm pulls in behind the shoulder and the body has rotated forward so that the head is now upward. The eyes then spot the water at the point of entry and the forceful reach downward for the entry is made with the arms and head. The legs continue lifting as the forward rotation is completed and the body is stretched for the head first vertical entry. The body remains in the pike position during the entire twisting movements (Fig. 15F).

V. 40 **Half Gainer, Half Twist, Layout With Forward One and One-Half Somersault, Tuck.**—Rise into the half gainer with arms spread in a layout position. If the twist is to the left, the left arm is thrown across in front of the chest and the left shoulder is lowered. The right arm remains partially extended along the longitudinal axis of the body with the elbow pressing backward. The legs lift up and the body turns over to a face-down position. The heels are then jerked toward the buttocks to start the rotation forward. The hands pull the legs into a tight tuck as the forward one and one-fourth somersault is completed. The untuck is made when the trunk is 30° below the horizontal. The arms shoot for the bottom of the pool and the legs are straightened and held together with the toes pointed at the vertical entry (Fig. 15G).

INDEX